The Subtlety of Sameness

The Subtlety of Sameness

A Theory and Computer Model of Analogy-Making

Robert M. French

A Bradford Book
The MIT Press
Cambridge, Massachusetts
London, England

This book was set in Palatino by Asco Trade Typesetting Ltd., Hong Kong and was printed and bound in the United States of America.

Library of Congress Cataloging-in-Publication Data

French, Robert M. (Robert Matthew), 1951–
   The subtlety of sameness : a theory and computer model of analogy-making / Robert M. French.
       p.   cm.
   "A Bradford book."
   Includes bibliographical references and index.
   ISBN 0-262-06180-5 (alk. paper)
   1. Artificial intelligence. 2. Analogy. I. Title.
Q335.F738   1995
006.3—dc20   95-8723
                                                     CIP

Contents

Foreword

If somebody asked me to design a book that would introduce the most important ideas in artificial intelligence (AI) to a wider audience, I would try to work to the following principles:

1. Go for details. Instead of presenting yet another impressionistic overview of the field, concentrate on the details of a particular AI model, so that the readers can see for themselves just how and why it works, seeing its weaknesses and boundaries as well as its showcase triumphs.

2. Model something we all know intimately. Choose a psychological phenomenon that is familiar to everyone—and intrinsically interesting. Not everybody plays chess or solves route-minimization problems, and although we almost all can see, unless we are vision scientists, we have scant direct familiarity with the details of how our visual processes work.

3. Explain exactly how the particular model supports or refutes, supplements or clarifies the other research on the same phenomenon, including work by people in other disciplines.

4. Give concrete illustrations of the important ideas at work. A single well-developed example of a concept applied is often better than ten pages of definition.

This book by Bob French all about his Tabletop model fills the bill perfectly, so when I read an early draft of it (I was a member of his Ph.D. dissertation committee), I encouraged him to publish it and offered to write a foreword. From its easily read pages, you will come to know the model inside out, not only seeing *that* it comes up with recognizably human performance but seeing—really seeing—*how* it comes up with its results. And what does it do? It does something we all do every day: it appreciates analogies. It creates them and perceives them, in a manner of speaking. The simple setting of the task is inspired: a game of "Do this!" whose point you will get in an instant, but whose richer possibilities are not only surprising, but quite inexhaustible.

You get to tackle all the problems yourself and think about them "from the first-person point of view." Something goes on in you when you do these problems. What on earth is it? It seems at first the farthest thing from mechanizable—"intuitive," quirky, fluid, aesthetic, quintessentially human—just the sort of phenomenon that the skeptics would be tempted to brandish, saying, "You'll never get a computer to do *this*!" Or, more cautiously, "You'll never get a computer to do this the way *we* do it!" If you are such a skeptic, you are in for a surprise.

Most AI programs model phenomena that are either highly intellectualized thinking exercises in the first place—like playing chess or constructing proofs—or else low-level processes that are quite beneath our ken—like extracting three-dimensional information about the visible world from binocular overlap, texture gradients, and shading. French's program, in contrast, models a phenomenon that is neither difficult nor utterly invisible but rather *just* out of reach to the introspecting reader. We can *almost* analyze our own direct experiences into the steps that French's model exhibits. AI workers love acronyms, and I hereby introduce the term AIGLES—almost-introspectible, grain-level events—as the general term for the sort of high-level psychological phenomenon French has modeled. If there *were* a Cartesian Theater in our brains, across whose stage the parade of consciousness marched, his would be a model of something that happens immediately backstage. (Those who join me in renouncing the all-too-popular image of the Cartesian Theater have a nontrivial task of explaining why and how French's model can avoid falling into that forlorn trap, but this is not the time or place for me to discharge that burden. It is left as an exercise for the reader.)

From the particulars, we can appreciate the general. French introduces, exemplifies, and explains some of the most important and ill-understood ideas in current AI. For instance, almost everybody these days speaks dismissively of the bad old days in AI and talks instead about "emergence," while waving hands about self-organizing systems that settle into coherent structures and so forth. (I myself have spoken of multiple drafts in competition, out of which transient winners emerge, a tantalizingly metaphorical description of the processes I claim are involved in human consciousness.) French provides a no-nonsense model of just such a system. When posed a problem, the answer it arrives at is "the emergent result of the interaction of many parallel unconscious processes" (p. 20). So here is a fine place to see what all the hoopla is about. You get to see how the currently popular metaphors—a batch of cooling molecules or a system of interconnected resonators coming to vibrate in unison, for instance—apply to an actual nonmetaphorical reality, a system engaged in doing some undeniably mental work.

His model also illustrates a version of "dynamic" memory structures, which deform to fit the current context, and it achieves its results by exploiting a "parallel-terraced scan." It accomplishes "implicit pruning," which must somehow be what we manage to do when we ignore the irrelevancies that always surround us. It does this by building (and rebuilding and rebuilding) the relevant structures on the fly, thereby avoiding at least some of the "combinatorial explosions" that threaten all AI models that have to ignore most of what they *could* attend to without catastrophically ignoring the important points. The central theme of the book is that the processes of producing mental representations and manipulating them are inextricably intertwined. As French puts it, "You *must* take the representation problem into consideration *while* you are doing processing." When you understand this paragraph in detail (and you will when you have read the book), you will have a good grip on some of the central ideas in recent AI.

These ideas are not just French's of course. His work grows out of the family of projects undertaken in recent years by Douglas Hofstadter's group at Indiana University and, as such, provides a fine demonstration of the powers of that school of thought in AI. Many skeptics and critics of AI from other disciplines have surmised there was something profoundly wrong about the hard-edged, inert (but manipulable) symbols of the "physical-symbol systems" of traditional AI, and hence they have been intrigued by Hofstadter's radical alternative: "active symbols." Active symbols sound great, but what are they, and how on earth could they work? This book takes us a few sure steps toward the answer. French provides a judicious comparison of his own work—which has plenty of its own originality—to that of others who have worked on analogy, in Hofstadter's group, in AI more generally, and in psychology.

If you don't already appreciate it, you will come to appreciate the curious combination of ambition and modesty that marks most work in AI and the work of Hofstadter and his colleagues in particular. On the one hand, the models are tremendously abstract, not tied at all to brain architecture or to the known details of such processes as "early vision." All the important questions in these research domains are simply sidestepped. That's modesty. On the other hand, the models purport to be getting at something truly fundamental in the underlying structure and rationale of the actual processes that must go on in the brain. That's ambition. Like more traditional AI programs, they often achieve their triumphs by heroic simplification: helping themselves to ruthless—even comical—truncations of the phenomena (more modesty), in order, it is claimed, to provide a feasible working model of the essential underlying process (more ambition). The reader is left, quite properly, with an unanswered question about just which helpings of simplification might be poisoned. Are any of these bold decisions fatal oversimplifications that could not possibly be removed without undoing the ambitious claims? There is something that is both right and deep about this model, I am sure, but saying just what it is and how it will map onto lower-level models of brain function is still beyond me and everybody else at this time, a tantalizing patch of fog.

French's program doesn't learn at all—except what it could be said to learn in the course of tackling a single problem. It has no long-term memory of its activities, and it never gets any better. This might seem to be a horrible shortcoming, but it has an unusual bonus: his program never gets bored! You can give it the same problem over and over and over, and it never rebels but always takes it in a fresh spirit. This is excellent for "rewinding the tape"—looking, counterfactually, at what *else* a system might do if put in the same situation again. Heraclitus said that you can never step into the same river twice, and this is particularly true of human beings, thanks to our memories. Aside from a few famous amnesiacs, we normal human beings are never remotely in the same state twice, and this seriously impedes scientific research on human cognitive mechanisms. Is investigating a system with total amnesia, like French's, a worthy substitute for non-doable human experiments, or does the absence of memory and learning vitiate his model? French shows that AI fell into a trap when it opportunistically separated the building of representations from their processing; will some meta-French soon come along to show that he fell into just as bad a trap by setting long-term learning aside for the time being? A good question—which is to say that no one should think that the pessimistic answer is obvious. In the end, at some level, no doubt just about everything is inextricably intertwined with everything else, but if we are to understand the main features of this tangled bank, we must force some temporary separation on them.

A standard conflict in AI is between the hard edges and the fuzzies, a conflict fought on many battlefields, and some of the niftiest features of French's model demonstrate what happens when you slide back and forth between hard edges and fuzzy edges. There are knobs, in effect, that you can turn, thereby setting parameters on the model to give you nice sharp edges or terribly fuzzy edges or something in between. Probability plays a deep role in French's model, which makes it imperative for him to test his model in action many, many times and gather statistics on its performance—something that would not be at all motivated in most traditional AI. But if you set the model so that some of the probabilities are very close to 1 or 0, you can turn it into what amounts to a deterministic, hard-edged model. Or you can explore the trade-off between depth-first search and breadth-first search, by adjusting the "rho" factor, or you can create what French calls a semi-stack, another fuzzy version of a hard-edged idea. This is a particularly attractive set of features, for one of the things we know about ourselves is that the *appearance* of determinism and indeterminism in our mental life is highly variable.

AI is a seductive field. Even a book as scrupulously written as French's may mislead you into ignoring deep problems or deficiencies in the model, or—a very common foible—it may encourage you to overestimate the actual fidelity or power of the model. Here, for the benefit of neophytes, are a few of the tough questions you should keep asking yourself as you read. (You will get a better sense of the genuine strengths of French's model by making sure you know just what its weaknesses are.)

French claims his domain, the (apparently) concrete world of Tabletop, is rich enough to "ground" the symbols of his model in a way that the symbols of most AI programs are not grounded. Is this really so? We viewers of Tabletop *see* the knives, forks, spoons, cups, bowls, and so forth, vividly laid out in space, but what does the model really understand about the shape of these objects? Anything? Does Tabletop know that a spoon, with its concavity, is more like a bowl than a knife is? *We* can see that a spoon is a sort of bowl on a stick, but that is utterly unknown to Tabletop. What other sorts of obvious facts about tableware are left out of Tabletop's semantics, and how could they be added? Perhaps it is here that we see most clearly what the model leaves out when it leaves out learning—in the real world of concrete experience. But what difference, if any, does this make to the groundedness of Tabletop's symbols? Is there some other sense in which Tabletop is clearly superior in "groundedness" to other programs? (I think the answer is yes. Can you see how?)

Tabletop gets its basic perceptual accomplishments for free. It cannot mistake a knife for a fork out of the corner of its eye or fail to see the second spoon *as* a spoon (if it ever directs its attention to it). Everything placed on the table is, as it were, legibly and correctly labeled according to its type. So what? (Might some of the combinatorial explosions so deftly avoided by Tabletop come back to haunt it if this gift were revoked? Again, so what?)

What would it take to add learning to Tabletop? What would it take to expand the domain to other topics? What would happen if you tried to add episodic memory? Could you readily embed Tabletop in a larger system that could face the decision of whether or not to play the Tabletop game, or play it in good faith? (A human player could get fed up and start giving deliberately "bad" answers to try to drive "Henry" into one amusing state of frustration or another. Is this a feature whose absence from Tabletop could be readily repaired, or would a model builder have to start over from scratch to include it?)

Finally, the granddaddy of all challenging questions for any AI program: Since this model purports to be right about something, how could we tell if it was wrong?

What sort of discovery, in particular, would refute it? The boring way of responding to this question is to try to concoct some philosophical argument to show why "in principle" Tabletop couldn't be right. The exciting ways are to be found down the paths leading from the other questions.

My raising of these challenging questions in the foreword is the most unignorable way I can think of to demonstrate my confidence in the strength and value of this book. Go ahead; give it your best shot.

Daniel Dennett

Acknowledgments

My interest in artificial intelligence can be traced to a very precise moment, to a day in 1981 when a gift from my father arrived in the mail for me in Paris—a gift that profoundly changed my life. The gift was a book called *Gödel, Escher, Bach*. It was both fun to read and fascinating to think about. One thing led to another, and a French colleague and I ended up translating it into French. During the two-and-a-half years that it took us to complete the translation, we worked closely with the book's author, Douglas Hofstadter. He and I got along splendidly, and it was agreed that I would return to the United States to do a Ph.D. in artificial intelligence with him. Thus, in the fall of 1985—with no formal training whatsoever in computers—I embarked on my graduate studies in computer science at the University of Michigan.

More than any other individual, Doug Hofstadter has helped shape my ideas about artificial intelligence and cognition. He has an inimitable way of seeing the essence of complex situations and conveying that essence to others. It was he who, in the early eighties, laid out the basic principles that guide the program described in this book. An ardent advocate of idealized domains, he also first suggested the microworld in which the program operates.

Melanie Mitchell and I were graduate students together, and this book is, in a sense, a sequel to her own, *Analogy-Making as Perception*. Over the years Melanie has been a continual source of intellectual stimulation and inspiration, help, friendship, and moral support. It is hard to imagine a finer person anywhere.

Special thanks to all those who contributed to the work in this book, in particular: Terry Jones: Terry saved me months of drudgery by writing a wonderful program that allowed me to simultaneously and maximally use all of our lab's resources to test Tabletop. Dan Dennett: Over the years, Dan has been an unflagging supporter of my work. His writings, like those of Doug Hofstadter, have served as my model of how one can put complex ideas into clear, readable prose. Gray Clossman: Whether he's explaining some obscure feature of LISP or telling you why manzanitas don't grow in Indiana, Gray makes everything seem clear and simple. Patrick Géhant: poet, Parisian, mathematician, computer scientist, climber, lover of literature, and *ami par excellence*. It was on his tiny T07 home computer that we first learned to program back in 1983. Jan Kuhl: after a wonderful decade in France, it was she who convinced me to quit translation and return to graduate school in computer science. Mark Weaver: Mark can be guaranteed to make insightful comments on everything from baseball to affirmative action, from Mark Twain to connectionism. A great friend, he contributed more to this work than anyone outside of my immediate research group. Stephen Kaplan: his course in neural models was the best course I ever had. His ideas and attitudes about science have influenced me deeply. Peter Suber: the first philosopher, lawyer, skier, professor, former stand-up comic, archer, hacker, cyclist, knot-enthusiast, camper, canoer, swimmer, and early-1900s-phone repairer I ever became friends with. David Moser: David is another one of those incredibly stimulating people who seems to do everything well. A writer and an artist, he is currently working as a jazz musician in Beijing while finishing his Ph.D. in Chinese. Alain and Pascal Chesnais, Benoit Hap, Renaud Dumeur, Jean-Daniel Fekete, and Jean-Alain le Borgne, friends at the now-defunct Centre Mondial de l'Informatique in Paris, first showed me what a "real" computer was (a DEC-20) and refused to let me sully it with Basic, forcing me to learn Pascal and LISP. Thanks also to Daniel Andler, Don Byrd, Jean-Luc Bonnetain, David Chalmers, Dany Defays, Kay French, Jim Friedrich, Liane Gabora, Mike Gasser, Françoise Géhant, Helga Keller, John Holland, John Laird, Sylvie Lachize, Gary McGraw, Jim Marshall, Jo and Françoise Montchaussé, David Rogers, Rich Shiffrin, John Theios and others I'm sure I've overlooked.

Thanks especially to Art Markman and Dedre Gentner for their careful reading of the original manuscript and for all of their extremely helpful suggestions. Thanks also Harry Stanton, who agreed to publish this book in the first place, and to Teri Mendelsohn, Sandra Minkkinen, and the others at MIT Press who actually made it happen.

Finally, I want to thank my family: My father, who first sent me *Gödel, Escher, Bach* and my mother, for whom these thanks must now go unread, who influenced my life more than any other individual through her love of books and never-ending curiosity about the world. Chuck, my brother and closest friend, who has always been an endless source of stimulating conversation and wrong ideas. My youngest brother, Roger, who has invariably been a font of common sense and good-natured fun. And thanks, most of all, to my wife Elizabeth. Before writing this book, I never really understood why authors lavished such abundant thanks on their spouses. Now I know. Thanks, Liz, tonnes.

Introduction

If only by definition, it is impossible for two things, *any* two things, to be exactly the same. And yet, there is nothing puzzling or inappropriate about our everyday use of "the same." We see nothing odd or wrong about ordinary utterances such as: "That's the same man I saw yesterday at lunch," or "We both wore the same outfit," or, "I feel the same way my wife does about abortion," or, finally, "That's the same problem the Americans had in Vietnam." What makes all these uses of "the same" (and this one, too) the same?

The answer is: analogy-making. And analogy-making is what this book is all about. Since no two things are ever identical, what we really mean when we say "X is the same as Y," is that, within the particular context under discussion, X is the *counterpart* of Y. In other words, X is analogous to Y. This book explores the complex mechanisms underlying everyday analogy-making, and it does so largely by means of a computer program called Tabletop.

To understand what Tabletop does, imagine two people seated directly across from one another at a small, perfectly ordinary table in a small, perfectly ordinary restaurant. (See the cover drawing.) The table is set as one might expect with knives, forks, spoons, plates, cups, and glasses. The two people's names are Henry and Eliza (after "the same" characters in *My Fair Lady*). At some point during their meal—perhaps to revive a flagging conversation—Henry proposes that they play a little game, and Eliza agrees. "Just do as I do," says Henry and touches his nose. Eliza touches her nose. He reaches across the table and touches her chin, she responds by reaching across the table and touches his beard. Aware that the other diners are beginning to stare, Henry proposes that they restrict themselves to objects on the table, and Eliza concurs. He touches the spoon on his side of the table and says, "Do this!" and she responds by touching the spoon on her side of the table. He touches his glass of Pepsi. She has no Pepsi, only coffee, but judges that to be good enough and touches her cup of coffee. Finally, he touches the piece of pie on his plate. Eliza fleetingly considers touching her coffee cup again because, after all, it is the only object on her side of the table that, like his piece of pie, is sitting on a plate, but then she decides against it and reaches across the table and touches his piece of pie.

Tabletop, the program, is designed to do "the same thing" Eliza does. Tabletop's world consists only of cups and saucers, silverware, salt and pepper shakers, and glasses on a tabletop. Making analogies in this world stripped of real-world complexities should be easy, or so you might think. I hope to convince you that this initial intuition is wrong, that the Tabletop domain of crockery and cutlery is indeed complex enough to be interesting. But even if you aren't convinced of that, I hope to show you that *the way in which* Tabletop makes analogies might, at least in theory, be applied successfully to the full-scale, real-world domains that must ultimately be tackled.

So the roadmap of this book is as follows. First, I will try to convince you of the ubiquity of analogy by means of examples from many and varied walks of everyday life. I think these examples will serve to convince you that analogy is not restricted to rarefied discussions of politics, science, and law. In fact, when you look closely, you'll notice just how often analogies occur, usually arising unbidden and without purpose, generally so mundane as to be almost invisible. Analogy, rather than being "merely" in the service of reason, is the minion of a far greater master, thought itself.

Next comes a description of the Tabletop domain. My hope here is to convince you that this domain is rich enough to be used to study the mechanisms of analogy-making. Then I will turn to a detailed account of how the program is actually put together. It is here that the philosophical rubber meets the computational road. I describe in detail how top-down processes interact with bottom-up agents, how parallelism and stochasticity pervade all levels of decision-making, how representations are built, how correspondences are made, and how the program finally chooses an answer. I then step you through one full run of the program and follow this with a close-up look the program's performance over several thousand runs on dozens of varying table configurations. Finally, the book examines a number of rival analogy-making programs and discusses their strengths and weaknesses.

By the end of this book, I certainly hope that you will have acquired a better understanding of analogy-making, both human and computational. But more important, I hope to have given you a better appreciation of our remarkable—yet largely unconscious and virtually automatic—ability to perceive one place or object or person or situation, however vast or insignificant, as "the same" as some other. It is this subtle ability, perhaps more than any other, that sets human cognition apart from any other on our planet.

Chapter 1

From Recognition to Analogy-Making:
The Central Role of Slippage

1.1 Introduction

Perhaps the most fundamental assumption underlying the research presented in this book is that the cognitive mechanisms that give rise to human analogy-making form one of the key components of intelligence. In other words, our ability to perceive and create analogies is made possible by the same mechanisms that drive our ability to categorize, to generalize, and to compare different situations. These abilities are all manifestations of what I will refer to as "high-level perception." Unlike low-level perception, which involves primarily the modality-specific processing of raw sensory information, high-level perception is that level of processing at which *concepts* begin to play a significant role.

High-level perception, in its simplest form, involves our ability to recognize objects (for example, a poppy in a wheat field) and relations between objects ("the book is *on* the table"). In its most complex form, it involves our ability to understand entire situations, such as a love affair or a civil war (Chalmers, French, and Hofstadter 1992). The assumption that all of high-level perception derives from a single set of mechanisms has far-reaching consequences for the computer modeling of intelligence in general and of analogy-making in particular. In this book, I examine these consequences in detail and describe and discuss a computer model of analogy-making based on these mechanisms.

Just as modeling intelligence requires an understanding of high-level perception, modeling high-level perception requires a deep understanding of concepts, with their blurry boundaries, their protean nature, and their ability to associate and interact with each other, to change in the face of contextual pressure, and to influence perception. For this reason, this book is as much about modeling concepts as it is about making analogies.

To explore explicitly the ideas that I believe underlie high-level perception, I have written a computer program, called Tabletop, that operates in a microdomain consisting of a small, imaginary table that is set with various plausible combinations of common table objects: knives, forks, spoons, cups, saucers, salt and pepper shakers, plates, and so on. The Tabletop program perceives analogies between various objects on the table.

This idealized world has, in spite of its diminutive size, a "real-world" flavor to it and was carefully designed to highlight many of the central mechanisms underlying human concepts and analogy-making. I will discuss these mechanisms shortly, but first let us take a closer look at some of the issues surrounding categories and concepts.

Tabletop differs from traditional analogy programs in a number of ways. Briefly, some of these differences are as follows:

- Traditional analogy-making programs are concerned with "exalted" analogy-making—e.g., reproducing famous scientific, literary, or philosophical analogies. Tabletop is a model of prosaic, everyday analogy-making; in some sense, the program only makes "trivial" analogies.
- Traditional analogy-making programs pretend to be operating in full-fledged domains. Tabletop admits to operating in a microworld, the better to isolate and study the mechanisms underlying analogy-making.
- Traditional analogy-making programs are, with few exceptions, given pre-packaged representations of two situations and are instructed to find the relevant correspondences. This approach, while not, strictly speaking, *wrong*, does not tackle the really hard part of analogy-making—namely, the problem of building the representations of the situations. Tabletop does build its own representations.
- Traditional analogy-making programs are serial and deterministic. Tabletop is largely parallel and stochastic.

The basic architecture underlying the Tabletop model has been implemented in an earlier program, Copycat, a computer model of analogy-making in a letter-string domain (Mitchell 1990; Hofstadter and Mitchell 1991; Mitchell 1993). There are, nonetheless, significant differences between Tabletop and Copycat. These differences are discussed at length in a later chapter.

1.2 *Slippage*

The term "slippage" (Hofstadter 1979) means, in its most general sense, the replacement of one concept in the description of some situation by another related one. The perceived similarities that engender slippage may range from the most superficial to the most abstract. Human metaphor usage, analogy-making, and counterfactualization are all products of the mind's ability to perform slippage fluidly. All analogies involve some degree of conceptual slippage, because they all involve comparing one particular entity to another, and no two objects or situations are *exactly* the same. Analogies involving slippages along highly abstract dimensions are generally, but not always, more interesting—deeper—than those that are made along more superficial dimensions.

Slippage is a fundamental component of a great many areas of cognition, ranging from translation to error-making in speech, from action slips to counterfactuals, from creative writing to humor, from poetry and politics to the recognition (and creation) of styles in art, music, literature, and so on.

Consider an example first discussed by Hofstadter, Clossman, and Meredith (1980) and again by Hofstadter (1985a). During Margaret Thatcher's twelve-year tenure as head of state of Great Britain, who was the "First Lady of Britain"? Let us start by considering the canonical definition of "First Lady." Webster's tells us that it is "the wife or hostess of the chief executive of a country." Does this mean that there was *no* First Lady of Britain? In a strict sense, yes. But when asked to designate the First Lady of Britain at that time, most people have no problem slipping those parts of the dictionary definition that are under stress. They often choose Denis Thatcher, the husband of Britain's chief executive. Thus, in this particular case, "wife" slips relatively easily to "husband."

Does this mean that the definition as given in the dictionary is inadequate and that it should be supplanted by a more comprehensive definition, such as "the spouse of the chief executive of a country"? No, because this definition would no longer convey the (normally central) notion of womanhood associated with the concept "First Lady." Significant pressures are necessary before we are willing to entertain the notion of a male First Lady." The dictionary definition merely provides an accurate *central* tendency of usage of the First Lady concept, whereas contextual pressures determine how that central tendency can be modified.

Depending on the pressures involved, the central-tendency definition can slip very far and yet still seem perfectly natural. For example, Herman B. Wells, president of Indiana University for almost four decades, was unmarried and often attended official university functions with his mother, who thereby became known throughout the university community as the "First Lady of Indiana University." Here, very little is left of the strict dictionary definition of "First Lady": "chief executive of a country" has slipped to "president of a university," and "wife" has slipped to "mother."

What are the implications of this for the definition of "First Lady"? Should we further weaken the original definition to include even cases like this one (e.g., "First Lady" means "person with a significant emotional tie to the director of a large administrative entity")? Can such attenuation of the original dictionary definition achieve the twofold goal of capturing the broad spirit of the concept as well as the original, narrower definition ("wife of a chief executive of a country")? If not, does this mean that it is impossible to define "First Lady," that we cannot know what "First Lady" means? Of course not; it simply means that the concept "First Lady," like all concepts, is fluid—that it can be adapted to a vast array of situations that no single, rigid definition can cover in advance.

1.3 Three Types of Slippage

In this section, I distinguish three types of slippage: export, transport, and import slippage. Using as the basis of discussion the "First Lady" example discussed in the previous section, I consider how we move from one situational framework to another—thus, making an analogy between the two situations—via three distinct types of slippage mechanisms (figure 1.1).

The first—*export slippage*—serves to carry us "upward" from the concrete framework of the first situation to an abstract schema. There are two key processes here: abstraction and variabilization. In the "First Lady" example, our concrete starting point is the canonical American concept of "First Lady"—namely, "wife of the president of the United States." In the upward leap to form an abstract schema, the concept "president" is replaced by the more abstract notion "chief executive" (abstraction), and "United States" is replaced by the variable "country X" (variabilization). Thus, the concrete notion "wife of the president of the United States" becomes, when exported from its native framework, the schema "wife of the chief executive of country X." (Note: Webster's in fact gives essentially this schema as the definition of the term. However, for most Americans the concept is narrower and more specifically America-centered.)

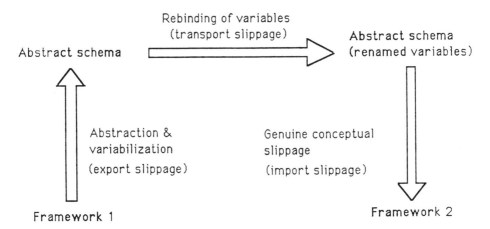

Figure 1.1
Various types of slippages

The abstraction process should ideally result in a concept at roughly the "basic level" as defined by Rosch and Lloyd (1978)—neither overly specific nor overly general. The earlier examples of highly attenuated "First Lady" definitions, such as "person with a significant emotional tie to the director of a large administrative entity," show the dangers of overgeneralization; on the other side of the coin, the dangers of too little generalization are obvious. The level of generalization whereby "president" slips to "chief executive," as here, seems just about ideal—poised roughly midway between dilution to the point of vacuity and narrowness to the point of rigidity.

The second type of slippage that takes place—*transport slippage*—is an attempt to adapt the successfully exported abstract schema to a new concrete framework. Specifically, it involves rebinding the free variables in the schema. In the "First Lady" example, this means replacing "country X" with "Great Britain."

The final type—*import slippage* (also called "conceptual slippage") (Hofstadter 1979; Hofstadter and Mitchell 1991)—is necessitated when some aspect of the exported and transported schema still does not apply to the target situation. This mismatch forces the aspect in question to "give," which means that one or more concepts in the original schema must be dislodged and replaced by suitable concepts that do apply. In the "First Lady of Britain" example, the need for import slippage arises because the prime minister in question happens to be female rather than male, and so the concept "wife of the chief executive" does not apply. What gives is the word "wife," and it slips into its conceptually nearest neighbor, "husband." This third type of slippage then completes the transformation of "wife of the president of the United States" into "husband of the chief executive of Great Britain."

One might well ask, "Why have this special import process? If 'wife' had just been abstracted upward to 'spouse' during the export stage, then there would have been no need to make an import slippage from 'wife' to 'husband' as one entered the target framework. Can't all the necessary slippages be made at the export stage?" The reply is that in any specific example, one can always argue a posteriori that the slippage in question could or should have been anticipated at the export stage. However, in practice, one always runs into bizarre target frameworks that require bizarre mental adaptations that one simply cannot reasonably be expected to have anticipated at the export stage. The abstract schema is not meant to be the most general imaginable version of the original notion but in some sense the most *reasonable* one—a generalized version but one that does not sacrifice the spirit of the notion purely for the sake of generality. For this reason, import slippage is an indispensable part of the process.

I examine these three types of slippage in more detail when I discuss a certain very simple category of analogies, called "me-too" analogies, in a later section of this chapter.

The continuum from recognition to full-fledged analogy-making is defined, to a large extent, by the amount of slippage, involved. In recognition or generalization, for example, only the first type of slippage involving abstraction and variabilization, is involved. One could plausibly argue that it is only when there is a transfer from one framework to another and subsequent conceptual slippage that we have true analogy-making.

1.3.1 Slippage and the Nature of Categories
"Philosophy matters," as linguist George Lakoff has put it succinctly, and it is unfortunate that traditional artificial-intelligence (AI) research has frequently ignored certain important philosophical issues related to the nature of categories—in particular, the philosophical (and psychological) literature on the impossibility, in general, of providing necessary and sufficient conditions for membership in any real-world category. AI researchers have typically treated these philosophical concerns as digressions at best, rather than as issues absolutely central to their research. To be sure, producing an artificial intelligence would be much easier if it were possible to discover and implement a set of necessary and sufficient conditions, however large, for every concept.

Lakoff (1987) refers to the view that it is possible to establish context-independent, complete definitions for concepts in terms of their properties and relations to other concepts—an underlying assumption of most AI research until very recently—as the "objectivist paradigm." "On the objectivist view," he writes, "reality comes with a unique, correct, complete structure in terms of entities, properties, and relations. This structure exists, independent of any human understanding." The problem is that such complete representations of reality are simply not possible. Just as it would have been difficult, if not impossible, to anticipate the application of the concept "First Lady" to the mother of a university president or to the husband of a prime minister, so it is with *all* real-world concepts.

I assume that concepts, such as "dog," "eat," and "First Lady," are all stored in long-term memory, whereas the corresponding representations of *instances* of these concepts are created, manipulated, and dissolved in short-term memory. The fluidity of concepts in long-term memory ("types," in the traditional language of AI) is mirrored in the flexibility of representations in short-term memory ("tokens"). As Chalmers, French, and Hofstadter (1992), have argued, the building up of representations of instances in short-term memory, essential for any cognitive task, cannot be made in isolation—for example, in some independent "representation-building module" that is independent of situation and context. Rather, representations in short-term memory must be structured in such a way that they can interact with the situation at hand, dynamically evolving and adapting themselves to it.

The most significant contribution, in my opinion, of the Tabletop project is that it is an attempt to implement this philosophy of fluid concepts and fluid representations. The representations that the Tabletop program develops of the objects in its world evolve dynamically as the program discovers more about the objects on the table and the various relationships among them. In addition, the activation levels and the distances between concepts in the program's conceptual network (its long-term memory) change as a result of the structures built in short-term memory.

Considerable attention will be devoted to mechanisms that allow this type of dynamic development of representations and concepts. For the moment, however, it is necessary to keep in mind only the central feature of Tabletop: its concepts are not rigid or static, and its representations of objects on the table are not fixed ahead of time. Rather, representations are shaped gradually by pressures created by the presence, types, groupings, positions, and orientations of the objects on the table, as well as by the relations among them. Likewise, concepts gain and lose activation and approach and recede from each other as the situation is perceived and understood.

The following two simple scenarios will serve as an introduction to the Tabletop project. In both cases you are asked to imagine that Henry is seated at a small table across from his friend Eliza.

In the first case there is a coffee cup directly in front of Henry and a second coffee cup directly in front of Eliza. Henry touches his cup and says to Eliza, "Do this!" She responds by touching the cup in front of her; she does not reach across the table and touch Henry's cup.

Let us describe what has happened using the terms defined above and shown in the slippage diagram (figure 1.1). First, variabilization transforms the concrete idea "the cup in front of Henry" into the schema "the cup in front of person X." (Abstraction is not needed in this case, because "cup" is already a basic-level concept in Rosch's sense.) Next, this schema is transported to the new framework (Eliza's side of the table) and becomes, en route, "the cup in front of Eliza." This is perfectly compatible with Eliza's situation, and so it is where things stop; she simply touches the cup in front of her. Eliza's response involves export and transport slippage but no import slippage (conceptual slippage).

Now we modify the example slightly. Suppose that instead of a cup, Eliza has a glass in front of her. As before, Henry touches the cup in front of him and says, "Do this!" In response, Eliza touches the glass in front of her.

Unlike the former scenario, this one does involve conceptual slippage. The same export and transport slippages as occurred in the previous scenario occur in the present one as well. However, there is an additional slippage in this example: "Cup in front of Eliza"—the transported schema resulting from the first two stages of slippage—cannot be literally applied on Eliza's side of the table, and so under this pressure it slips to the close notion "glass in front of Eliza." This is real conceptual slippage, since the concept "cup" was dislodged, and then it slipped to the closely related concept "glass."

In both of these scenarios, it is important to note that the slippages occur unconsciously. The notion that all of these processes occur at a subcognitive level is one of the recurrent themes in this book.

If our desire to classify, categorize, label, and understand is the driving motor of metaphor and analogy, slippage is the means by which we accomplish this smoothly, almost invisibly. Slippage is so deeply a part of the mechanisms of thought that, unless explicitly alerted by the use of words like "literally" (compare the expression "Do this!" with "Do *literally* this!"), most people are completely unaware that anything like analogy-making is actually going on when they respond, for example, to a "Do this!" challenge.

This is an important point and emphasizes the ubiquity of conceptual slippage at all levels of human thought. Even though Tabletop is in the business of doing only "simple" analogies—what could be simpler than finding correspondences between objects on a table?—I believe that the mechanisms underlying such prosaic analogy-making are the same as those that allow us to make more grandiose analogies, such as seeing Afghanistan as the "Vietnam of the Soviet Union." This point has been argued at length by Hofstadter in *Metamagical Themas* (Hofstadter 1985a).

Our perception of a given category as being the same as, or similar to, another is a direct consequence of our being able to sense, by means of some internal, intuitive metric, how "far apart" categories are. Algorithms designed to calculate conceptual distance date back to Thurstone (1927). In the early sixties, Roger Shepard (1962) developed a spatial model of conceptual similarity that relied on the now widely used technique of multidimensional scaling. Many other investigators have studied the question of conceptual distances between categories (Tversky 1977; Smith and Medin 1981; Nosofsky 1984), and, even though a number of significant problems with spatial similarity models have arisen (Tversky, 1977; Goldstone, Medin, and Gentner 1991), the basic notion of a metric on the space of categories is almost universally accepted—indeed, it proves central to the notion of slippage. The closer together two categories are in an individual's mental "category space," the more likely the one is to slip into the other. A second notion of paramount importance in the present model is that the distances between categories vary depending on context.

1.4 The Importance of Context

Before any discussion of the importance of context, it is important to clarify the notion of "situation." Situations can be anything from simple objects like an apple or a snowflake to complex events like a civil war or an attempt to fly to the moon. I argue that humans are doing essentially the same thing when they recognize two different apples as both being members of the category "apple" or when they describe Afghanistan as the "Vietnam of the Soviet Union" (or even when they recognize that recognizing two apples as being essentially the same and calling Afghanistan the "Vietnam of the Soviet Union" are, in essence, the same thing). This point is similar to one made by Glucksberg and Keysar (1990), who propose that metaphors are comprehended via a more elementary process of categorization.

Context is intimately and integrally a part of the representation that we build of a situation. Representations in short-term memory would, presumably, be derived from the corresponding concepts in long-term memory. I believe, however, that it is impossible to design "context-independent" representations of real-world objects or situations to be used in the computer equivalent of short-term memory. The hope of those who do not share this point of view is that a single (possibly gigantic, very complex) representation of, say, a table could be brought from long-term memory into short-term memory and be used, unmodified, by the program for whatever situations it happens to be facing.

For example, suppose a program were equipped with a context-independent set of criteria of the following sort to allow it to recognize tables:

- has three or more legs
- has a flat, horizontal surface at its highest point
- is made of a hard material, such as wood, metal, or plastic
- is bigger than a bread box
- weighs less than a ton
- was made by human beings

In such a case, there would be certain objects that, although clearly perceived by human beings as tables, would never be classified as such by the program. For example, if a large rock in an Alpine meadow were covered with a tablecloth and set with silverware, Wedgwood china, candles, and a large platter of roast duck and roast potatoes, it would certainly count as a table, even though under most circumstances it would be indistinguishable from any other Alpine rock.

The number of possible ways in which a "single" situation can be viewed is so vast that it is implausible—and probably impossible—that the mind could store in long-term memory a single gigantic structure that would anticipate all possible ways that situation might have to be represented in short-term memory. It is far more reasonable to assume that representations in short-term memory are built by borrowing on the fly from the store of concepts in long-term memory, and that their size and content are functions of the context in which they are found. Three short examples will suffice to illustrate the centrality of context in representation-building.

1. The representation of "dog" that is built in short-term memory when I am talking about a pack of dogs is more skeletal than the representation of "dog" I use if someone says to me, "Think of a dog." In the latter case, my representation is more complete, having features like eyes, a shiny coat, a wet nose, a wagging tail, drooping ears, a loud bark, and so on. Perhaps this representation in short-term memory of "dog" is deeply influenced by the dog I once had as a child. However, in the expression "a pack of dogs," all but a few of the details in "dog" vanish, leaving a sparser representation, to be sure, but one that is perfectly adequate for the purposes of understanding the expression.

2. Assume you are reading a travel brochure about summer vacations in Italy and you come across the following heading: "Florence, the San Francisco of Italy." Central to the representation of Florence that would be built in short-term memory would be the notion of cultural attractions, pretty scenery, and so on. However, the representation of Florence that you would build had you seen the identical sentence in a magazine for gay people would be very different: it would undoubtedly focus on facts about the social acceptance of homosexuals. Then again, had it appeared in a magazine for cyclists, it would have conjured up images of hilliness.

3. I had just hung up the phone after talking to a friend in Belgium. We had been speaking French, and therefore French was still active in my mind. I picked up an American news magazine and began reading an article about incendiary bombs. In the article I came across the expression "aimable clusters" and it puzzled me. I kept thinking, "I wonder what's so *friendly* about them? Must be military irony." (*Aimable* is a very common French word meaning "friendly.")

But it was only when I thought, "Shouldn't that be spelled 'amiable'?" that it hit me that the word I was looking at had nothing to do with friendliness but was, in fact, "aim-able," meaning "can be aimed." There could be no doubt that the French-language context had caused that particular error in my interpretation of the word "aimable."

There is nothing unusual about these examples. They are perfectly normal outcomes of a mental architecture in which concepts adapt to context.

1.5 The Continuum from Recognition to Analogy-Making

Although the research presented in this book deals with analogy-making, the work is best viewed as part of a broader research endeavor—namely, presenting a unified framework in which categorization, recognition, and analogy-making can be seen as being, if not precisely the same, related in a very deep and essential way. They are all types of high-level perception and, I believe, are a product of the same underlying mechanisms.

At first blush, it would seem that recognizing one's husband with his beard shaved off (or recognizing one's husband at all) has very little in common with making an analogy between the United States involvement in Vietnam and Soviet involvement in Afghanistan. But if we examine this more closely, we see that the two vary along a single common dimension—namely, degree of slippage. Small amounts of slippage are perceived as categorization (*very* small amounts of slippage are, in fact, not perceived at all—we say that two situations are "literally" the same under those circumstances, even though, strictly speaking, this is of course not possible), whereas large amounts of slippage, especially when conceptual slippage is involved, are perceived as analogy-making.

At this point I wish to make clear a distinction that is important to any discussion of analogy-making. When people talk about analogy-making, they generally mean one of two things: either they mean retrieving from memory (or constructing) some situation that bears some resemblance to the one under discussion (Roger Schank refers to acts of retrieval of analogous situations as "reminding incidents" [Schank 1983]) or they mean recognizing the similarity between two already-given situations. In the latter case, no new situation is retrieved from memory.

In the case of reminding experiences, the expression "That reminds me of ..." is a device usually designed to focus attention on particular aspects of a situation—those aspects that, presumably, the speaker feels are most important. In essence, the speaker is saying, "The essential features of the present situation are really the same as the ones in this other situation." The mechanisms of this type of memory-retrieval process, however interesting, are not the subject of this book. I am concerned, rather, with the mechanisms underlying the recognition that two *already*-given situations are "the same." From now on, therefore, when discussing analogy-making I will be referring to the recognition, and not to the retrieval, of analogies.

Viewing everything, from the most elementary recognition tasks to the most abstract analogies, as being simply different forms of a single cognitive process allows us to better appreciate why there may be general agreement in the recognition of, say, a specific object as a member of the category "apple" (only a small degree of "slippage," constituted, in this case, by a very slight divergence between the concept "apple" stored in long-term memory and the representation in short-term memory of a particular apple) but significant disagreement over the validity of the statement "Mikhail Gorbachev is the Abraham Lincoln of the Soviet Union" (because of both leaders' overriding desire to hold their countries together). In the latter case, many facets of each situation have to slip in order to make this particular analogy, and each of these slippages (an analogy in its own right) carries with it some risk of disagreement. For example, in order for the Gorbachev-Lincoln analogy to work, "the pre–Civil War United States" must slip to "the Soviet Union in 1990." In order for *this* analogy to work, "the antebellum South" must slip to "the non-Russian western republics of the Soviet Union, especially the Balkans." Obviously, there is much room for disagreement with each of these analogies. In short, the greater the total number and importance of slippages in an analogy, the greater the potential for disagreement over its validity.

As I have already said, there is a metric on the space of concepts in each human mind. Although no two such metrics are identical, they generally have enough resemblance to allow communication among individuals (Hofstadter 1979, pp. 373–379).

A fundamental and simple principle of conceptual slippage is that the smaller the distance between two concepts, the more likely people are to slip the one into the other. Another fundamental, and equally simple, principle is that any particular context temporarily brings some concepts closer together. When these two principles are combined, they imply that in each specific context, certain slippages are facilitated.

For instance, if you happen to spill coffee on your shirt after dinner, you might think, "Good thing I wasn't drinking tea—tea stains" ("coffee" slips to "tea") or "Good thing that wasn't spaghetti sauce: it *really* leaves a stain" ("coffee" slips to "spaghetti sauce"). On the other hand, if you had just changed the oil in your car before having your coffee, you might think, "Good thing that wasn't dirty motor oil" ("coffee" slips to "motor oil"). In this case, even though the *default* conceptual distance between "motor oil" and "coffee" is quite large, the context of having just changed your oil brought them temporarily closer together, because both coffee and dirty motor oil are black and hot (motor oil is usually changed when warm or even hot).

The frightening Tylenol murders of a decade ago, in which an anonymous killer somehow managed to introduce cyanide into the painkiller in the gelatin capsules, provide another good example of conceptual slippage (Hofstadter 1985c). The Food and Drug Administration reacted to these horrifying murders by requiring certain products (and not others) to be packaged in new, safer ways. The pharmaceutical industry, in particular, was required to adopt new packaging procedures. The fruit-and-vegetable industry, on the other hand, was not; the FDA apparently felt that this industry was much less at risk than the pharmaceutical industry. Why? Because Tylenol is a painkiller and it therefore made sense (in the logic of conceptual slippage) to assume that if a deranged individual were going to attempt to commit the "same kind" of murder, he or she might tamper with Bayer aspirin (conceptually very close to Tylenol capsules) or Contac capsules (i.e., cold remedies, which are still conceptually relatively close to Tylenol capsules), or even with Pepto-Bismol tablets (i.e., general remedies for when you are feeling ill). However, few people in the FDA felt that would-be killers would be likely to slip "Tylenol capsules" to "oranges" or to "apple cider," even though, strictly speaking, it would have been as easy, if not easier, for someone to inject cyanide into an orange or into a bottle of juice as to tamper with a bottle of cold pills.

1.6 The Ubiquity of Analogy

The best way to illustrate the ubiquity of conceptual slippage in human language, thought, and action is to present a number of examples of slippages, ranging from ordinary to exalted. Many of these examples are, in fact, so prosaic that at first glance it is hard to recognize the conceptual slippages involved. And that is precisely the point. We will return to some of these examples during the course of this book.

1.6.1 A Brief Taxonomy of Slippages and Analogies

To attempt to present a detailed taxonomy of slippages and analogies, even if this were possible, is beyond the scope of this book. I do, however, present a number of broad categories of analogies and slippages.

Recognition This involves slippage along the smallest number of dimensions. An individual apple is recognized as belonging to the category "apple." There is, of course, never an exact "pixel-by-pixel" match between any instance in the world and the corresponding concept in long-term memory, but the divergence is so small that the instance observed—a McIntosh apple, say—is automatically and effortlessly recognized as an apple. In an adult mind, the recognition of the McIntosh as an apple adds nothing new to the concept "apple" in long-term memory. There is "slippage" in the sense of an imperfect match with the representation in long-term memory, but there is not a large enough divergence for *concepts* (like identifiable features) to be slipped.

Generalization Assume that the only corn you had ever seen was sweet corn. Whenever you saw an ear of sweet corn, it would be recognized as the concept "corn." Nothing new is added to the concept of corn in long-term memory by seeing yet another ear of sweet corn. However, the first time you encountered multicolored Indian corn, there would be a significant divergence between the instance in the world and the prior concept in long-term memory. But "Indian corn" matches the already-existing concept of corn along enough dimensions for it to be incorporated into the category "corn." There is slippage of the concept "yellow" to "multicolored," and the concept of corn is thereby enriched. Henceforth, whenever you see ears of Indian corn, you will recognize them as belonging to the category of corn.

Superficial similarity This notion is due to Gentner, Forbus, Falkenheiner, and other researchers involved in the Structure-Mapping Engine research (Gentner 1983; Falkenheiner et al. 1989). The idea is that only "superficial" attributes of the two situations in correspondence are mapped to one another—for example, color, size, temperature, weight, and so on—and that at a deep, abstract level, the situations still have little or nothing in common. Situations that share merely superficial similarities are not recognized by Forbus, Falkenheiner, and Gentner as being analogous. *Real* analogies—or, at least, good analogies—according to this view, require mappings between *relations* in each of the corresponding situations. Holyoak and Koh (1987) have also addressed the issue of surface similarity in the context of analogical transfer.

Pluralization Pluralization lies on the boundary between category-making (i.e., generalization) and analogy-making. Consider the question "Do you have any Melanie Mitchells in your research group?" Not only is a new category created ("people having the characteristics of Melanie Mitchell") but there is an implied analogy between Melanie Mitchell and other people. Some pluralizations are so firmly established that the original individual is hardly remembered other than as defining the name of the category. For instance, "He is a real Casanova" or "Don Juans are a dime a dozen in Hollywood." Not too many people know much about the original Casanova or Don Juan—but that does not matter. All one *needs* to know about Casanova is that he was a real Don Juan (and vice versa).

Pluralization is probably closer to the categorization end of the spectrum than to the analogy-making end. However, there is a closely related phenomenon illustrated by the sentence "President Clinton is another John Kennedy," in which there is more of a feeling of making a genuine mapping between two distinct entities at roughly the same level of abstraction (as opposed to a mapping between an entity and an abstract category). This form of pluralization seems closer to full-blown analogy-making in the sense that Gentner et al. define it.

"Me-too" analogies The name comes from the following paradigmatic example of a me-too analogy. Two friends are having a beer together. One says, "I'm going to pay for my beer." The other replies, "Me, too." Clearly the latter individual does not mean to pay for the *friend's* beer but rather for his *or her own* beer. In me-too analogies, the mapping between the two separate frameworks is so obvious that people seldom even recognize that this is a form of analogy-making. This is arguably analogy-making at its most prosaic and has much in common with many of the Tabletop analogy problems that form the basis of this book. These analogies involve unconsciously extracting a template from one situation (often centered on someone else) and automatically applying it to another situation (often centered on oneself). One of the central characteristics of me-too's is their spontaneity. This type of analogy has been discussed extensively by Hofstadter (1991).

Supertranslation These are very similar in flavor to pluralizations, except that they are characterized by the template: "*B* is the *A* of *Y*," which means that in framework *Y*, *B* plays "the same" role as *A* plays in an unspoken but implicit framework, *X*, presumed to be obvious from context. Two examples are Lenin's remark "Coal is the bread of industry" and the advertising slogan "Stolichnaya is the Cadillac of vodkas." It might appear that the supertranslation "*B* is the *A* of *Y*" is nothing more than the "proportional" analogy "*A* is to *X* as *B* is to *Y*." However, the special feature of supertranslations, unlike pluralizations, is that they imply that the role of *A* in framework *X* is *so* obvious that it does not even need *hinting* at—not even to the extent of naming *X* at all. Thus the role of *A* is in effect genericized in the act of supertranslation. For example, if one were to call Bobby Fischer "the Einstein of chess," this would implicitly convert Einstein the *individual* into a kind of generic, very close in feeling to calling someone "another Einstein" or referring to the "Einsteins of the next few centuries." Einstein's particular discipline of physics is, in such cases, considered not only obvious but, in fact, quite irrelevant.

Caricature analogies This type of analogy is used in explaining a complex or hard-to-understand situation, or in attempting to convince somebody of a controversial point. Caricature analogies are usually retorts to a viewpoint the speaker finds silly and wishes to ridicule. Consequently, they often begin, "Oh, come on! *That* would be like," followed by a completely hypothetical situation made out of a combination of stereotypes and extreme cases. For example, in response to someone's saying, "Edward Teller is the greatest physicist of all time," someone might indignantly reply, "Oh, come on! That would be like saying *Salieri* [sneering tone at this point] was the greatest composer of the classical period!" In an ideal case, the manufactured analogous situation is always hypothetical, simple, very clean, and manufactured from stereotypes or extreme examples (e.g., Hitler, Einstein, Marilyn Monroe, Cadillacs, Mount Everest, a million dollars, the Empire State Building, etc.). Ideally, a caricature analogy also highlights just the properties of the original complex situation that its inventor wants to stress and is constructed in such a way that the mapping between it and the original situation is patently obvious, thus hopefully preventing hearers from feeling the similarity is forced. Unfortunately, however, this is usually the place where caricature analogies break down.

Explanatory analogies This type of analogy has the same purpose as caricature analogies do except that the analogous situation is not a hypothetical and extremely simple one deliberately manufactured from stereotypes and extreme examples but is a genuine, factual situation. For example, a gay male might say to a heterosexual male friend, "I feel about Jim the way you feel about Sally." Or someone might say, "The secession of the Baltic States from the Soviet Union is like the secession of the South from the Union in 1861." In each case, a hard-to-understand situation is explained (or understood) in terms of a situation that may be equally complex but is more familiar and better understood.

Reminding incidents One situation reminds us of another situation stored in long-term memory. The retrieval of the latter situation from memory is triggered by some set of salient (generally, but not always, abstract) characteristics of the first situation. These analogies are most closely related to explanatory analogies, because the situations retrieved are not hypothetical, manufactured examples but real examples from our experience. However, explanatory analogies, unlike simple reminding incidents, have a purpose—generally, to persuade someone of something or to clarify some situation. Reminding incidents usually have no explicit explanatory purpose, even if they might be used subsequently to explain a particular situation. At the time they occur to us, there is no thought of purpose.

1.6.2 A Collection of Examples

In this section, I present some of my favorite examples of analogies of various sorts, drawn from my own collection and those of a few friends. The intention of this list is to give readers a feel for the ubiquity of analogy-making. In particular, I hope readers will come away with the feeling that analogy-making is a very large superset of what is classically considered to be analogy-making (e.g., the "exalted" analogies involving the Iran-contra affair and Watergate, Afghanistan and Vietnam, the Rutherford atom and the solar system, and so on). Thus, many of the examples below involve mappings so prosaic that they would rarely, if ever, be thought of as analogies. Yet all of the following examples essentially differ along only one dimension—namely, the amount of slippage that they involve.

We begin with a group of analogies in which the amount of slippage is so small as to be almost unnoticeable. Many people would dispute that the term "analogy" should be applied to them at all.

- A child learns to recognize her mother. This is recognition in its purest form. The same image of the child's mother never appears on the child's retina twice, and yet she learns to recognize her.
- A child learns to recognize the image in the mirror in front of him as being an instance of the concept "me." This is a case of generalization, because the child extends his concept of himself to include the image in the mirror in front of him. There is a slippage of the child's concept of self to the concept of his image in the mirror.
- A closely related example that requires slightly more slippage is when a child learns to use the pronouns "you" and "me" correctly. This is harder than it may seem, since adults around a child refer to the child either by name or as "you." It is therefore not uncommon for very young children to believe initially that "you" *always* refers to themselves. They do this, presumably, because they (incorrectly) slip their name to the pronoun "you." When a parent says to a child, "Susan, you are such a good girl!" the child associates "you" (rather than the pronoun "me") with "Susan," her name. She will be likely to come out with utterances like "You are hungry now," meaning that she herself is hungry.
- Someone refers to another person by a name taken from literature: "Alice became a real Miss Haversham after her divorce"; "Andrew is a real Scrooge." These are quintessential pluralizations in that an individual is being treated as (or converted into) a category. It is of no importance whether the original individual is fictional or real.
- Someone says that Jonas Salk, the discoverer of the polio vaccine, is "no Watson and Crick." This example of pluralization is particularly interesting because it groups "Watson and Crick" together as a single entity suitable for mapping onto a single individual. Such a one-to-many mapping may seem surprising, but it is more common than one might suspect. The following examples may sound more familiar: "If I were the computer science department, I sure wouldn't give her tenure" and "If I were his parents, I wouldn't buy him a bicycle until he was a little older."
- Here is an example that lies somewhere between generalization and analogy-making. Most physicists would consider the red shift, used to determine the speed at which a galaxy is receding, to be a trivial generalization of the Doppler effect. The red shift, they would claim, simply *is* the Doppler effect, applied to electromagnetic waves. And yet, it is equally accurate to view this as an insightful analogy because of the slippages ("sound" slips to "light," "air" to "vacuum," and, if one knows more physics, "longitudinal" to "transverse"). Understanding the red shift as the Doppler effect involves making an analogy between waves that require air (or some material medium) to propagate and waves that need no medium at all. This is a deep slippage.

The following is a series of six me-too analogies intended to illustrate increasing amounts of slippage in the same template. Each of these examples involves effortless, spontaneous slippage. In the progression from the first me-too example to the last, there is an increasing amount of slippage, of the export, the transport, or, especially important, the import (conceptual) variety.

- A friend and I are drinking beer of the same brand (say, Coors). She says, "I like Coors." I reply, "Me, too." The only slippages here involve variabilization to "X likes Coors" and then the transport of this schema to my framework, giving "I like Coors."
- A friend and I are again drinking Coors beer together. She says, "I like this beer." Since I know we are both drinking the same brand, I take her remark as a reference to the brand in general rather than to just her particular glassful of it, and I reply, "Me, too." This is just like the previous example except that there is abstraction in addition to variabilization—specifically, "this beer [the one that I am drinking this very moment]" was abstracted to "Coors beer."
- A friend and I are drinking beer, but this time *not* of the same brand. She says, "I like this beer." I reply, "Me, too." This is slightly more complex, because we are referring not to the brand but to the specific glassfuls in front of us. Thus there is an additional slippage of *her* instance of beer (i.e., the beer in her glass) to *my* instance of beer (i.e., the beer in my glass). In other words, the original utterance is first slipped into the schema: "X likes the beer in front of X" and then this is transported to my framework by rebinding the variable X to "me." There is a bit more slippage than in the first example, because there are two occurrences of the variable X in the schema, both of which have to be rebound.
- A friend and I are having a beer. She says, "I'm going to go pay for my beer." I say, "Me, too." In this case, *her* beer slips to *my* beer. This is very much like the former example in which "in front of" is replaced by "belonging to." The amount of slippage is the same as in the previous example.
- My friend is drinking a beer, and I am drinking a Coke. She says, "I'm going to go pay for my beer." I say, "Me, too." Here, the same export and transport slippages as before happen, but also, because of the mismatch between the schema and my framework, "beer" slips to "Coke," as the schema comes down from its abstract plane to my concrete situation. This is the first instance of conceptual slippage in this series, and it produces the following idea in my mind: "I am going to go pay for my Coke." But rather than say that, I simply say, "Me, too." The analogy is made unconsciously—both by me in generating this remark and by my friend in understanding it.
- My friend and I are at a local bar. She is having a beer, and I have just eaten a plate of French fries. She says, "I'm going to go pay for my beer." I say, "Me, too." In this last case, the conceptual slippage of "beer" to "French fries" starts to become a little strained (or humorous) but would still not require the least explanation to be understood. The only difference between this scenario and the one involving paying for a Coke is that the conceptual distance between "beer" and "French fries" is considerably greater than between "beer" and "Coke."

The next example is another me-too analogy involving a rather different type of situation. However, it illustrates exactly the same principles as in the series above.

- Matt, a teenager, says to his girlfriend, Susan, "You know, my father is always calling me 'Dave' and my brother 'Matt.'" Susan replies, "Oh, yeah—mine does that, too." In this me-too analogy, Susan certainly does *not* mean that *her* father confuses Matt with his brother Dave. Nor does she mean that her father calls her "Dave" and her brother "Matt." In fact, she does not have a brother—she has a sister—and she means that her father often accidentally swaps her name, "Susan," and her sister's name, "Joan."

The most likely explanation of this remark is that abstraction and variabilization produced in Susan's mind the abstract schema "X's father often reverses the names of X and X's brother." Transport slippage then put this into Susan's framework by re-binding the variable X to "Susan," giving, "My [Susan's] father often reverses the names of me and my brother." Finally, because this transported schema still did not quite fit the particular situation, a conceptual slippage completed the process, replacing "brother" with "sister."

In the following analogies, the canonical slippages are *refused*. It is worth noting that our expectations for the natural slippages are so strong that when they are refused or when some alternate slippages are made, their very unexpectedness sometimes makes us laugh (Hofstadter and Gabora 1990).

• Signs put up by the California Highway Patrol warn drivers, "Watch your speed—we are." When we read this sign, the normal me-too slippage in the second sentence—that is, the one that gives the interpretation "We, the police, are watching our own speed"—is the one that first occurs to us. But this interpretation clearly does not fit the context of the police preventing speeding. The normal slippage is thus refused in order to understand the sign. It is quite possible that the intent of the sign is not just to warn but to mildly amuse drivers and thus to reduce the sternness of the image attached to the police in general.

• A friend was visiting her family in Plainfield, Indiana, a suburb of Indianapolis. They were talking about how grade schools had changed over the years. Her mother, who grew up in Newark, New Jersey, remarked, "When I was a schoolgirl, we used to take day trips to New York. It's really a shame they don't do that sort of thing in the schools here." My friend replied, "Mom, they couldn't do that—New York's too far!" At the time, this seemed like an amazing reaction, given that the obvious parallel would seem to be to take day trips to Indianapolis, not New York City. However, my friend later explained what had run through her mind. She said that for a fleeting instant, she had had the image of taking schoolchildren to Indianapolis, but that in her mind, Indianapolis was so dull compared with New York City that the whole idea just did not work for her—it simply was not analogous. She then flirted for a split second with the idea of taking Plainfield schoolchildren on field trips to Chicago or Cleveland, but those cities seemed only a bit better than Indianapolis, and, besides, they were already so far away that one might as well simply go the whole distance. And so she made a remark that made her appear amazingly literal-minded, whereas beneath the surface there had in fact occurred quite a bit of fluid thinking.

• Someone pointed out to the psychologist George Miller that an orange crate in a field covered with a tablecloth, dishes, glasses, and flatware would make a pretty good table. Miller refused the analogy, saying "An orange crate is an orange crate; it is not a table" (Cognitive Neuroscience Summer Institute, Dartmouth, 1990). In other words, Miller refused to slip "orange crate" to "table" even though the presence of a tablecloth, dishes, and so on, on the crate would seem to make this slippage an extremely natural one. What did Miller mean by this refusal? He meant that the slippage from "orange crate" to "table" was just too much for him to make under any circumstances. For Miller, the orange-crate-to-table slippage would presumably make as much sense as dressing a dog up as a little child and claiming that the dog had become a little child. But certainly an orange crate is not an inviolate conceptual entity in people's minds. Even if the concept "orange crate" could not slip to "table," could it at least slip to "toy box"? This certainly would seem plausible.

Would Miller refuse to acknowledge that a saw under certain circumstances could be a strong member of the category "musical instrument"? And could a glass partially filled with water be a musical instrument? Are so-called "beanbag chairs" *in fact* beanbags and not chairs after all?

• Translation can be thought of as analogy-making between languages. The role of the translator is, insofar as is possible, to slip form and content in one language into "the same" form and content in another. The completely interwoven nature of form and content in poetry is precisely what makes it so hard to translate. It is very hard to find ways of slipping both form and content in such a way that both are satisfactorily preserved at once.

The bread and butter of sports on radio or television is caricature analogies. The following simple and colorful example gives us a clearer idea of just how dangerous it was for a pitcher to pitch fastballs to Hank Aaron.

• Curt Simmons, a catcher for the St. Louis Cardinals, once said of the player who hit more home runs than any other person in baseball history: "Trying to sneak a fastball by Henry Aaron is like trying to sneak the sun past a rooster" (Coffey 1983). Here, "Hank Aaron" slips to "a rooster," "a baseball" to "the sun."

Supertranslation is one of the most common rhetorical devices in attempts to persuade or to make vivid, and in other forms of argumentation. Here are some examples of supertranslation.

• Daniel Lambert, an Englishman who lived at the turn of the nineteenth century, was world-famous for his enormous weight: he measured 5 feet 11 inches and weighed 739 pounds. George Meredith, the famous Victorian poet and writer, once referred to London as "the Daniel Lambert of cities." Herbert Spencer, the Victorian social philosopher, called one of his contemporaries "the Daniel Lambert of learning."
• One of the largest German artillery pieces in World War I was nicknamed "Big Bertha." Then in World War II, the particularly sensitive microwave early-warning system developed by the British was called "the Big Bertha of radar." This is an instance of supertranslation, fitting the template, "*B* is the *A* of *Y*," where *A* has some particularly salient feature within its own domain (in this case, tremendous firepower) that is used to illustrate just how salient *B* is within *its* domain, *Y*.

A significant current in analogy research (Kedar-Cabelli 1985) assumes that analogy-making must be purpose-driven. However, reminding incidents generally seem anything but purpose-driven. They simply happen; they are not designed to explain, clarify, contest, or focus attention on a particular aspect of a situation. The examples below illustrate reminding incidents. All of them are clearly analogies between two situations, and none of them had any particular purpose. Nonetheless, after the fact, one could certainly use them as explanatory analogies in certain situations.

• I was discussing the supposed burning of the library at Alexandria in 642 and the reputed justification for it offered by the Moslem religious leader Caliph Omar, which was the following: either the knowledge was already in the Koran and consequently would be preserved anyway, or else it was not in the Koran, was therefore irrelevant, and ought to be destroyed. (The claim that he really said this, it turns out, was pure fabrication by thirteenth-century Christian theologians to vilify the Moslems, a practice in vogue at the time because of the recent Crusades.) In any event, this reminded me of the sack and massacre of Béziers by the Catholics at the beginning of the thirteenth century. The commander of the Catholic forces asked the local abbot how he and his men could distinguish heretics from Catholics. "Kill them all!" the prelate said. "God will sort them out." Thus in my mind, the "good books," whose contents were contained in the Koran and were thus not really destroyed by the fire, slipped to the "good people," whose souls would be preserved in Heaven in spite of dying at Béziers.

• Walking through a small village in the south of France early one morning, I disturbed a sleeping dog that awoke and began barking, arousing other dogs, who in turn began barking, until soon every dog in the village was barking its head off. I was reminded of spreading activation in a Hebbian cell-assembly. "Dog" slipped to "neuron," "village" slipped to "cell-assembly," and "contagious barking" to "spreading activation." Note that this reminding incident could, in a future discussion, very well be used as an explanatory analogy.

• I had to replace a lug bolt on the wheel of my car. The shiny new bolt stood in distinct contrast to the three other dull, slightly corroded bolts. The new bolt reminded me of a gold front tooth.

• I was showing a friend around Paris. When I pointed out the Tour Montparnasse, a huge skyscraper, I commented that its being built had caused a huge uproar about destroying the Paris skyline. I mentioned that a law was subsequently passed to prevent any other skyscrapers from being built and that this whole episode reminded me of the bombing of Hiroshima and Nagasaki. This explanatory analogy (and reminding incident) mapped the Tour Montparnasse, the first true skyscraper ever built in Paris, to the first two A-bombs ever dropped on cities. The severe damage done to the Paris skyline corresponded to the severe damage done to the cities of Hiroshima and Nagasaki. And in both cases, the severity of the damage prevented a repeat of the cause of the damage—in one case, the building of more skyscrapers in Paris; in the other, the dropping of more atom bombs.

• I was discussing the advantages of big cities with a foreign friend, and the topic of violence and other big-city problems came up. It spontaneously occurred to me that cities are like axiomatic reasoning systems, in that both are self-undermining. As soon as a city becomes big enough to be interesting, insoluble problems arise precisely because of its size. Similarly for axiomatic systems: Kurt Gödel showed that as soon as any such system becomes big enough to have any reasonable amount of power, insoluble problems arise precisely as a result of its power.

The following pair of examples illustrates the notion of what Gentner has called "superficial similarity." She would not consider these to be genuine analogies, since for her the sine qua non of an analogy between two situations is structure-mapping—in other words, mappings from relations in one situation to relations in the other. An alternate view, the one presented in this book, is that slippage (i.e., schema extraction plus transport slippage plus conceptual slippage), rather than structure-mapping alone, constitutes the basis of analogy making. The following two examples exhibit slippage—even if these slippages are between certain "superficial" aspects of each situation—and, as such, have the right to be called analogies.

- "The plane cruised through the night like a sliver of ice." (King 1986) Because of its silver color and long, narrow shape, an airplane bears a superficial resemblance to a sliver of ice. None of the deeper, "structural" properties of ice (the fact that it is used to cool things, melts, and becomes water, etc.) or airplanes (that they transport people, are fancy technical machines, etc.) are mapped in this analogy.
- Bob is called "a real giraffe" by his classmates. Here the only mapping is between two "superficial" characteristics of Bob and giraffes—namely, their height. (Almost the only salient thing for people about giraffes is their height.) On the other hand, what if Bob were called "a real wolf"? We would presumably be mapping the particular role that a wolf plays in its environment (predator of other animals) to the role that Bob plays in his social environment ("predator" of women). For Gentner, the first example would probably not be considered an analogy, whereas the second would. In the view that holds that slippage is the defining criterion of analogies, both of these examples would be analogies; the first would be a shallower analogy, but no less of an analogy for that.

One final analogy illustrates the fact that sometimes even though structural mappings may be entirely appropriate, the analogy nonetheless fails because of some other semantic constraint not reflected in the structure of the situations.

- Edmond Rostand's play *Cyrano de Bergerac* tells the story of the flamboyant poet-chevalier Cyrano, whose distinguishing feature was his very long nose. On *Saturday Night Live*, a black Cyrano was portrayed as having a very *wide* nose. Here "white" slipped to "black." And since the stereotypically big Caucasian nose is long, whereas the stereotypically big black nose is wide, a parallel and concomitant slippage of "long" to "wide" was carried out (personal communication from David Touretzky). We laugh because this slippage not only is unnecessary but violates the very essence of the character of Cyrano, whose most salient feature, independent of his skin color, the time period in which he lives, or the country he defends, is his *long* nose—one upon which birds can perch, as he himself says. It would be somewhat akin to making Père Goriot an indifferent father, Don Quixote a hard-bitten cynic, or Don Juan a gay recluse. In each case, no matter what the reason for the transformation, we have destroyed the essence of the original character.

1.7 Subcognitive Processes

As was pointed out in several cases above, analogies often bubble up, unbidden, from the depths of the unconscious. Even when one feels that one is consciously constructing an analogy (as in a caricature analogy), the "ingredients" are handed up to the conscious mind from an unconscious source below. It seems beyond dispute that the processes responsible for the generation and the comprehension of analogies are subcognitive and that the power of analogy making deeply depends on the parallel subcognitive nature of the brain.

The notion of myriad interacting subcognitive processes giving rise to high-level cognitive behavior is fundamental to this research. The issue of whether or not it is necessary for computer models of intelligence to be based on highly parallel subcognitive processes is arguably the most important philosophical question in AI research today. It is an issue that has divided the AI community relatively cleanly into two camps. This book is based on the unambiguous belief that programs will never achieve the flexibility of human cognition unless their behavior, like human behavior, is the emergent result of the interaction of many parallel unconscious processes.

The existence of inaccessible subcognitive processes is not a new idea in cognitive psychology. It dates at least from the early years of this century. Perhaps the first explicit recognition of the existence of subcognitive processes was made in about 1906 by the Würzburg introspectionists, headed by Oswald Külpe. The introspectionists realized that pure association alone, rather than any conscious process, was responsible for certain high-level cognitive acts. They believed that appropriately trained subjects could describe all of their high-level cognitive acts in terms of lower-level—but still conscious—processes (called "judgments") that constituted the basic substrate of cognition. The celebrated counterexample that brought the entire movement to a halt was Külpe's own instant translation of "Homo cogitat" into "der Mensch denkt." Külpe was incapable of describing any lower-level processes involved in his act of translation. The only reasonable conclusion that could be drawn was that there were processes acting below the perceptual threshold and that these processes beyond the reach of introspection were responsible for the translation. This realization brought a sudden end to their attempt to analyze cognition through introspection (Humphrey 1963).

Oddly enough, Sigmund Freud's highly influential theory of the unconscious motivations of human behavior did not inspire a counterpart in experimental psychology. Quite to the contrary, the behaviorist movement, with its explicit banishing of all notions of internal representations or processes, took hold. Gradually, however, by the end of the fifties, introspectionist-like protocols had returned to the fold of serious experimental psychology and were incorporated in early attempts to do cognitive modeling by means of computers. An especially noteworthy example of such reliance on protocols is the General Problem Solver (GPS) of Newell, Shaw, and Simon (1959).

Although Newell, Shaw, and Simon recognized the existence of subcognitive processes in human cognition, they denied that these processes needed to be included in a model of intelligent behavior. Theirs was a deterministic, top-down approach to artificial intelligence, an approach that held sway for two decades, through the sixties and the seventies. It is interesting to note that Walter Reitman, who originally worked with Newell, Simon, and Shaw, chose to deviate somewhat from the GPS approach in his Argus program (Reitman 1972), in which he made explicit use of simulated parallelism and associative mechanisms to control the flow of his program. More recently, work by connectionists (Rumelhart and McClelland 1985) has had an eroding effect on the notion that low-level processes are of no importance in producing high-level cognitive behavior. Connectionists maintain that the appropriate level at which the modeling of cognition should be studied is *below* the symbolic level described by Newell, Shaw, and Simon (in which, in essence, objects in the world correspond to symbols in a program) and *at or above* the level of neurons (many connectionists, rejecting the facile mapping of neurons onto their units, equate a unit with a Hebbian cell-assembly) (Smolensky 1988).

Tabletop, like its predecessor, Copycat (Mitchell 1990; Hofstadter and Mitchell 1991; Mitchell 1993), lies squarely between these two camps. Instead of being driven either in a rule-based, top-down way like GPS or in a purely bottom-up way like most connectionist models, Tabletop combines both top-down and bottom-up processing. These two types of processes continually interact, gradually allowing the program to build up a representation of the problem at hand.

The following chapters will give the details, in terms of both their philosophical justification and their actual implementation, of the Tabletop architecture and the microworld in which the Tabletop program runs.

Chapter 2
The Tabletop Microdomain

2.1 Microdomains in Analogy-Making

Microdomains have fallen out of favor in the AI community. This is particularly true in the case of research in analogy-making. Over twenty years ago, Thomas Evans (1968), one of the first people to attempt to model human analogy-making on a computer, used a microdomain—geometric shapes in various dispositions—but since that time, researchers have concentrated almost exclusively on real-world domains for modeling analogy-making.

At least on its surface, most current research in computer modeling of analogy-making involves real situations filled with real-world concepts and interactions among them. For example, Winston modeled analogy-making between stage plays and the real world (Winston 1975); Falkenhainer, Forbus, and Gentner's Structure-Mapping Engine (SME) constructs mappings between the solar system and the Rutherford atom, or between heat flow and water flow (Falkenhainer, Forbus, and Gentner 1989); Thagard and Holyoak's ACME discovers an analogy between midwifery and Socrates' teaching methodology (Holyoak and Thagard 1989); Kedar-Cabelli uses real-world situations in which goals are important (Kedar-Cabelli 1985); and so on. With the exception of Hofstadter and Mitchell's Copycat (Hofstadter 1984; Mitchell 1993) and Hofstadter and Meredith's Seek-Whence (Meredith 1986), computer modelers of analogy-making have eschewed microdomains. This, in my opinion, is an error.

Consider the way physics has progressed. To study the properties and behavior of matter in motion, Newton made great strides by treating bodies in space as points and ignoring the notion of friction. Progress in physics, whether it has involved the study of gases, electricity, heat, or subatomic particles, has always relied on the use of idealized models. Idealizations are used so that one does not have to take into account, at least initially, of all the myriad influences that might mask the essential properties being investigated. Once some of these properties have been described, the idealizing constraints on the system can gradually be relaxed to allow one to study the problem in a more general setting, in order to perfect the model.

This would seem to be an eminently reasonable way for the computer modeling of analogy-making to proceed. This "isolate-and-idealize" methodology was the justification for the letter-string microdomain used in the Copycat project. Just as in physics, far too much is going on in real-world analogy-making—for example, there are hundreds of thousands of categories involved, any of which might interact—for one to be able to develop a good understanding of basic mechanisms while remaining in unsimplified domains.

The Copycat domain was one of the first explicitly idealized domains to be used in the computer modeling of analogy-making since Evans's work in the late sixties. (The integer-sequence-extrapolation domain in Hofstadter and Meredith's Seek-Whence project was another.) In what follows, I will begin with a brief explanation of the Copycat domain. This will be followed by a detailed description of the Tabletop domain. One of the primary advantages of the latter domain is that it has more of a real-world feel to it. Tabletop is an attempt to move closer to real-world analogy modeling. Even so, Tabletop is still a far cry from the real world; the Tabletop domain is simple and very restricted. It does, however, use concepts (e.g., "fork," "knife," "cup," "salt shaker") that are slightly more "blurry-edged" and real-world than the concepts used in Copycat (e.g., "A," "B," "successor," "predecessor," "first," "last"). Most significantly, the relationships among concepts in the Tabletop domain are harder to formulate than those in the Copycat domain.

Let us begin by taking a brief look at the Copycat domain.

2.2 The Copycat Domain

The basic objects in the Copycat domain are the letters of the alphabet. Analogy problems in this world involve strings of letters, and all problems have the following form:

> "If **letter_string_1** changes to **letter_string_2**,
> then what does **letter_string_3** change to?"

An example of this type of problem would be this:

> "If **abc** changes to **abd**,
> then what does **pqr** change to?"

This is written, in short form, as

> **abc** ⇒ **abd**
> **pqr** ⇒ ?

Here, **abc** is called the "initial string" and **pqr** the "target string." The challenge is to "do the same thing" to the target string as was done to the initial string. The answer in this case seems fairly straightforward—namely, **pqs**. But this answer is not the only one possible. It is the answer one would give if one perceived the transformation of **abc** into **abd** in terms of the rule "change the rightmost element to its successor." If, on the other hand, we decided (unlikely, but possible) that the original transformation rule was "change the rightmost element to **d**," then we would give **pqd** as the answer. Even more unlikely (but still possible), if we concluded that the rule was "change all **c**'s to **d**'s," this would result in **pqr**. Or what if somebody thought the rule was "change the whole string to **abd**" (highly improbable, but still not absolutely impossible)? This rule would result in the answer **abd**. Finally, there are answers, like **xjxx**, that would never be given by any human. A logician might argue that this answer is every bit as "correct" as **pqs**, because rules certainly exist that would map **abc** to **abd** and **pqr** to **xjxx**. One such rule is "**a**'s and **b**'s always remain the same, **c**'s map to **d**'s, **q**'s map to **j**'s, and everything else maps to **x**, except **r**, which maps to **xx**." This rule, although "mathematically correct," is completely lacking in psychological plausibility and is therefore unacceptable.

People have evolved mechanisms that allow them to recognize regularities in their environment. These regularities include successorship (in the Copycat microdomain, for example, **b** is the successor of **a**), sameness (e.g., **kkkk**), alternation (e.g., **ababab**), and so on. We impose structure on the letter strings in the problem on the basis of these perceived regularities: we tend to group certain letters and not others, notice certain relationships and not others, find certain correspondences between letters (and groups of letters) and not others, and so on. These groupings, relationships, and correspondences are not, technically speaking, "right" or "wrong"; rather, they reflect the concepts present in our mind and the relationships between them.

In Copycat, Mitchell and Hofstadter studied how a particular set of concepts and relationships applied to letter-string analogy problems. In the Tabletop world, I will examine how concepts and the relationships among them are brought to bear on the various configurations of objects on the table. But whether it is the Copycat microdomain, the Tabletop microdomain, or some truly real-world domain that is being studied, it is a central tenet of this work that the underlying *mechanisms* of analogy-making are essentially the same, differing only in the number and complexity of the concepts and relationships involved.

This claim leads to the obvious question of the feasibility of scaling up. In Copycat there are only about fifty concepts—and this number includes the twenty-six letter categories—that play any role in the solution of a problem. The number of concepts in Tabletop is roughly the same, although, obviously, the concepts and the relationships among them are different.

Could the underlying architecture of these programs, at least theoretically, scale up to much larger domains—for example, those with a thousand, or even a hundred thousand, categories? Since this is one of the most important questions about this architecture, I will postpone detailed discussion of it until a later chapter. Suffice it to say that, unlike many other architectures designed to do computer modeling of analogy making (Winston 1975; Holyoak and Thagard 1989; etc.), the Copycat architecture has been designed specifically with scaling up in mind. In fact, it is probably fair to say that the Copycat architecture was inspired by the goal of scaling up. Its various mechanisms—in particular, those that allow it to focus its resources—should allow this architecture to scale up.

2.3 The Tabletop Domain

Tabletop does not attempt to discover analogies between political situations, concepts in science, or plots in literature. Rather, it operates in a microdomain called the Tableworld, consisting of ordinary table objects on an ordinary table. Imagine two people, Henry and Eliza, seated at a small table facing each other. Henry touches some object on the table and says to Eliza, "Do this!" Eliza must respond by doing "the same thing." In other words, she must find the object (or, possibly, the group of objects) that, from her vantage point, seems to correspond most closely to the object that Henry touched. She is required to touch a physical object. She is not free, for example, to simply touch a location on the table, although, strictly speaking, this could be a reasonable thing to do under some circumstances.

A human Eliza intuitively takes into account a number of factors when making her choice. These factors include the positions and orientations of the objects on the table, the categories to which they belong, their sizes, their functional associations with other objects (for example, cups and saucers are related in a way that cups and plates are not), and their participation in groups on the table. Each of these factors exerts some pressure on her decision. Some pressures are relatively context-independent (for example, the category to which an object belongs is not dependent on the categories, positions, and functionalities of the other objects on the table). Other pressures (such as the participation in groups) are evoked by the situation itself and cannot reasonably be anticipated either by a human Eliza or by a program simulating Eliza. Rather, they emerge gradually as the person or program develops a representation of the configuration of objects on the table. Finally, it is important to emphasize that Eliza, unlike a real human being, is not influenced by having done previous Tabletop problems. She begins each problem as if it were the first Tabletop problem she had ever seen.

2.4 Sample Problems

The best way to appreciate the often-subtle interplay of the various competing pressures is by considering a series of sample problems. I hope that by the end of this series the reader will begin to appreciate some of the complexity and subtlety of this domain. The objects on the table will be taken from the following palette of objects:

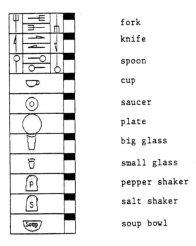

fork

knife

spoon

cup

saucer

plate

big glass

small glass

pepper shaker

salt shaker

soup bowl

Figure 2.1

Two series of problems are presented. There is a first series of thirteen table configurations followed by a second series of six. Each of the sets of problem constitutes a (roughly) escalating series, in which pressures present in the first problem are systematically varied, and new pressures are introduced and also varied.

Figure 2.2 shows the simplest possible table configuration. A single cup is on the table in front of Henry. Henry touches this cup. Eliza's response, the only possible response, is to touch the same cup.

In figure 2.3, by far the most likely response is for Eliza to touch the cup in front of her. In this case, there are two pressures: literal sameness (i.e., to touch Henry's cup) and position on the table. The latter pressure swamps the former, and she will generally touch the cup in front of her. Notice that it is not impossible for her to decide to touch the cup in front of Henry. While this is not excluded a priori from the set of

Figure 2.2

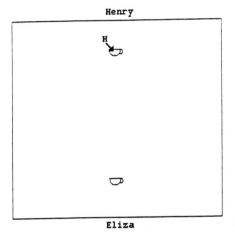

Figure 2.3

possible responses of either a human Eliza or the tabletop program, it is a very un-likely answer.

In figure 2.4, there is a new pressure: category membership. A cup and a glass are not members of exactly the same category but are, nonetheless, conceptually close in the sense that both objects are used for drinking liquids. This nonidentity puts a little more pressure on Eliza to reach across the table and touch the cup in front of Henry, but generally not enough for her to do so very often.

In figure 2.5, the object in front of Eliza is, in this context, radically different from the cup in front of Henry. The position pressure that would encourage her to touch the object closest to her is, generally, more than matched by the pressure produced by the differences in category membership. She will thus most often opt to touch the cup in front of Henry.

Although cups and saucers do not belong to the same category, they are strongly associated because, like knives and forks, they are used together. There is therefore

Figure 2.4

Figure 2.5

greater pressure in figure 2.6 for Eliza to touch the object in front of her than in the preceding situation, but perhaps a bit less than in figure 2.4.

In figure 2.7 aside from literal sameness (which is always a pressure), the two competing pressures are category membership and position on the table. In this situation, the chances are good that Eliza would touch the cup on her side of the table, diagonally opposite the touched cup.

There is a new pressure in the table configuration of figure 2.8—namely, "belonging to a group." Both the glass at the bottom and the touched cup at the top are part of a group of objects. With respect to the previous configuration, this makes it more likely that Eliza will touch the glass in front of her.

In figure 2.9 there is a good possibility of mapping the "bunch of objects to the right of the touched cup" onto the "bunch of objects to the right of the glass," even though the groups are not the same either in number or in makeup. This increases the

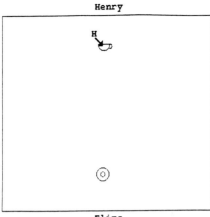

Figure 2.6

Figure 2.7

Figure 2.8

Figure 2.9

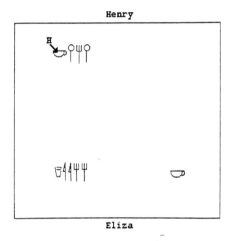

Figure 2.10

pressure on Eliza (relative to what it was in figure 2.8) to touch the glass on her side of the table.

In figure 2.10, there is a group of silverware to the right of the touched cup and another group of silverware to the right of the glass on Eliza's side of the table. Even though the groups are very dissimilar in composition, there is a good possibility that each of these collections will be grouped as "silverware" and then that the two of them, as such, will be put into correspondence. This further increases the pressure for Eliza to touch the glass, rather than the cup, on her side of the table.

In the configuration in figure 2.11, not only are there groups around the touched cup and the glass, but the groups are quite similar. For one thing, they have the same number of objects. For another, the objects surrounding the cup and the glass are the same, even if they are not arranged around the two objects in exactly the same way. This further increases the pressure on Eliza to touch the glass.

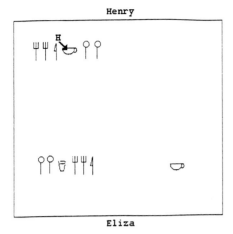

Figure 2.11

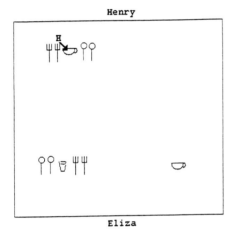

Figure 2.12

Take close note of this problem. We will be seeing it throughout the course of this work. It will serve to illustrate many of the features of the Tabletop architecture.

In figure 2.12, not only are the groups the same size but the subgroups (two forks, two spoons) are in corresponding positions on either side of the touched object and the glass. The overall pressure for Eliza to touch the glass is even stronger than in the previous configuration.

The glass in front of Eliza has now been replaced by a saucer, in figure 2.13. Does this shift the balance of pressures to favor the isolated cup? Possibly, but not necessarily; this is because, as was pointed out above, even though cups and saucers do not belong to the same category, they are conceptually related as "objects that are used together."

In figure 2.14, the replacement of figure 2.13's saucer by a saltshaker shifts the overall pressures even more significantly to the isolated cup in the lower right-hand

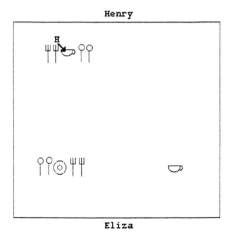

Figure 2.13

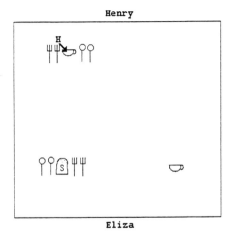

Figure 2.14

corner. In spite of the considerable pressure coming from the fact that the saltshaker and the touched cup are surrounded by identical groups of objects, the fact remains that a saltshaker and a cup are conceptually very dissimilar and have no obvious relationship between them, such as "used together."

This concludes the first series. We now go on to the second series, which is essentially the one referred to as the "Blockage" series in chapter 5 of this book.

Figure 2.15 is very much like the configuration in figure 2.4. The addition of a spoon to that configuration is unimportant. As before, Eliza will most probably touch the glass in front of her. If not, her only other reasonable choice would be to touch Henry's cup—certainly not to touch his spoon.

In figure 2.16, the spoon in the upper right-hand corner has been replaced by a glass. At first blush, the glass adds nothing "concrete" to the table configuration, no

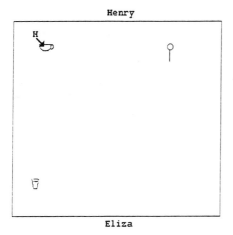

Figure 2.15

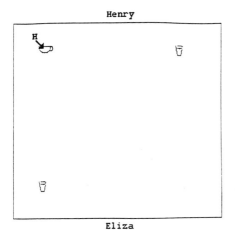

Figure 2.16

more than the spoon did: It is isolated from the other objects; its position on the table means that it certainly is not a likely candidate to be the object touched by Eliza; and, because it is isolated, it does not play a role in grouping. But something un-anticipated happens. Even though Eliza's attention is focused on Henry's cup rather than on the glass in the upper right-hand corner, she might nonetheless devote enough attention to it to notice a correspondence between that glass and the one in front of her. (She would certainly have noticed this correspondence had Henry touched his glass instead of his cup.) If so, this correspondence will then form part of her view of the tableworld. The two glasses will be seen as "grouped," in the sense that they correspond to each other. Eliza will be somewhat more hesitant to break this group by touching the glass on her side of the table.

The reason for this is that the cup/glass and the glass/glass correspondences are competing with one another. We humans are not capable of seeing the small glass in the lower left-hand corner of the table as corresponding *simultaneously* to both Henry's cup and the small glass in the upper right-hand corner of the table, any more than we can see both interpretations of the Necker cube simultaneously. We there-fore choose one correspondence or the other. If we choose to put the small glasses into correspondence, then we cannot also put Henry's cup in correspondence with Eliza's glass. This new, unanticipated pressure makes it considerably more likely that Eliza will wind up simply touching Henry's cup than in figure 2.15.

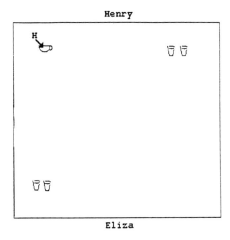

Figure 2.17

In figure 2.17, Eliza is much more likely than in figure 2.16 to notice that there are two identical pairs of objects on the table, diagonally opposite one another. Because of this stronger pairing, she is much more likely than she was in figure 2.16 to touch the cup that Henry originally touched.

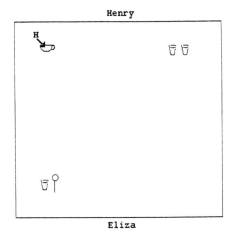

Figure 2.18

The two diagonally opposite groups in figure 2.18 are not identical any longer, so the resemblance between them is considerably weaker. These two groups may well not be perceived by Eliza as corresponding. This shifts the balance of pressures back to favoring the glass in front of Eliza.

Figure 2.19

In figure 2.19, there is very little likelihood that Eliza will put the saltshaker-plate group into correspondence with the glass and spoon. Thus, under these circumstances, she will be strongly inclined to touch the glass near her.

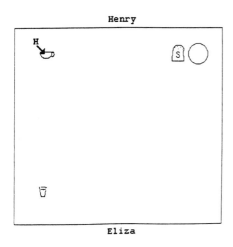

Figure 2.20

In figure 2.20, there is virtually no possibility that Eliza will see the group in the upper right-hand corner as corresponding to the glass in the lower left-hand corner. This means that the pressure is once again extremely strong for Eliza to touch the glass rather than Henry's cup.

This series of problems serves to give the flavor of the Tabletop microdomain. The problems illustrate the major types of pressure that can arise in this microdomain, and, in particular, they demonstrate that certain pressures can emerge that were un-anticipated at the outset. Figures 2.16 and 2.17 clearly illustrate this: correspondences that a priori have nothing to do with (i.e., are nowhere in the vicinity of) the touched object are discovered and ultimately come to play essential roles in determining the object to be touched.

These problems were designed to bring out and isolate certain general abilities or mechanisms necessary for analogy-making, which include the following:

Grouping of various parts comprising a situation This includes grouping objects (i) physically, because they are physically close together, and (ii) conceptually, because they belong to the same, similar, or related categories.

Generalizing to the correct level of abstraction This is related to conceptual group-ing (referred to above). Should we describe a particular object as a "cup" or, more generally, as a "liquid holder" or, still more generally, as "crockery"? This is an all-important decision when attempting to determine what corresponds to what in the two situations to be compared.

Ignoring the irrelevant ("implicit pruning") This is one of the key dimensions of analogy-making. A given situation almost always has a great many potential descriptions, a few of them relevant to the analogy to be made, most of them not. It is not good enough to attempt to enumerate all possible descriptions and then winnow out the bad ones. This technique is neither psychologically nor combinatorially plausible. Consider, for example, figure 2.10. It is likely in this problem that the silverware to the right of the touched cup and the silverware to the right of the glass on Eliza's side of the table will be grouped and put into correspondence. In this case, the number of pieces of silverware is irrelevant, as is the fact that there is a fork between the two spoons in the group on Henry's side of the table, or that there is a fork inside the group on Eliza's side of the table, and so on, and so forth, ad nauseam.

Consider another example, in which an isolated cup is directly in front of Henry, a second isolated cup is directly in front of Eliza, and three small groups of silverware are in the upper right-hand corner of the table. Not only is the lo-cation of the silverware very poor with respect to the touched cup in front of Henry, but the category "silverware" is not relevant to the problem at hand. The program should be able to ignore—not consider, then reject—the small groups of silverware. (This is why the term "implicit pruning" is used.)

In problem solving, humans operate in the same way. People focus on what is important and do not even notice the irrelevant. One example is navigating in a big city. It has been shown (Kaplan 1983) that people move from "land-mark" to "landmark" (for example, in Paris, some of these might be Notre Dame Cathedral, the Opéra, and the Place de la Bastille) and are frequently incapable of recalling anything between landmarks, even though the amount of time that they were exposed to the landmarks was probably considerably less than the time they were in the vicinity of the "irrelevant" buildings.

Focusing the program's resources This is related to the ability to ignore the irrele-vant. It is essential that the program have mechanisms to focus its resources in order to allow it to overcome problems of combinatorial explosion. These mechanisms, arguably the most important of the program, will be discussed in detail later. In general, the program must be endowed with mechanisms that give it a tendency to explore avenues that seem to be promising before exploring less promising avenues, without, however, completely squelching the exploration of unlikely pathways.

The basis for this exploration strategy is the way in which humans operate when confronted with a novel situation: we first explore the most likely avenues, and, if this fails to produce satisfactory results, we gradually expand our exploration to include the a priori more unlikely possibilities. Notice, though, that we humans do not do this in a deterministic or even systematic way. A common example among computer scientists is tracking down a nonobvious bug in one's code. Even though the chance that the problem is due to a bug in the operating system is extremely small, after a few unsuccessful attempts to ferret out the bug, even experienced programmers start to entertain the notion that, rather than their code's being at fault, it might be the operating system.

An authentic personal example of the interplay of top-down and bottom-up pressures in a situation of unpredictably expanding search happened to me one summer while I was fixing an old air conditioner on the porch of my home. At one point a small chisel about the size of a short pencil slipped out of my hand. If I had dropped the tool straight downward from the point where I had been using it, it would have fallen directly onto the grass about three inches below the air conditioner. As soon as I noticed that the tool was no longer in my hand, I looked for it in the most obvious place—namely, the grass immediately below where I was working. But there was no tool.

"How can that be?" I thought. "Perhaps I put the chisel in my other hand and dropped it farther from the air conditioner." So I expanded my search to the area below my right hand. Still no chisel.

"Maybe I put it in my pocket, but just don't remember doing so," I thought. So I checked. No chisel.

"Perhaps I put it back in the tool box," I mused, wondering at the same time why I would not have remembered doing so. But I checked anyway. Still no chisel.

Then I thought, "Just go back and look *carefully*." So I did. I went over every square inch of grass in a three-foot radius from the point where it had slipped from my hand. *Still* no chisel.

Then bottom-up thoughts even farther out on the fringe started coming. "Maybe a mole took it and carried it down its hole." This was immediately countered by a top-down, scientific, rational thought: "That's ridiculous." But then an inner voice said, "OK, you're right, that *is* ridiculous. *So where's the chisel?*"

Next I got a fork from the kitchen and dug through all of the earth within a three-foot radius of the air conditioner and pulled up every last bit of grass and vegetation. But still there was no chisel.

Even stranger explanations bubbled up. "Perhaps I struck a very strange blow to the chisel, causing it to leap out of my hand (unnoticed by me, however), sail through the air, and go down the drainpipe four feet from the air conditioner." Highly implausible, said my top-down, rational control mechanisms, but I could not escape the simple fact that the chisel had completely disappeared. So I stuck my hand down the drain, way down the drain. Still no chisel.

Then really weird thoughts started arriving, each time countered by top-down knowledge about how the world (presumably) worked, each time rebutted by the cold, hard fact that the chisel was nowhere to be found.

"What if it slipped off into another dimension …?"
"Cut it out. That's completely crazy."
"So where's the chisel, huh?"
"Hey, what if space aliens took it?"
"Now that's a super-crazy thought, Bob."
"Just tell me where the chisel is, then."
"Maybe God took it. That sure would be an interesting proof of God's existence. A bit disappointing, though, to become a true believer because of a silly little chisel. You would think the Lord would be slightly more grandiloquent about the whole thing."
"Cut it out. This is insane."
"Uh, so where's the chisel?"

Finally, I noticed a few horizontal cooling slots a few inches above the air-conditioner bolt I had been trying to chop off. I had an immediate paradigm shift. I knew without looking that the chisel had to have slipped inside the air conditioner above the bolt. Suddenly I felt incredibly foolish for having gone way, way out in my search space—so far out as to imagine fleetingly, if not consider seriously, space aliens and new dimensions to the universe as having caused my chisel to vanish.

2.5 Problems That Are Not Part of the Tabletop Domain

One of the goals of the project was to try to develop a microdomain that had a real-world feel to it. This meant that each of the table configurations had to be reasonably realistic, in the sense of looking like a real table that was set with plates, cups, saucers, saltshakers, pepper shakers, and silverware. In other words, this was not a patterns-and-shapes domain in which just *any* configuration was permissible. In a real-world situation, you would not find the objects on a table arranged in the shape of a Christmas tree or in strange, alternating patterns, for example. Figure 2.21 shows two disallowed table configurations.

2.6 Analogy Recognition versus Analogy Retrieval

What I mean by analogy-making is not necessarily what everyone thinks of when they talk about making analogies. The problem is that when many people refer to analogy-making, they are referring either to analogy *retrieval*, a memory-retrieval process whereby one situation brings to mind another situation stored in memory, or to analogy *construction*, whereby a fictional situation analogous to a given one is manufactured.

It is safe to say that it is virtually impossible to have any conversation of substance without some appeal to analogy retrieval or analogy construction. Analogies serve as a means of calling attention to a particularly important aspect of a situation. Typically, the retrieved (or constructed, fictional) situation is, by design, free of some of the confusing aspects of the generally more complex situation under discussion.

For example, a graduate student in the department where I work was killed in a caving accident, and a friend of his told me, "His parents suspect there must have

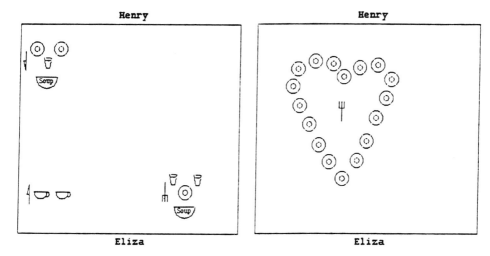

Figure 2.21

been a defect in the rope." As a person with many years of experience in handling ropes in the context of mountaineering, I replied, "That's like discovering some problem with your program and immediately suspecting the operating system." The purpose of my comment was to highlight the improbable nature of the parents' assumption and was immediately understood as such. In addition, my analogy served to give an indication of just *how* improbable I thought the defective-rope scenario was.

A number of researchers are concerned with analogy retrieval, among them Schank (1983), Gick and Holyoak (1983), Carbonell (1983), and Thagard (1989). Although their ideas are certainly related to the research described in this book, they have more to do with questions of memory storage and retrieval than with the issues I wish to deal with. The research I will be describing is concerned not with the organization of memory but with high-level perceptual processes (perceiving concrete things at abstract levels, perceiving relationships among objects, etc.) and with representations and correspondences between representations.

In Mitchell and Hofstadter's Copycat; in Falkenhainer, Forbus, and Gentner's SME; and in Thagard and Holyoak's ACME, among others, the program is *given* the two situations between which it must discover correspondences. There is no question of retrieval. This is true also in Tabletop, except that the two situations between which mappings will be formed overlap and blur on the table. There is, in some sense, only one situation, although people easily and intuitively break it into two situations (e.g., the objects on Eliza's half of the table and those on Henry's side of the table) unless the table configuration is a very strange one. In any event, memory retrieval is not a part of the Tabletop analogy-making process.

Much as I believe that the process of representation cannot be divorced from the process of analogy-making (Chalmers, French, and Hofstadter 1992), other researchers believe that the process of analogy-making cannot be divorced from the processes of analogy retrieval and construction. By contrast, it would seem to make sense to investigate analogy retrieval separately from analogy recognition, and this intuition is shared by numerous researchers studying the computer modeling of analogy-making. Only time will tell whether this will turn out to be correct or not, but I feel it is necessary to highlight these two different approaches to studying ostensibly the same phenomenon, in order to make clear the distinction between my work on analogy-making (i.e. analogy *recognition*) and other work being done in analogy retrieval and analogy construction.

2.7 Intra-domain versus Inter-domain Analogies

Most highly creative analogy-making occurs between situations in domains that appear to be remote from each other. (Note, however, that the overwhelming majority of analogy-making is of the completely banal sort: recognizing an apple as a member of the category "apple," uttering a me-too analogy as described in chapter 1, etc.) In these very creative analogies, the Rutherford atom is mapped to the solar system, water flow is mapped to electrical current, and so on. Even in the Copycat world, each problem involves two clearly distinct "domains"—namely, the initial string and the target string. Although both domains involve letters of the alphabet, they may be radically different from each other on other levels. For example, in the problem "If **abc ⇒ abd**, then **mrrjjj ⇒ ?**" **abc** and **mrrjjj** are so different from each other that they are like two domains conceptually very far apart. Thus, in Copycat, one can crudely simulate the conditions described above for highly creative analogy-making.

In the Tabletop domain, on the other hand, domains do not come so cleanly defined. There is simply a table with a set of objects on it seen from two different perspectives, suggesting to most people a breakup roughly (but not necessarily exactly) halfway across the table.

Since the initial situation and the target situation are one and the same in Tabletop, there is always the possibility of doing *literally the same thing*, a possibility not afforded in most analogies. This is comparable to a situation in which your friend says, "I'm going to pay for my beer," you reply "Me, too," and then you proceed to pay for *his* beer. Although unlikely, this scenario could occur under certain circumstances. Several examples of this basic theme are given in chapter 1 (e.g., the California Highway Patrol sign that reads, "Watch your speed—we are").

Initially, many people do not even think of the "Do this!" challenge as being analogy-making, any more than they think of "Me, too" remarks as being analogy-making. In most people's minds, the word "analogy" evokes lofty comparisons between highly intellectual domains. It does not include such prosaic things as touching objects on a table, or replying "Me, too" when your drinking partner says he is going to go pay for his beer, or determining which cheek to wipe when your girlfriend, pointing to her left cheek, tells you that you have splattered spaghetti sauce on yourself "right here."

One of the assumptions underlying the Tabletop architecture is that, although the analogy problems that the program solves are of the most prosaic sort, the *mechanisms* of representation-building and correspondence-building that go into solving these problems are identical to those used in solving "loftier" cross-domain analogies.

2.8 Learning

As indicated briefly at the end of section 2.4, the Tabletop program is not a learning program in the sense of learning over a long time span—in other words, it does not improve its performance based on past experience with a number of problems. This is not to say that this type of long-term learning is incompatible with Tabletop's archi-tecture; in fact, it might turn out to be relatively easy to implement. But, for the mo-ment, there is no attempt to model long-term learning.

Tabletop does not even improve its performance on already-tackled problems. No long-term learning mechanisms are built into the program that would, for example, adjust default conceptual distances in the Slipnet in reaction to a particular problem. This was a conscious design decision based on the belief that the mechanisms of learning can be investigated separately from the mechanisms of analogy-making. The work reported in this book is an attempt to model the flexibility of human concepts and, in particular, to model how flexible concepts interact in analogy-making. It is not an attempt to model how concepts originate or develop.

Although the program does not do long-term learning, it is quite reasonable to say that the program engages in short-term learning over the course of a single problem. At the beginning of a particular run, the program knows nothing about the particular configuration of objects on the table. It goes through a "learning process" in the sense that it quickly begins to perceive and adapt to the table configuration that it is presented with: it notices objects and groups of objects, builds representations for them, discovers correspondences, keeps some correspondences and rejects others, activates certain concepts, adjusts conceptual distances, and so on. In this sense, it is clearly learning about its environment. But when the run is completed, everything is reset to "zero" for the next run.

2.9 Goals of the Tabletop Project

The goals of this project must be defined, at least in part, with respect to the prior accomplishments of Hofstadter and Mitchell's Copycat project. Copycat and Table-top were written largely concurrently, although the work on Copycat had begun in earnest about two years before Tabletop and was completed in 1990. There is an ab-stract architecture common to both projects, which was discussed continually for at least two years in our research group. It is therefore reasonably accurate to say that Copycat and Tabletop are "the same project in different domains." In light of this, it is important to point out the major differences between Tabletop and Copycat.

2.9.1 The Issue of "Reasonable" Answers

Many of the fundamental demonstrations concerning the underlying architecture have been clearly and elegantly made by Mitchell (1993). In some sense, the Copycat microdomain lends itself to a more fine-grained analysis of the effects of certain mod-ifications of the architecture. For example, consider the following Copycat problem:

abc ⇒ **abd**
mrrjjj ⇒ **?**

Possible answers to this are **mrrkkk**, **mrrjjk**, **mrrjjjj**, **mrrddd**, and **mrjjd**, not to mention less plausible answers, such as **mrrjjj**, **abd**, and so on.

On the other hand, Tabletop problems generally have only one or two reasonable answers—sometimes three, but no more. For example, consider figure 2.11 again. This problem has only two reasonable answers and one implausible—but nonethe-less possible—answer. The two plausible answers are for Eliza to touch the glass in the lower left-hand corner or the cup in the lower right-hand corner. The implausible (but possible) answer is for Eliza to touch the cup Henry touched. Any other answers would seem strange indeed. For this reason, some of the detailed statistics-gathering done in the Copycat project does not make sense for Tabletop, simply because the limited number of plausible answers does not allow significantly different responses to be recorded when various parameters are changed. In Mitchell's program, adjusting certain conceptual pressures by slightly changing a problem in a number of different ways resulted in varying percentages of each of, say, six or seven different answers to a particular problem. In Tabletop this is not possible.

One of the goals of the Tabletop project is to demonstrate that the type of architecture used for the Copycat domain would also work for the Tableworld, a domain closer to the real world than that of Copycat. In order to demonstrate this, I will show how the program solves a variety of problems in a psychologically realistic way.

In the Copycat world, the question often arose as to how one could be sure that various answers produced by the program were "reasonable." How did Mitchell and Hofstadter *know* that a particular result was reasonable? A number of tests with subjects produced results (Mitchell 1993) that corresponded, by and large, to Hofstadter and Mitchell's personal intuitions (often based on aesthetics) about the answers to various problems.

In Tabletop, the distinction between "reasonable" and "unreasonable" answers is somewhat more obvious: people are apparently better able to visualize a real table and select an outcome than for the Copycat domain. Virtually no one asks, "How do you know that that is a reasonable answer?" for the Tabletop domain, whereas Mitchell and Hofstadter have been constantly asked this question. For those few Tabletop problems in which there might have been some doubt, I will refer to the statistics gathered from experimental subjects.

2.9.2 Differences with Respect to Copycat
For all its similarities to Copycat, Tabletop explores certain conceptual territory that Copycat did not, and certain aspects of its architecture are designed to handle subtleties Copycat could not handle. This section describes these differences.

> *Blurrier categories* The categories in Tabletop have more of a real-world feel to them than those in Copycat. Although *in principle* there is no difference at this level, the Tabletop concept network contains far more ISA links (indicating membership in one category in another [Quillian 1968]) than the Copycat concept network does. In Tabletop, a single category is often associated with a number of different superordinate categories (e.g., a "soupbowl" is a "liquid holder," but it is also a "food holder" as well as "crockery"; a "knife" is "silverware" as well as a "sharp object"). The way in which activation spreads and link lengths shrink must take these differences into account.
>
> *Real-valued object locations* Tabletop is a continuous two-dimensional world. The notion of physical proximity among objects, irrespective of how the objects are related conceptually, plays only a minor part in the Copycat world, but it figures very significantly in the tabletop world. In particular, groupings in Tabletop can arise on the mere basis of objects' being physically close to one another on the table, although, of course, conceptual closeness can also play a crucial role in grouping.

No rigid compartmentalization In Copycat, mappings are made between a specific initial string and a specific target string. For example, in the problem

abc ⇒ abd,

pqr ⇒ ?

no mapping can be made between the **a** and the **c** in **abc**. In Tabletop, on the other hand, any particular object or group of objects can, at least theoretically, map to any other object or group of objects. This is because in Tabletop there are no boundaries between situations, as there are in Copycat (e.g., between **abc** and **pqr**, above); there is really only one situation in which all of the groupings and mappings occur.

The problem of a single node with multiple activations This problem is best explained with a real-world example. Suppose you are visiting a friend in Detroit, Michigan, and you wish to go to Ann Arbor. You ask for directions, and your friend replies, "Just go west on I-94." You happen to know that in the parking structure where you are parked, both the west exit and the east exit provide equally quick ways of getting out of the structure. But, even though the concept "west" is still active in your mind from your friend's directions, this does not affect your selection (or only minimally so) of exit from the parking structure. But how can this be, if there is only one "west" in the concept network of your brain? It would seem that if "west" were active, this should give a significant boost to the likelihood of choosing the west exit over the east exit. But this certainly does not seem to occur. Furthermore, we cannot argue that the concept "west" is simply not active at all, because as soon as you leave the parking structure, "west" is clearly active as you get on I-94. Are there, then, in reality any number of different "west" concepts—one for interstate highways, another for parking structures, and so on? How can we account for the seeming paradox of having only one concept "west" (i.e., a single collection of neurons), which has a specific level of activity in one situation and yet is active at an entirely different level for a situation "within" the first situation? Is it possible that we have many nonoverlapping patterns of neural activity that correspond to various instances of the concept "west"? Or is there possibly an alternative solution?

This problem arises in Tabletop as follows. Consider figure 2.22.

Assume that the program has established correspondences between the two silverware groups and between the two cups, as shown. The concept "mirror symmetry" will then be active because of the presence of two correspondences between diagonally opposite corners of the table. This is analogous to the activation of "west" by the direction "Just go west on I-94." What happens, though, when the program "enters the parking structure"—in other words, when it begins to examine the correspondences *within* the two silverware groups that correspond? Given that the concept "mirror symmetry" is active, should we expect the program to attempt to map the objects within these two silverware groups in a "mirror-symmetric" way? Should there be pressure to map the knife group in the upper left-hand group to the single knife in the lower left-hand group (i.e., the mirror-symmetric mapping within silverware-group-to-silverware-group correspondence)? Although there might be a slight pressure to do so, I have tested human subjects on similar problems, and there

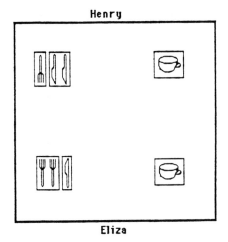

Figure 2.22

would appear to be little evidence of this. This means there is a problem, to wit: The concept "mirror symmetry" should be active, and yet it apparently exerts little or no influence on the way in which the structures at the lower level are built.

I will suggest a solution to this problem, which I call the "problem of a single node with multiple activations" due to the fact that a single node must to be able to maintain different levels of activation simultaneously.

Competition that is less destructive In Copycat, competitions between structures are fatal for the loser. A structure may take a long time to evolve, but if it goes head-to-head with another structure and loses, it is destroyed, and if it is ever to exist again, it must be rebuilt from scratch. In Tabletop, by contrast, structures that lose competitions are penalized but not destroyed. In Tabletop, the distinction is made between the Workspace, where essentially all of the structures that have been built are present, and the more elite Worldview inside it, where only the currently perceived structures are present. Work on memory savings dating back as far as Ebbinghaus (1886) would suggest that this approach is more psychologically realistic than the Copycat approach. Or consider the famous ambiguous drawing of the "young woman/old woman" (Hill 1915). In general, the first time we see this drawing, we see one of the interpretations but have a difficult time "seeing" the other one. However, once we have seen the competing representation, it becomes much easier to switch back and forth. Even though we can perceive only one of the representations at any given time, the fact that we can retrieve the other one much faster with practice proves that some of the structure allowing us to perceive it remained intact.

Overcoming the problem of "urgency explosion" on the Coderack The Coderack, one of the fundamental data structures in the tabletop architecture, is designed to implement simulated parallelism of the many small tasks (called "codelets") from which an answer will gradually emerge. A problem called "urgency explosion" was observed in Tabletop, and a solution to this problem was conceived and implemented. An analysis is given as to why, in Copycat, particular constraints on how codelets produced follow-up codelets caused this problem to go undetected and why, in Tabletop, it caused significant problems.

A "local" way of determining computational temperature Temperature in Tabletop, although serving the same purpose as temperature in Copycat, is derived in a more emergent manner than in Copycat. I will explain Tabletop's temperature-determining algorithm in detail, discussing the advantages and difficulties with respect to the Copycat algorithm.

Chapter 3

The Architecture of Tabletop

3.1 Background

It would be impossible to discuss the architecture of Tabletop without reference to its ancestors and relatives, and especially without referring to one program in particular: Mitchell and Hofstadter's Copycat (Mitchell 1990; Hofstadter and Mitchell 1991; Mitchell, 1993). The underlying architectural principles of both Copycat and Tabletop were described in the "Copycat Memo" (Hofstadter 1984). Over the next five years, these basic design principles were modified and refined through extensive discussion in Hofstadter's research group.

Prior to Copycat, three programs had been written that implemented some of the principles discussed in the Copycat Memo: Hofstadter's Jumbo (Hofstadter 1983), Meredith's Seek-Whence (Meredith 1986), and Defays' Numbo (Defays 1986). I will give an overview of Jumbo and the Copycat Memo below, indicating their respective contributions to the mechanisms of the Copycat and Tabletop programs.

Tabletop and Copycat are explicit attempts to implement a particular abstract architecture in different domains. The major difference is that the Tabletop project, conceived of some three years later, is an attempt to bring the Copycat architecture into a somewhat more real-world domain. The underlying architecture of Tabletop is therefore on a deep level the same as the Copycat architecture, but it has been modified and augmented as appropriate to fit the exigencies of the new domain. In many ways, the conceptual forerunner of Tabletop and Copycat was a program developed by Hofstadter (Hofstadter 1983), called Jumbo.

Jumbo solved anagram problems in a nontraditional way without recourse to dictionary look-up. A particular anagram problem was done by a large number of small "codelets"—functions, or small pieces of code, designed to build or break groups of letters. These codelets gradually built up hierarchically structured groups of letters that represented plausible candidate answers to the anagram problem given to the program. One of the key principles of this program was the competitive, stochastic nature of codelet-running.

Jumbo was typically given a number of "jumbled" letters, from which it produced a single plausible English-like word. Unlike dictionary-search anagram programs, Jumbo was completely unconcerned with producing real words. The program was endowed with knowledge only about the plausibility of certain letter groupings in English. It knew, for example, that *ough* was a much more plausible grouping of the four letters *o, g, u,* and *h* than, say, *ouhg*.

The program operated in a bottom-up fashion, constructing pseudowords by building up smaller structures, testing those structures against its knowledge of consonant or vowel clusters in English, breaking those structures if necessary and rebuilding others, using newly built groups of letters as components of larger groups, and so on. By means of this gradual process of building and breaking, small and large structures evolved and linked up with other structures in a hierarchical manner, and eventually English-like pseudowords emerged.

The process of grouping various letters based on our implicit knowledge of cluster frequencies in English is a process that we do all the time when we are reading text. Usually, though, the process is done so automatically that we do not realize it is taking place. On occasion, however, we follow a highly attractive route to a hierarchical structure that, though plausible, is not an English word; we then have to explicitly break the already-built groups. For example, I once saw the word "shelflist" on a sign. In English, *fl* is a very common syllable-initiating consonant cluster. For me, this fact once imposed an initial parsing of the entire word as "shel-flist." Note that both major pieces are perfectly reasonable English-like syllables. It just so happens that neither of them corresponds to anything in the dictionary. But "shel-flist"? I could not figure it out. I happened to be in a library, however, and as I puzzled over the word, it suddenly occurred to me that I had to break the "flist" group. Once the *f* had migrated over from the initial cluster *fl* (of "flist") to attach itself instead to the *l* of *shel*, thus making a final consonant cluster of *lf*, I was home free: "shelf-list"!

I have had similar experiences with words like "misled" and "beribboned," and I am sure that everyone has at one time or another had a similar experience. The point is that one must sometimes be willing to break old structures in order to produce new and better ones, but in the real world it is often not clear when to do so or which structures need to be broken. For instance, I might have stopped puzzling over the sign in the library, satisfied that "shel-flist" was simply some word I did not understand, promising myself that I would look it up in the dictionary some day.

3.2 *The Parallel Terraced Scan and the Necessity of Stochastic Processing*

Perhaps the central feature of the Jumbo architecture is a strategy that became central to both the Copycat and Tabletop programs: the *parallel terraced scan*. The basic idea is that of "exploration proportional to promise," which means that if a promising solution seems to be evolving, the program devotes more of its resources to developing that solution than to other, less promising ones. This is closely related to the exploration-versus-exploitation problem discussed by Holland (1975). For the purposes of illustration, it is worth examining a particularly simple example of this problem, the "two-armed-bandit problem."

Assume we have a slot machine with two payoff slots, one paying at the rate of three to one, the other at two to one, but we do not know which slot pays at which rate. We have a very large number of tokens, and we wish to maximize our winnings. If we knew a priori which slot paid the most, we would, of course, put all of our tokens into that slot. Since we do not know which one is the better-paying slot, we have to use some of the tokens to explore the environment. Initially, we put tokens into both slots at random; then, as we begin to suspect that one of the slots is paying more than the other, we devote more of our resources to that slot and less to the other slot. However, even if we have a pretty good idea that we have discovered the good slot, we cannot be absolutely certain. We must therefore continue to check the "bad" slot from time to time. The more sure we are of having identified the "good" slot, the less we need to test the "bad" slot (exponentially less, it turns out). And the less we explore the bad slot, the more resources we can devote to exploitation of what we believe to be the good slot.

It is also important to notice that we are not obliged to play the slots serially. We can, in fact, put tokens into the slots in a completely parallel manner (feeding one slot with our left hand, for example, and the other with our right hand).

This reliance on parallelism and biased randomness is the underlying principle of the parallel terraced scan. Like the water filling the lake behind a newly dammed river, any number of different "fingers of exploration" move outward simultaneously into various gullies at different speeds, depending on the contour of the gully bottoms.

Jumbo performs its exploration and structure building in just such a "many-armed-bandit" fashion. Codelets—small functions—that make or break groups of letters are "hung" on a data structure called the Coderack. Each codelet has an *urgency*—a real number that determines the likelihood of its being executed. One by one, codelets are selected from the Coderack in a biased, random manner—that is, chosen randomly but with biases determined by their urgencies. Virtually never are choices made deterministically. The higher the urgency of a particular codelet, the greater the likelihood that it will be executed. Both the number of codelets on the Coderack and their urgencies depend on the program's prior processing.

Codelets are not entirely independent of each other in the sense that the evaluations and group-building that they do depend on what has already been built up. Let us look, for example, at how a group of letters is built and put into the program's work space, to be considered then as one of the groups of letters to which other groups can be attached. Some candidate set of letters is selected randomly (but with biases) from the jumbled set of input letters. This set goes through three stages of evaluation, each successive stage representing more stringent criteria by which to judge the quality of that group of letters.

Each of these evaluations is carried out by a separate codelet. An initial codelet "grabs" a set of letters from the input set and makes a very superficial evaluation of the potential "glom" (the term comes from the colloquial verb "to glom," meaning to stick separate things together to form a single entity) of letters formed. The (probabilistic) outcome of this evaluation is either to stop (i.e., throw the letters back) or to hang on the Coderack a follow-up codelet that will continue the evaluation. When this second codelet runs (and it may take a while before it is chosen; in fact, it might never be chosen at all), it performs a somewhat more detailed and resource-costly evaluation of the quality of the glom. Based on this evaluation, it either throws the letters back or, like the first codelet, posts a further follow-up codelet to the Coderack that will continue the evaluation process. If, after the third evaluation, the glom has still not been rejected, it is then put into the program's work space as one of the building blocks of the anagram being created. This is how the resulting anagram emerges from the "primordial soup" of input letters.

The process can be compared to the selection of one person for a job from among an overwhelming number of applicants, say, one thousand. Clearly, it would be too costly in terms of both time and resources to examine each dossier carefully. So a first-pass, easily evaluated criterion is selected—for example, number of publications. On the basis of this single criterion, the number of candidates can be cut down to, say, two hundred. Although a number—even a considerable number—of highly qualified candidates may be passed over, this cannot be avoided. Such fallibility is an inevitable consequence of any search strategy with time and resource constraints. Now that the original number has been reduced to two hundred, a somewhat more rigorous, resource-intensive criterion can be used—for example, the letters of recommendation of these candidates will actually be read. Each person on the ten-member hiring committee will then be given the files of twenty candidates and will select three candidates on the basis of their letters of recommendation. This reduces the total set of candidates to thirty. For these thirty, one or two papers included with their files might be read and more minute factors considered (what their salary requirements are, how much experience they have had, and so on). On the basis of this evaluation, the original thousand is winnowed down to, say, just five. These candidates, finally, are brought to the institution, invited to give job talks, invited to dinner, and so on. A considerable amount of time and resources is now expended on this final phase of the selection process until, ultimately, a candidate is chosen.

This is a real-world example of the parallel terraced scan: the candidates' records are examined in parallel, the selection criteria become progressively more costly in terms of time and resources as the search continues, and fewer and fewer candidates are allowed to move up the hierarchy toward the final selection.

Let us return to Jumbo. What if the program builds up some small gloms, but whenever it tries to continue the process toward completion by grouping the given gloms and the unglommed letters, the combinations it finds are rejected by the program's evaluation criteria?

For example, suppose the program is given as input the letters **a**, **b**, **g**, and **n**. Assume that it has reached a point in its processing where it has found a perfectly reasonable three-letter glom: **bag**. This passes all the evaluation tests and is put into the work space as one of the groups of letters to be used in forming the anagram. The workspace thus consists of **bag** and **n**. So suppose it tries to create the glom **bagn**; since **gn** is a very rare syllable-ending consonant cluster, this does not pass the chain of evaluation. Then it might try **nbag**. The same thing happens, since **nb** is not an initial-consonant cluster in English. It is rejected. Then what? In a standard AI program, the program might make its retreat through deterministic backtracking, but Jumbo has no deterministic backtracking strategy. It relies instead on a mechanism called *computational temperature*. So let us leave the program for a moment with its work space containing **bag** and **n** and see how it will deal with this problem.

Computational temperature is the other major mechanism introduced by Hofstadter in the Jumbo architecture, even though it was not fully implemented in the actual program. It is a feedback mechanism that has a direct effect on the urgency of a codelet. Temperature, in essence, tells the program the extent to which a codelet's urgency will bias the codelet's chances of being selected to run. Very low temperatures imply that the program will respect urgencies in an almost deterministic manner. In other words, if one codelet has an urgency of 30, another 70, the latter will virtually always be chosen at very low temperatures. As temperature rises, the likelihood that the former codelet will be chosen increases. At very high temperatures, the selection of either codelet is almost equally likely, the actual difference in urgency being of little consequence.

The temperature at any moment is a function of how close the program thinks it is to having produced a reasonable pseudoword. The better the structures so far built up are, the lower the temperature, and the worse the structures, the higher the temperature.

This notion of temperature has often been compared to the notion of temperature used by Kirkpatrick and others (1983) in a process they called "simulated annealing." There are several important distinctions, however. One is that the standard simulated-annealing algorithm has a fixed "annealing schedule." In other words, the amount of randomness in the program decreases according to a predetermined schedule, independent of the results of the processing that has taken place. Although this annealing schedule can be modified, it is not part of a feedback loop. Unlike computational temperature in Jumbo, Copycat, or Tabletop, the temperature in a simulated-annealing algorithm changes purely as a function of time rather than as a function of the quality of partial results of the program's processing.

Another distinction between Jumbo's temperature and simulated-annealing temperature is that the latter is very strictly based on the Boltzmann distribution in statistical mechanics, and accordingly it requires an energy variable and controls only probabilities dependent on this variable. By contrast, temperature in Jumbo, Copycat, and Tabletop is based less strictly on the physics image of temperature and hence can be more freely adapted to control many diverse aspects of the program. Temperature affects not only the selection of codelets but virtually all situations in which multiple choices are possible.

Jumbo will try, perhaps many times, to group **bag** and **n**, and will fail. As it continues to try—and fails—the temperature of the system goes up. "Breaker" codelets, which normally have a very low urgency, become ever more likely to run as the temperature rises. Sooner or later, a breaker codelet will run, breaking the glom **bag** back into its constituent letters. From that point on, the program is free to try again. In a second or third attempt, it may come up with the gloms **ba** and **ng** and produce the high-quality word candidate "**bang**."

Both the parallel terraced scan and computational temperature play significant roles in the Tabletop architecture, although the implementation of temperature is significantly different than in either Jumbo or Copycat.

But a key element was missing from the Jumbo architecture, one that was subsequently incorporated into both Copycat and Tabletop. This missing structure was an associative network of permanent concepts that interacted with the codelets. Hofstadter laid out the basic ideas of this type of network, called the Slipnet, in the Copycat Memo (Hofstadter 1984), which is discussed below.

3.3 Copycat

The idea for the Copycat project was first described by Hofstadter (1984). It is difficult to tease apart the contributions to the Tabletop project of ideas from Hofstadter's original plan, Mitchell's Copycat implementation of that plan, and the many discussions within Hofstadter's research group of the underlying architecture. These discussions spanned five and a half years and covered virtually every aspect of the architectures of these programs.

In the Copycat Memo, Hofstadter described the letter-string microdomain discussed in chapter 2. This document advocated a particular approach to computer modeling of analogy-making. The Memo consists of two major axes: a high-level analysis of analogy-making and the description of an architecture compatible with this analysis. The high-level analysis consisted of enumerating a number of psychologically plausible mechanisms, such as overlapping concepts, "halos" of concepts surrounding a particular concept, distance between concepts, conceptual slippage, and so on—mechanisms that Hofstadter proposed formed the basis of human analogy-making. Thereafter the Memo describes in considerable detail an architecture designed to implement these mechanisms.

The overarching theme of the Memo is that analogy-making consists of recognizing one situation ("situation" being used in the general sense of the word: an apple is a situation, and so is a civil war) as being "the same as" another. In making an analogy, we "slip" certain aspects of one situation into the corresponding aspects of another situation. This can involve very complex situations (e.g., slipping "love affair" to "political alliance") or comparatively simple ones (e.g., any of the me-too analogies in chapter 1). As I have said elsewhere, every concept in our mental-concept network is surrounded by a halo of other, related concepts. At the core of analogy-making is perceiving one of the concepts in the halo as being "the same as" the central concept under the pressures induced by the particular context. For example, consider the concept "beer." In the conceptual halo of "beer," we would find "wine," "Coke," "French fries," and so on. The examples in chapter 1 in which one person says that she is going to pay for her beer and the other replies, "Me, too" are specific examples of how "beer" slips to various concepts in its conceptual halo. The Copycat architecture provides a set of mechanisms that allow this type of conceptual slippage to be achieved.

3.3.1 Details of the Basic Copycat Mechanisms
The basic features that Hofstadter proposed to implement his ideas of conceptual slippage are the following:

A network of "fixed" concepts called the Slipnet The concepts in the Slipnet have various default distances between them; activation spreads between concepts in inverse proportion to the distance separating them; and the distances, rather than being fixed, vary dynamically during processing. The activation of any concept decays over time as an inverse function of the concept's abstractness (Hofstadter referred to this abstractness as the "semanticity" of a concept; Mitchell chose to call it "conceptual depth"). There was to be continual interaction between the Slipnet and the Workspace (or Cytoplasm, as Hofstadter called it).

A Workspace called the Cytoplasm In the Cytoplasm, all the representational structures needed to perceive the situation are gradually built up. As in Jumbo, possible groupings of letters, descriptions of letters and of groups of letters, as well as correspondences between letters and letter groups, and so on, would be made in the Cytoplasm. An example from the Copycat domain will serve to illustrate this. Assume the program is given the letter string "**abbccc**." Initially, it has no parsing of this string into "chunked" entities, but as it runs it will most likely produce the structure **a(b b)ccc** and then **a(b b)(ccc)**. Under these contextual pressures, a little like peer pressure, the program may ultimately come to view the **a** as a group as well, a "degenerate" group containing just one letter. This will lead to the following parsing of the initial string into the three groups **(a)(b b)(ccc)**. The building of this representational structure—in this case, the three groups of letters **a**, **b b**, and **ccc**—occurs in the Workspace.

Codelets These are small semi-independent functions that carry out all of the processing, including the following kinds of actions: finding relationships between letters, building descriptions of letters, building groups, finding correspondences between letters (or groups), and sending activation to specific nodes in the Slipnet on the basis of the presence of specific letters, types of relationships noticed, and types of new structures built.

The Coderack This is the "staging ground" for the codelets. As in Jumbo, the Coderack is where codelets are posted and from which they are selected to run.

Continual interaction between the Slipnet and the Workspace This has already been discussed. This is an essential feature of the architecture; it is how the program implements the notion that there must be permanent top-down/bottom-up interaction.

Competition among structures Different groupings of letters compete continually with other groupings. In a similar fashion, correspondences between letters (and groups of letters) also continually compete with one another. All structures have a *salience*, a value that indicates how much they stand out, how much they need to be attended to by codelets.

Parallel terraced scan This has been discussed in the context of the Jumbo architecture.

Computational temperature Again, the philosophy of temperature was identical to that of Jumbo. Mitchell and Hofstadter have discussed this in detail elsewhere (Mitchell and Hofstadter 1989; Mitchell 1993).

Local processing There was to be no global executive. All results (i.e., the answer to the analogy problem that the program is given) should emerge from a continual interaction and running of codelets. The actions of codelets are affected in a top-down manner by the Slipnet, but in no sense is there a "conductor" orchestrating their actions.

(Simulated) parallelism Codelets to perform many different tasks hang on the Coderack waiting to be executed. Any codelet can, at least theoretically, be chosen to run at any time. The effect of running a particular codelet might be a change in activation levels in the Slipnet, an increase or decrease in computational temperature, the creation or destruction of a structure in the Workspace, or some other change. These factors then affect the running and actions of subsequent codelets on the Coderack. This type of processing might reasonably be compared to time-sharing, which can be considered a sort of simulated parallelism. Assume that an operating system wishes to time-share two large jobs. Each job can be thought of as being broken into many little pieces that are run during the short time slices allotted by the operating system. The processing done during a single time slice is much like the processing done by a single codelet. However, in contrast to an operating system, in Copycat there are no large predefined jobs; there are only little independent pieces of code, one of which is probabilistically chosen to run during each individual time slice.

Reliance on stochastic mechanisms The Copycat architecture is fundamentally stochastic. Virtually *all* decisions are made in a stochastic manner.

Integration of representation-building and correspondence-finding There is no separation of the processes of building representations and finding correspondences between elements of different representations. This sets the program apart from virtually all other analogy-making programs, since in these programs, attention is focused only on finding correspondences between entities whose descriptions are given, prepackaged, to the program. A fundamental tenet of Copycat and Tabletop is that it is impossible to separate the process of representation-building from the process of correspondence-building (Chalmers, French, and Hofstadter 1992).

All these architectural features were implemented in Mitchell's Copycat program as well as in Tabletop. There are, of course, differences in the way in which certain features have been implemented in the two programs, especially at the level of how competitions are resolved and how temperature is determined, but conceptually the architectures of Copycat and Tabletop are very close. Certainly the philosophy of the two programs, as expressed in the mechanisms used in their implementation, is identical.

Copycat became a real, functioning program, in 1990. Its author was Melanie Mitchell (Mitchell 1993). The program consisted of approximately eleven thousand lines of Lisp code and effectively transformed the Copycat Memo, a theoretical document of what should work, into a real program demonstrating that the ideas, in fact, did work. The development of a second program, Tabletop, to implement the ideas of the Copycat Memo in a more "real-world" domain began in 1987, about two years after work on the Copycat program had already begun.

3.4 Tabletop

Tabletop is a comparatively large program. In all, it consists of over twenty-six thousand lines of code, over twice the length of Copycat. One might worry that this increase in program size could be due to the fact that the Tabletop domain seems more realistic than the Copycat domain. Put another way, if this is to be a general architecture for cognition, are we not experiencing an unacceptable blowup in size? If twenty-six thousand lines of code are required to solve problems in the Tabletop microdomain, how many would be required for an even larger and more realistic domain? In short, will this architecture scale up?

The answer to this question would seem to be that as the domain size grows, the number of lines of code will increase, probably roughly in proportion to the number of concepts in the program's Slipnet. (The number of codelet types is essentially proportional to the number of concepts in the Slipnet, and it is these functions that occupy the most space in terms of lines of code.)

However, the specter that haunts AI is not whether the *physical size* of a program will grow as a function of the complexity of the domain but whether the program will experience a combinatorial explosion of *run time* due, for example, to exponentially increasing searches, and so on. The Tabletop architecture is designed specifically to avoid the problem of a combinatorial explosion of run time, which means that, at least theoretically, this architecture should scale up.

The fact that the Tabletop architecture has been explicitly designed with the problems of combinatorial explosion in mind puts it in stark contrast with certain current analogy-making programs (e.g., that of Thagard and Holyoak [1989]). The way in which codelets run (i.e., certain codelets engendering other codelets, codelet selection probabilities varying according to urgency, codelets selecting structures to act on the basis of the salience of those structures, etc.) allows the program to (probabilistically) focus its resources very sharply and sensitively. In other words, this architecture incorporates a powerful mechanism for probabilistically focusing attention: important activities—whether simple exploration, representation building, or correspondence construction—tend to get done before less important ones. The interaction between the Slipnet and the Workspace allows the program to dynamically adapt its resources to those aspects of the situation it has judged to be important.

Tabletop, like Copycat, consists of three main components: the Slipnet, the Workspace, and the Coderack. As in Copycat, the Slipnet is a permanent concept network, and the Workspace is a theater of operations. Swarms of codelets, like an army of soldiers, pilots, diplomats, engineers, and doctors, are dispatched stochastically from the Coderack to the scene, where they go to work on the Tabletop problem, observing the table, building and breaking structures, sending activation to the Slipnet, and attempting to discover correspondences between pairs of objects (and groups of objects). Gradually, fewer and fewer new, good structures and correspondences between objects are discovered. At this point, the program begins to conclude that, possibly, it has found the best way of looking at the situation that it is going to find, the temperature begins to fall, and, eventually, a codelet will run that says, "OK, stop and designate as answer whatever is currently mapped onto the touched object." And this completes the run.

The objects in the Tabletop world are pieces of silverware, cups, saucers, plates, soup bowls, drinking glasses of two different sizes, saltshakers, and pepper shakers. These objects can be placed anywhere on the table. The forks, knives, and spoons have four possible orientations. All objects have a size; they are not simply point objects.

In what follows, we will examine in detail each of these three structures. In addition, I will discuss my algorithm for determining computational temperature and will subsequently compare it to the Copycat implementation of temperature.

3.4.1 The Slipnet

The Slipnet is a model of human concepts and conceptual associations. One of its principal purposes is to provide a means of achieving conceptual slippage, the key cognitive mechanism underlying this approach to analogy-making. Another is to focus and guide processing in the Workspace. The Slipnet is a node-and-link network, each of whose nodes represents the "core" of a particular concept. In the Tabletop Slipnet, for example, the nodes have names like "cup," "saucer," "fork," "knife," "spoon," "plate," "saltshaker" (the most concrete concepts), "liquid holder," "food holder," "sharp object," "identity," "group," "used together," "opposite," "diagonal symmetry," "mirror symmetry," "left," "right," "end," "middle," and so on. Each concept has a fixed degree of *conceptual depth*, also sometimes called *semanticity*, a real number that represents roughly where the concept lies on the continuum of concepts, ranging from the most concrete, such as "cup," "fork," and "plate," to the most abstract, such as, "eat from object," "similar shape to," and "opposite from." In the Tabletop domain, for example, the concept "cup" has less conceptual depth than the concept "liquid holder," which, in turn, has less conceptual depth than the concepts "similar to" and "opposite." Conceptual depth is intended to correspond roughly to the distinctions made by Rosch and others (1976). The concept "armchair," for example, would have less conceptual depth than "chair," which in turn would have less than "furniture."

At any given time, each node in the Slipnet has a particular level of activation. The amount of activation of each node is determined by three factors:

> 1. Activation added by low-level perceptual agents (codelets) whenever an *instance* of the particular concept is discovered or noticed in the work space.
> 2. Activation added by activation-spreading from nearby concept nodes in the net itself.

3. Decay of activation, the rate of which is a function of the conceptual depth of the node. The idea is that highly "semantic" or abstract concepts, once active, will continue to influence the perception of a situation longer than concrete concepts.

Let us briefly consider the consequences of the third point—namely, that the more abstract a node is (in other words, the greater its conceptual depth), the more slowly it loses activation. This means that nodes representing very concrete concepts lose activation quickly and, as a result, must receive new activation continually to remain active. On the other hand, more abstract nodes lose activation slowly and, as a result, can reach high levels of activation more easily and can remain active longer than less abstract nodes. This means that very "semantic" nodes will, in general, play a more important role in the overall process of analogy-making than more "syntactic" nodes, which will tend to be less active. The "abstractness principle," in which more abstract relationships are favored over less abstract ones, so crucial to Dedre Gentner's theory of analogy-making, is thus a natural consequence of decay rates' varying according to conceptual depth. However, in this architecture, the bias toward using more abstract concepts is just one factor in determining the quality of an analogy and can be overridden by other aspects of the situation.

Links between nodes in the Slipnet are of only two types: ISA links, in the tradition of Quillian's semantic networks (Quillian 1968), and labeled links. ISA links are links that designate category membership—for example, "robin ISA bird" and "bird ISA flying animal." For labeled links, the *label* indicates the type of relationship that the link encodes. Each label is itself a concept and hence is represented by a node.

Every link in the Slipnet also has a *length*. The conceptual distance between any two nodes in the Slipnet can be calculated as a function of the lengths of the links connecting them. One crucial feature of the Tabletop Slipnet that sets it apart from other semantic network architectures (with the exception, of course, of Copycat) is the length of any labeled link varies dynamically as a function of the activation of the link's label node. This feature allows the Slipnet to adapt to the specific situation (i.e., the analogy problem) with which it is presented.

As surprising as it may seem, the need for a malleable conceptual network in which the distances between concepts can vary according to context has been considered to be either irrelevant or unnecessary by some researchers. I think that a single example will clearly point out that this view is erroneous.

In France, laws aimed at preventing underage drinking exist, but they are rarely, if ever, enforced. In addition, everyone must have on their person their National Identity Card. A driver's license is needed only when one is operating a motor vehicle. Therefore, in the minds of nineteen-year-old French college students, the concepts "beer" and "driver's license" are very distant. The activation of one would certainly not activate the other. But were a French college student to go to the United States for a year, the conceptual distance between "driver's license" and "beer" would soon be radically altered. Henceforth, in the new context of thoughts about an American university, the activation of the concept "driver's license" *would* activate "beer" and vice versa. This indeed implies a change in the Slipnet structure. Note that this change is not necessarily a permanent one. When the "American university" context decays, the original, long default distance returns. In other words, these changes do not involve a permanent, context-independent shortening of the distance between "beer" and "driver's license" (example provided by Jean-Luc Bonnetain).

This example is useful in that it clearly illustrates the necessity for a malleable concept network, but it is perhaps misleading in that it could give the impression that such malleability is a rather exotic feature of cognition. Not all changes in Slipnet distances require modifications of context as radical as the one suggested in the example—in fact, most do not. Concepts move closer together all the time. For example, whenever one situation makes us realize, "Hey, that's like ...," the two concepts involved in the "that's like" utterance are brought conceptually closer together. We are continually seeing old information in a somewhat different light and relating it to new concepts, thus changing, however slightly, the distances in our concept network.

The Copycat and Tabletop Slipnets contain many instances of the abstract structure shown in figure 3.1.

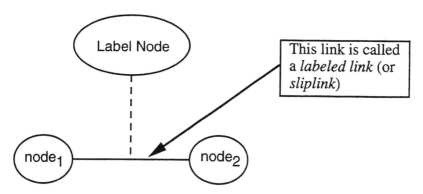

Figure 3.1

This abstract link-and-node structure is used to represent the relation between two concepts. Two examples taken from the Copycat world are "**A** [is the] **successor** [of] **B**" and "**successor** [is the] **opposite** [of] **predecessor**." The corresponding link-and-node representations are shown in figure 3.2.

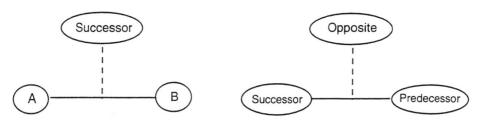

Figure 3.2

In the Copycat Slipnet, these two pieces are "hooked up" as in figure 3.3.

This type of structure recurs throughout Copycat's Slipnet. At one time, it seemed that this type of structure alone would also be sufficient for Tabletop's Slipnet architecture. This assumption turned out to be inaccurate, and the work of correcting it led to certain changes—notably, the incorporation of ISA links—in the design of both the Slipnets.

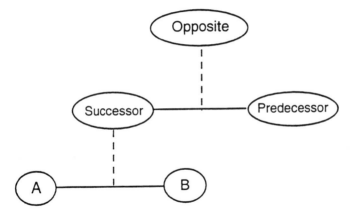

Figure 3.3

Up to now, conceptual distance has been considered to correspond to a metric on our space of concepts. I now wish to give an equivalent but alternate definition in terms of conceptual slippage:

> The conceptual distance between two concepts measures how easily the first concept can be replaced by ("slipped to") the second in the context under consideration.

The conceptual distance between a given pair of concept-core nodes in Copycat is completely controlled by the level of activity in the label node. This is illustrated in figure 3.4.

Because connectionist networks (see, for example, Rumelhart and McClelland 1986) make use of nodes, links, and spreading activation, many people erroneously

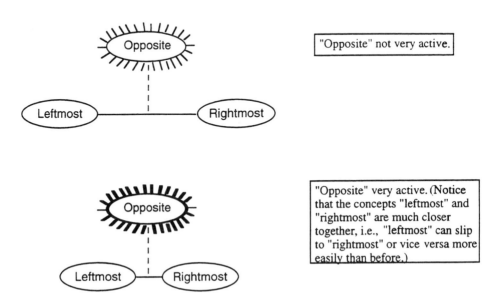

Figure 3.4

assume that when one says "net," one must mean "connectionist net." Once people have made the incorrect assumption that the Slipnet must be a connectionist network, albeit perhaps a localist one, they impose on the Slipnet their connectionist under-standing of how activation must spread, and this invariably leads to problems.

In keeping with the work done by Roger Shepard (1962) on multidimensional scal-ing, in which he established a means of measuring the "distance" between concepts, we refer to distances between concepts in the Slipnet. This is also in keeping with the commonsense notion of conceptual distance. Most people would agree, for example, that the concept "snake" is closer to the concept "worm" than it is to "refrigerator"; that "car" is closer to "bicycle" than to "civil war"; and so on. Thus people do have an intuitive notion of conceptual distance. This notion is implemented in the Tabletop Slipnet by means of links (or series of links) of various lengths. The length of the path between two concepts represents the default distance between them. For example, in Tabletop, the link between "knife" and "fork" is quite short, whereas the path (i.e., a series of simple links, since there is no direct link) from "knife" to "salt-shaker" is very long.

In Tabletop's Slipnet, activation spreads from one concept to another in a manner inversely proportional to the distance between the two concepts. If one compares this to a connectionist network, distance can be likened to the reciprocal of weight, rather than weight itself. Specifically, in a connectionist model, the activation passed from one node to the next is the product of the first node's activation and the weight of the link connecting the two nodes. By contrast, in the Slipnet, the amount of acti-vation spread is (essentially) inversely proportional to the distance between concepts, although, of course, the node cannot spread more activation than it possesses. Thus, the closer two concepts are in the Slipnet (i.e., the shorter the lengths of the links be-tween them), the greater the amount of activation spread from one to the other.

The original design of the Tabletop Slipnet was identical to Copycat's original Slipnet in that it used only relational links. For example, in the original implementa-tion of the Tabletop Slipnet, the label on the link between "fork" and "spoon" was "utensils that go in mouth." The problem, however, was that this did not fit the rela-tional formalism corresponding to Copycat's nodes and labeled links. We would have to have had "fork [is the] utensils that go in mouth [of] spoon," which, obviously, did not make sense. Many of the labels in the original Tabletop Slipnet were ISA links, for which relational labeling was inappropriate. This is not to say, of course, that *no* relational links belong in Tabletop's Slipnet. They certainly do. For example: "[a] knife [is] used with [a] fork," "[a] cup [is] used with [a] saucer," and "[a] saucer [is] smaller than [a] plate." It turned out, though, that in Tabletop's Slipnet, this type of relational structure occurs less frequently than ISA links do. The overriding difference, then, between Tabletop's Slipnet and Copycat's Slipnet was that ISA links are more com-mon in the former. As could be expected, certain new problems arose with this design because it relied so heavily on ISA links.

ISA links first appeared in Ross Quillian's computer implementation of a semantic network in the late sixties (Quillian 1968). In his net, markers rather than activation passed from node to node. In that system, either a node was "on," indicating that it had been marked, or it was "off." For Quillian, a marked node "activated" (i.e., marked) nodes directly connected to it. For example, if we had "John ISA person ISA living thing," marker-passing would proceed from "John" to "person" to "living thing." In these original semantic nets, there was no notion of conceptual distance.

Essentially, if a marked node was connected to a second node, a marker was passed from the first to the second, otherwise not.

By contrast, in the Copycat and Tabletop Slipnets, no markers are passed; rather, activation is spread. The amount of activation spread from one node to another is inversely proportional to the conceptual distance between the two nodes.

But what happens if there are multiple pathways between a given pair of nodes? The following simple diagram, figure 3.5, illustrates this:

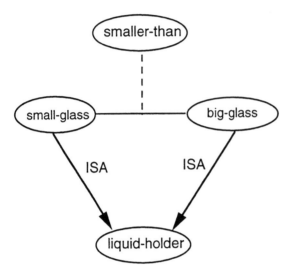

Figure 3.5
Multiple pathways between "small glass" and "big glass"

How do we calculate the conceptual distance between two nodes joined by pathways of differing types and differing lengths? The answer to this question led to the generalization of the Copycat Slipnet, the heart of which is the following premise: All pathways contribute to reducing the conceptual distance between nodes; the amount of activity spread between nodes is a function only of the conceptual distance between the nodes. Activation can be thought of as radiating between nodes: The closer the two nodes are together, the more activation is radiated from the "warmer" node to its neighbor.

All pathways between a given pair of nodes, regardless of their component links' types, help determine the conceptual distance between those nodes. Once this conceptual distance has been calculated, we can then determine the amount of activity that should radiate between the two nodes in question. The clearest way to understand this is first to visualize all the pathways used to derive the conceptual distance between two nodes, A and B, and then to show exactly how the computation is done. Assume the pathways in figure 3.6 connect the nodes A and B.

How do we calculate the conceptual distance between A and B? The formula for computing conceptual distance is inspired by the formula used to calculate the resistance of several resistors connected in parallel. In electronics, the basic idea is that each additional pathway between two points *lowers* the total resistance between those two points. Similarly, in the Slipnet, each additional pathway between two

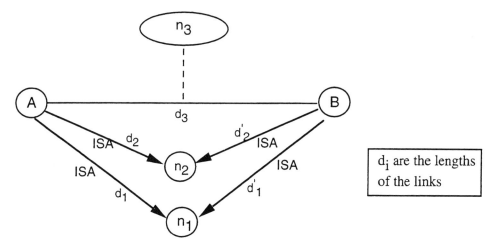

Figure 3.6
Slipnet indicating a number of pathways between two nodes A and B

nodes decreases the conceptual distance between the nodes. This stands to reason if one considers that if two nodes have many pathways joining them through ISA links and labeled links, they are more similar than two nodes that do not.

To return to the analogy with electricity, consider the circuit element in figure 3.7. Its total resistance is given by the formula

$$R = \frac{1}{\frac{1}{r_1} + \frac{1}{r_2} + \frac{1}{r_3}},$$

where r_1, r_2, and r_3 are the resistances of the individual pathways. Now consider the chunk of an abstract Tabletop-like Slipnet above. By analogy, it would seem logical that the distance from A to B should be the following:

$$\text{Distance}_{A,B} = \frac{1}{\frac{1}{d_1 + d'_1} + \frac{1}{d_2 + d'_2} + \frac{1}{d_3}},$$

where d_i is the distance between A and r_i, d'_j is the distance between n_i and B.

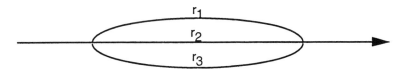

Figure 3.7

Once the conceptual distance between two nodes has been calculated, it is easy to determine how much activation will spread from one node to the other. Assuming that the distance from node A to node B is $d_{A,B}$, then the amount of activation that spreads from A to B is proportional to the activation of A divided by $d_{A,B}$.

In the Slipnet, activation decays as a function of the conceptual depth (abstractness) of the concept in question. In the Tabletop Slipnet, for purposes of simplicity, there are three levels of abstractness. The following heuristics are used to decide how abstract a particular concept is. Nodes that represent the categories of the actual objects on the table (e.g., "cup," "fork," and other basic-level categories [Rosch 1976]) are the least abstract. Categories at the second level of abstraction are those that contain the first-level categories (e.g., "crockery," "silverware," "sharp objects"). This second level of abstraction also includes the categories of possible relationships among the first-level categories (e.g., "used with": a knife is used with a fork; "bigger than": a plate is bigger than a saucer; "neighbor": cup_1 is the neighbor of $fork_3$; "left": cup_1 is to the left of $fork_3$). Finally, at the level of highest abstraction come concepts that are typically superordinates of concepts at the second level, or that might be relations between relations at the second level (e.g., "opposite": "left" is the opposite of "right"; "direction": "left" is a direction).

Activation may be sent to parts of the Slipnet by codelets when they run. If a node in the Slipnet is sent activation by a codelet very early on (i.e., if an instance of that concept was noticed) and if no instance of the same concept is noticed again, this would indicate that the concept is probably not very important and should therefore not remain active. Since all nodes lose activation through decay, the node will thus tend to return to dormancy unless it is resupplied with activation either from other active nodes (i.e., spreading activation) or from codelets examining the table. The greater the conceptual depth of a node, the less its activation will decay with each cycle.

The activation levels of concepts in the Slipnet reflect the presence of instances of those concepts in the Workspace. If both of the concepts joined by a labeled link play an active role in a correspondence—for example, if the leftmost object of one group is mapped to the rightmost object of a second group, so that "left" slips to "right"—then activation is sent to the label node associated with that link. (In addition, whenever both of the concepts joined by a labeled link are active, a small amount of activation is also sent to the label node.) This will then shrink the length of *all* of the links labeled by the label node. For example, the concepts "fork" and "knife" are joined by a link labeled "used together." If the slippage from "knife" to "fork" is part of the description of one of the analogical mappings, this will spread activation to the concept "used together." But the concept "used together" also labels the link joining the two concepts "cup" and "saucer." Because "used together" is active, not only will the link between "knife" and "fork" shrink but so will the link between "cup" and "saucer." This is the way the Slipnet modifies its structure to reflect context.

The Tabletop Slipnet contains forty-six nodes representing the following concepts. These concepts are possible descriptors of the objects, groups of objects, and other structures on the table: cup, saucer, plate, knife, fork, spoon, saltshaker, pepper shaker, small glass, big glass, soup bowl, sharp object, silverware, crockery, liquid holder, food holder, eat-from object, receptacle, buccal object (i.e., can be put in the mouth), open object, closed object, sameness, opposite, bigger than, smaller than, similar shape to, used with, symmetry, mirror symmetry, diagonal symmetry, group, neighbor, direction, left, right, above, below, horizontal, vertical, position, end, middle, number, one, two, three, many. There are three distinct link types:

> *Labeled links* These are links controlled by label nodes like "opposite," "used with," "bigger than," "smaller than," and so on.

ISA links These are standard ISA links between categories and their super-ordinate categories—for instance, "cup ISA liquid holder."
Has-member links These are the opposite of ISA links—for instance, "liquid holder HAS-MEMBER cup."

The number of nodes and link types could, of course, be increased, but the algorithm governing activation spreading and decay would remain unchanged.

3.4.2 Codelets and the Workspace

The Copycat Workspace was originally called the "Cytoplasm" in Hofstadter's 1984 Copycat Memo, an allusion to the seething activity of thousands of enzymes building and breaking structures simultaneously throughout the cytoplasm of a cell. In much the same way that applying the term "genetic" to genetic algorithms is appropriate even though there is considerable simplification of real genetic processes, it is instructive to liken the Tabletop Workspace to a cell's cytoplasm. This is because of the image that is evoked of how the codelets act on the table situation under consideration. It is useful to think of a raw, unstructured table configuration as being immersed in a "seething broth" of codelets qua enzymes, all of which are attempting to help build the representation of the table configuration. In particular, the image conveyed is one of parallel, local activity of codelets, resulting in a high-level product, much like enzymes collectively producing a new strand of DNA.

Codelets   Codelets are small pieces of code that perform certain simple actions. In Tabletop, there are approximately thirty different codelet types. Typically, a codelet searches for (or builds) some particular kind of structure associated with some specific concept in the Slipnet. For example, there are *find-group* codelets, whose job it is to look for groups of objects. When such a codelet finds a group, it sends activation to the "group" node in the Slipnet. There are also *find-neighbor* codelets, which look for the neighbor of a particular object. If a neighbor is found, activation is sent to the "neighbor" node in the Slipnet. Then there are *find-end* codelets, which look at the ends of groups. Whatever category of object such a codelet finds on the end of a group, it sends activation to that category in the Slipnet and also to the concept "end." (Note: Tabletop cannot handle completely amorphous groups. For groups that have clear horizontal or vertical ends, it will find them. However, for more amorphous groups, it will conclude that certain objects are horizontal or vertical end objects, even though we humans might think that they are very weak or questionable end objects. For example, consider a U-shaped group of objects. Even though we would clearly perceive both objects at the ends of the U to be the end objects of this group, the program will choose only one as the upper end object.)

There are also *find-same-obj* codelets. Such a codelet is given as its argument a particular object (or group of objects) and looks for an identical copy of the given object (or group of objects). If the codelet succeeds in finding an identical object (or group of objects) elsewhere on the table, it sends activation to the concept "sameness."

Specifically, codelets are posted to the Coderack when

- The activation of a particular concept in the Slipnet is high; codelets associated with that concept are posted to the Coderack (e.g., when the concept "group" is sufficiently active, *find-group* codelets are posted to the Coderack).
- A particular codelet runs and succeeds in doing the task for which it was designed; this codelet then posts a new set of codelets to the Coderack (e.g., if

find-group finds a group, it will post a number of codelets designed to explore the structure of the group that has just been found).

An active concept in the Slipnet dispatches codelets to look for instances of itself in the Workspace. For example, if the "group" concept is active, codelets will be dispatched that search for groups in the Tableworld. If one of these codelets succeeds in finding a group, this causes more activation to be sent to the concept "group" in the Slipnet. This amounts to a signal to the system to hunt for even more groups; thus more codelets are sent out to look for groups. Eventually, however, as the rate of group-finding falls (i.e., the rate of change of activation of "group" decreases) and less activation gets sent to "group"—and thus the activation of "group" decays—fewer codelets will be sent out to look for groups. Eventually, the program will thus cease looking for groups, which can be taken as a tacit conclusion that there are probably no more groups to be found on the table.

This process is rather like that used by a person who wants to pick all the apples from a tree. Initially, it is easy to see the apples. She will look first in the most salient places on the tree (e.g., on the outer, leafy branches). The sight of apples remaining in the tree will encourage her to look for more. As the number of apples in the tree gets smaller, she will start to look in less likely places (e.g., on the lower branches, closer to the main trunk). Gradually, as fewer and fewer apples remain, it becomes harder to determine if there are any left at all. Ultimately, there will come a point when she will peer into the tree several times and decide that she has gotten all the apples. But did she really get them all? Probably, but not necessarily. But in the end, the energy (to say nothing of eyestrain) involved in attempting to find any additional apples becomes prohibitive and she stops looking. (The difference, of course, between this and Tabletop is that the apple picker makes a conscious decision to stop hunting for apples, whereas in Tabletop, the decision is tacit.)

The group-finding codelets find groups on the table in a similar way. It is true that some groups may be missed, but on the other hand, the program does not expend needless energy covering every last metaphorical square centimeter of the table to make sure that every single group has been found, even those that have very little chance of playing any role in a potential analogy. In an approach like this, which does not rely on systematic search, as group-finding codelets increasingly fail to find groups, fewer of these codelets run, until finally none run at all. The program has then "decided"—without any single codelet's seeing the whole table, any more than the person below the apple tree could take in the entire tree at one time—that it has found all of the groups on the table, or at least all groups worth looking for.

This might seem somewhat strange at first blush. Why not allow the program to search the table systematically to make sure it has found *all* groups? In short, the answer is scaling up. That is, such a brute-force technique would lead to unacceptably costly and psychologically unrealistic performances in scaled-up situations.

3.4.3 *Structure-building and the Discovery of Descriptions*
Initially, the program explicitly knows only the location and object type of the touched object. The concept in the Slipnet corresponding to the type of the touched object is highly activated. It is not aware of the other objects, their positions on the table, their groupings, and so on. Such things will be discovered during the run of the program.

The table is divided into nine regions like a tic-tac-toe board, although the boundaries between regions are intentionally blurry. In other words, an object that is actually in one region but very close to a region boundary may sometimes be considered by the program to be in the adjacent region.

Because Tabletop builds its representations gradually, it initially represents a newly discovered group of objects in a "gestalt" manner. In other words, no representation is built for the individual objects comprising the group; rather, when a particular codelet discovers a group, it does two things: (1) sends activation to the concept "group" in the Slipnet and (2) posts new codelets to the Coderack that will, if they run, further examine the newly found group for more details about its components, internal structure, and the like. For example, these newly posted codelets will include ones that look for the objects on the ends of the group, others that determine the neighbors of the various objects in the group, still others that scan the group for "sameness groups" inside it (see figure 3.8), and so on.

Consider the group of objects in figure 3.8.

Figure 3.8

Notice that there is theoretically a huge range of groupings that *could* be made. For example, the cup and the knife could be grouped, and then this group could be grouped with the fork immediately to its left. Or the cup could be grouped with the spoon to its right, and then that group could be grouped with the fork-knife group to the left of the cup, and so on. However, even though there is no reason in principle that Tabletop could not make these groups, it very seldom does so. It will almost always discover "sameness groups" (i.e., groups made up of identical objects—the spoon-spoon group and the fork-fork group, in this case). It will usually see groups whose objects share a common ISA category ("shared-ISA groups"). So, for example, the program will generally build silverware groups or crockery groups but will do so less often than it will build sameness groups. And it will only very rarely build groups whose objects have nothing in common. This is why one will not often see a cup-spoon grouping in the representation built by Tabletop of the above set of objects.

The process of "understanding" the initial "gestalt" group is, in some sense, the reverse of distinguishing individual objects, a key goal of standard vision programs. The goal in Tabletop is not to separate objects from each other but to group them into conceptually organized, coordinated sets of items.

There are a number of *find-group* codelets initially on the Coderack, giving the program an initial built-in bias to look for groups of objects. There are also *pick-salient-object* and *pick-salient-correspondence* codelets initially on the Coderack. These codelets simply pick an object (or group of objects) or a correspondence between objects (or groups of objects) for further processing. Such codelets have a probabilistic bias toward picking objects and correspondences of high salience over ones having lower salience. This notion of salience is such an important one that it deserves closer attention (see the next section).

Certain concepts in the Slipnet—in particular, the concept "opposite" and the category of the touched object—are active initially. "Opposite" is active because, given that Eliza is sitting opposite Henry, there should be a natural tendency to look for groups and examine objects on the opposite side of the table from Henry. Activating "opposite" encourages just that.

The Salience of Objects   On the table, certain objects (and correspondences between objects) are more salient to people than others. In Tabletop, the *salience* of an object (or correspondence) is a variable that determines how much attention the program will tend to pay to that object (or correspondence). Salience plays a key role in focusing the program's attention during a run and thus in ensuring that the architecture will be able to scale up to real-world domains. *Pick-salient-object* codelets are continually picking objects in proportion to their salience (for human beings, this corresponds to consciously noticing the objects) for further processing. The calculation of an object's salience takes into account many factors that tend to make an object stand out from the rest of the objects on the table. These factors are as follows:

> *Activation of the concept corresponding to the type of the object* For example, if a certain number of spoons have been noticed by the program, the concept "spoon" will be active. This will contribute to the salience of *all* spoons and make them more likely to be noticed than objects whose types are less active.
>
> *Proximity to the touched object* Objects close to the touched object (usually the most salient object on the table) are noticed preferentially because of this proximity.
>
> *Extremal position in a group of objects* Objects at the ends of a group are, in general, more likely to be noticed than objects in the middle of a group (unless, of course, the concept "middle" is much more active in the Slipnet than the concept "end," in which case the default preference for objects on the ends of groups can be overridden).
>
> *Preferred regions with respect to the touched object* Studies I ran on human subjects showed that certain regions are favored *a priori* as places to look for an object corresponding to the touched object. If the touched object is in a corner, for example, the most favored region is diagonally opposite the touched object, and the next most preferred region is directly opposite the touched object.
>
> *Groups versus simple objects* Groups of objects compete for attention with single objects. Groups are given salience points simply for being groups, which constitutes a pressure in favor of looking at them over simple objects.
>
> *Whether or not the object corresponds to another object* An object's salience increases if it has been mapped to another object on the table (specifically, if the object is part of a correspondence in the Worldview, which is the program's current perception of the central structures on the table, a notion described in detail below).
>
> *How often the object has been part of a correspondence that has won (or lost) a competition* Each time a correspondence competes to become part of the Worldview and wins, bonus points are awarded to the two objects making up the correspondence. Objects in losing correspondences lose points.

Composition of the groups of objects Certain additional factors are taken into consideration in determining the salience of groups of objects:

- *Repetition of objects*: If all the objects in a group are of the same type (i.e., it is a sameness group), this increases the group's salience.
- *Common superordinate category*: If all the objects in a group have the same superordinate object category (e.g., they are all "silverware" or "crockery"), this increases the salience of the group. (These groups are referred to as "shared-ISA groups.")
- *Size*: Larger groups are favored over smaller groups.

Each of these factors determines a real number, and these numbers are summed to determine the salience of the object. The salience of an object thus varies according to how well developed its description is. For example, at the beginning of a run, there are no objects, in correspondence with other objects, and no relations between objects have been found yet. In this case, then, this factor contributes zero to all calculations of salience. However, as soon as it is noticed that a particular object corresponds to another in the Worldview (i.e., the program's current perception of the table), this will increase the salience of both objects. In other words, salience is a dynamic quantity that changes as the program develops its picture of the Tableworld.

The program progressively elaborates a representation of the current Tabletop situation. The first focus of attention of the program tends to be objects whose corresponding concept node in the Slipnet is very active. For example, if Henry touches a cup, the Slipnet concept "cup" will become very active, which means that the program will, at least initially, be more likely to focus attention on cups than on other objects whose corresponding concepts are less active. Activation will subsequently spread to other objects that are conceptually close to cups (e.g., glasses), and the program will focus on these objects. It will explore for other objects and relationships in the neighborhood of these "active" objects. Thus, the initial focus on salient objects will have a subsequent influence on the relational structure that is discovered. So, in the above example, the program will start to test for possible correspondences involving cups and glasses, examine the table for possible neighbors of these salient objects, and so on. The type of "progressive alignment," whereby early focusing on object attributes will lead to and influence the discovery of subsequent relational structure has been observed in children as they learn to represent their world. As Kotovsky and Gentner (1994) point out, "the child starts out making concrete comparisons. . . . Because the child can recognize similarity present in these stimuli, they are able to align the relational structure of the stimuli." Further, Gentner, Rattermann, and Campbell (1993) report what they refer to as a "relational shift: a shift from early attention to common object properties to later attention to common relational structure."

What constitutes high-level structure in the Tabletop world? Correspondences between objects (or groups of objects) are high-level structures, much as groups of objects are high-level structures. They are rated by the program in much the same manner as are objects or groups of objects. A correspondence is defined by its end objects. Its rating is a function of three types of factors: static factors, dynamic factors, and a "bonus" factor.

The static evaluation of a correspondence consists of those factors that do not depend on the relation of that correspondence to the other correspondences in the

Worldview. The dynamic evaluation is a rating of how well the correspondence fits into the current Worldview. The bonus is awarded each time the correspondence wins a competition to get into (or to remain in) the Worldview. Correspondences that lose competitions lose points. The bonus factor in the evaluation of correspondences is designed to model the well-established phenomenon of representational inertia (Kaplan and Kaplan 1982), whereby previously established representations are favored a priori over new representations of data. The longer we humans maintain and use a particular representation, the harder it becomes to dislodge it (James 1892).

The static factors involve, for the most part, slippages that "support" the correspondence. For example, if "leftmost" is one of the descriptors of a particular object and "rightmost" is one of the descriptors of the object to which it corresponds, then we say that the *right-left* slippage "supports" the correspondence. When a concept slips to itself (e.g., *right-right*), this is a degenerate case of the notion of slippage, called an *identity*. The two "objects" in correspondence may be either simple objects—e.g., a fork—or chunked groups of objects—e.g., a group consisting of a fork, a knife, and a spoon. All of the static factors taken into consideration in evaluating correspondences are as follows:

Salience of the two objects that make up the correspondence The higher the salience of the objects (see previous section), the more points are awarded for the correspondence.

Simple-object/group-of-objects slippages The program favors either group-group or simple-object-to-simple-object slippages. If the "group" node is active, the former are favored over the latter; if the "isolated" node is active, the latter are favored; both of these slippages are preferred over group-to-simple-object slippages.

End/middle location slippages The program favors mapping an object on the end of one group to an object on the end of another group or, alternately, an object in the middle of one group to an object in the middle of another group.

Position slippages These are slippages of the descriptions of the positions within their respective groups of the objects making up the correspondences. For example, the first object might be located on the left end of one group and the second object on the right end of another group. This will produce a left-right slippage. The value of this slippage depends on how active the "diagonal symmetry" and "opposite" nodes are, these concepts being the ones that link the two concepts "left" and "right" in the Slipnet. (The activation of the concepts "opposite" and "diagonal symmetry" also depends on how many other correspondences in the Worldview have "opposite" and "diagonal-symmetry" slippages.)

Same or similar object type Points are awarded based on how conceptually close the types of the two corresponding objects are in the Slipnet.

Number-of-objects slippage Points are awarded based on the slippage of the number of objects making up the first object of the correspondence (one, if it is a simple object; otherwise, the size of the group if there is a group of objects) to the number of objects making up the second object in the correspondence. For example, the conceptual distance between "two" and "two" in the Slipnet is less than the distance between "one" and "two." For this reason, the first slippage ("two" to "two") would be awarded more points than the second ("one" to "two").

Same or similar ISA description (applies specifically to shared-ISA groups) If both objects connected by a correspondence are shared-ISA groups, the program compares them. Points are awarded on the basis of how conceptually close the ISA description of one group (e.g., "silverware") is to that of the other. The closer they are, the more points are awarded.

Same-objects slippage (applies specifically to groups) If the object types in both groups making up the correspondence are the same (e.g., both groups consist of a fork, a knife, and a cup), points are awarded to the correspondence.

Orientation slippage (applies specifically to groups) If both groups are linear, there can be horizontal-horizontal, vertical-vertical, or horizontal-vertical slippages. This works in the same way as the position slippages.

The dynamic part of the evaluation of a correspondence can be done only when there are other correspondences in the Worldview. This evaluation is based on the following considerations:

Whether or not the correspondence contains the touched object If it does, it is given a special status, a "Hobj correspondence" (for Henry's object), and receives points.

Whether or not the correspondence is a neighbor of the current Hobj correspondence Two correspondences are considered neighbors if the end objects (i.e., the objects that the correspondence maps onto one another) of one correspondence are the neighbors of the end objects of the second correspondence.

Whether or not the correspondence is the neighbor of one of the correspondences in the Worldview Being a neighbor of a non-Hobj correspondence in the Worldview is worth fewer points than being the neighbor of the Hobj correspondence, but if a correspondence is close to a correspondence already in the Worldview, this nonetheless increases its salience somewhat.

Bonus points in the evaluation of a correspondence are awarded on the basis of *whether a correspondence wins or loses a competition*. The salience of a correspondence in the Worldview is increased each time it wins a competition with a rival trying to take its place. Any correspondence that loses a competition has its rating decreased. The psychological justification for this "the strong get stronger, the weak get weaker" philosophy has been discussed in the previous section.

In much the same way as the salience of objects is determined, the points from the static and dynamic evaluations and from the winning or losing competitions are added together. This determines the strength of a particular correspondence.

3.4.4 Competing Structures and the Worldview
In both Copycat and Tabletop, when a new structure is proposed, it is evaluated with respect to the structures already built. In some cases, the proposed new structure will have to compete with an already-existing structure. For example, in Copycat, the third **a** in the string **aaabc** might be described as belonging either to the subgroup **aaa** or to the subgroup **abc**, depending on various other groupings already found, but it cannot be described as belonging to both **abc** and **aaa** simultaneously.

Psychological plausibility does not allow a single object to belong simultaneously to two rival subgroups at once. There may be competing descriptions of reality, but at any given time, only one of these descriptions belongs to our *perception* of the situation. For example, there are clearly two possible competing descriptions of the line drawing called the Necker cube. However, at any given moment, one sees it in just one of those ways. Similarly, for the famous ambiguous drawing of the young woman and the old woman (Hill 1915), we are incapable of perceiving both representations simultaneously. The same principle applies to ambiguous newspaper headlines, such as "Milk Drinkers Turn to Powder" and "Squad Helps Dog Bite Victim" (Cooper 1980). When we conceptualize one of the meanings (for example, "a squad of people helping a dog bite some innocent person"), we are thereby blocked from envisioning the other high-level interpretation (namely, "a rescue squad providing medical care to a person bitten by a dog"), and vice versa. The mutual exclusivity is total.

It is to simulate this human inability to perceive a situation in two conflicting ways simultaneously that the program must choose which subgroup (**aaa** or **abc**) the middle **a** belongs to. Now, if in other strings the program has already found the sameness groups **ppp**, **ddd**, and **mmm** and no successor groups like **pqr**, then it is very likely to group the three **a**'s together and to describe the third **a** in **aaabc** as belonging to **aaa**. Conversely, if it has elsewhere found the repetition groups **pqr**, **efg**, and **xyz** and no sameness groups, then it is very likely to describe the third **a** in **aaabc** as belonging to **abc**.

Competition in Tabletop works in the same way as in Copycat with one exception. In Copycat, competition is a "gladiatorial" process: structures that lose competitions are "killed"—that is, are eliminated entirely from the Workspace. Thus, regardless of how much time and energy were required to build a particular structure, if that structure loses a competition with another one, it is broken, and the program, in order to get a new one like it again, has to build the structure up from scratch again. This may not pose too serious a problem if the structures involved are relatively small, as they are in Copycat and Tabletop, but in more complicated domains, this type of policy is neither practical nor psychologically plausible. (As long ago as the late nineteenth century, Ebbinghaus (1885) demonstrated subconscious memory "savings" of this type.) Competition among structures in Tabletop is a more "sporting" process: although losers are penalized for losing, they stay in the game.

To understand the difference between Copycat-style destructive competition and Tabletop's more sporting style, consider the young woman/old woman figure. Regardless of whether we see the old woman or the young woman first, it invariably takes us a while to see the other figure, but eventually we do see it. Thereafter, when our perception flips back to the first interpretation, it is easier to see the second interpretation a second time. Eventually, we can flip back and forth between the two interpretations with no trouble. This is presumably because we maintain a somewhat active (although below-conscious-threshold) representation of the second figure in our brains. However, in a Copycat-like implementation of vision, the second representation would be destroyed, having lost the competition with the first representation. This view would imply that it would be no easier to reconstruct the second representation each time. That this is clearly not the case in humans argues for a perceptual architecture that does keep rejected representations around for some time, even if they are not highly active.

All the resources of the program are devoted to building up the Worldview. The Worldview is a set of noncontradictory mappings of objects and groups of objects onto one another. In this context, "noncompeting" (sometimes called "noncontradictory") means that no object can simultaneously correspond to two or more different objects. (Note that this does not prevent one object from being mapped onto a chunked group of two or more objects. A fork, for example, could very well be mapped onto a chunked group of two forks.) This also means that if the program maps a group of objects, **A**, onto another group of objects, **B**, as wholes, then the individual objects inside **A** can map only to objects inside **B** and not to some other object elsewhere on the table. (Correspondences in the Worldview are always indicated by solid lines connecting objects or groups of objects.) A set of noncompeting correspondences (i.e., no object or group of objects is the end object for two distinct correspondences) is illustrated in figure 3.9.

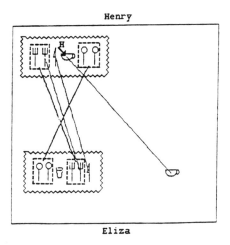

Figure 3.9
Noncompeting correspondences

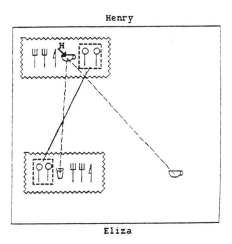

Figure 3.10
Directly competing correspondences: the cup-glass and the cup-cup correspondences. They compete, and one of them will emerge a winner.

The incorporation of correspondences into the Worldview is a three-stage process: correspondence creation, initial testing, and competition. A correspondence will not even be created unless certain not-too-stringent conditions are met—for example, the objects in question must not be in the same group. Once created, the correspondence will be evaluated on the basis of a set of more rigorous conditions. Again, the outcome of this evaluation is a probabilistic one: there is no rigid evaluation threshold above which the correspondence passes and below which it fails. If the correspondence passes this test, it can then proceed to compete with any conflicting (in the sense shown above) correspondences in the Worldview so far developed.

Figure 3.11 shows an example of a competition between a correspondence in the current Worldview (indicated by the solid line between the touched cup and the isolated cup in the lower right-hand corner of the table) and a rival correspondence (indicated by the dashed line between the touched cup and the small glass).

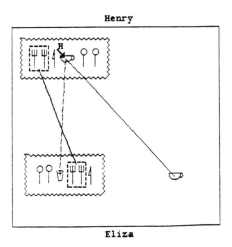

Figure 3.11
Competition between a correspondence in the Worldview (solid line) and a proposed rival correspondence (dashed line)

The proposed new correspondence must compete with any conflicting correspondences already in the Worldview. The way in which such competition works is as follows: All the conflicting correspondences are temporarily removed (subjunctively) from the Old Worldview, and the new correspondence is temporarily inserted (subjunctively) in their place to form the Rival Worldview. The Rival Worldview is evaluated according to the criteria given in the section on determining the salience of correspondences between objects. The probabilistic winner of this competition between the Rival Worldview and the Old Worldview is then installed as the new Worldview.

Once the winning Worldview has been chosen, the rating of each of the correspondences in that Worldview is improved and the rating of the losing correspondence is lowered. In other words, winning a competition improves the chances of the winner the next time it competes. Similarly, it becomes a little harder for the loser to compete the next time around. The loser, although not in the Worldview, remains nonetheless in the Workspace with the potential to compete again.

In Copycat, structures that lose competitions are simply removed from the Workspace and must be entirely rebuilt in order to have another chance. In Tabletop, structures (like old soldiers) do not die, they just fade away. In other words, each time a structure is involved in a competition and loses, its salience rating drops until finally, if this happens enough times, it gets removed from the Workspace. In addition, the salience ratings of objects that are part of losing correspondences are decreased, of winning correspondences, increased. This applies not only to correspondences but, in particular, to various conceptual groupings of objects. It would be reasonable to maintain a record of the age of a particular structure, even though this is not presently implemented in Copycat. If a structure remained inactive for a long time (i.e., was not part of a correspondence in the Worldview, or occasionally competed to get into the Worldview, or was not part of building new structures, etc.), then it would be removed from the Workspace. (Note that once a correspondence is removed from the Workspace, any codelets that might have this correspondence as one of its parameters would, if selected to run, simply "fizzle," i.e., have no action at all.)

Let us return to the example of the letter string **aaabc**. In Copycat, the program will allow only one possible interpretation of the string at a time: either **(aaa)(bc)** or **(aa)(abc)**. These two interpretations will compete and one will win and "kill" the other, which will then be removed from the Workspace. In Tabletop, by contrast, the winner would be put into the Worldview (and its rating would be enhanced by dint of winning the competition) while the loser would remain in the Workspace (and its rating would be lowered after losing the competition). Because the losing structure remains in the Workspace, the program does not have to go to the trouble of rebuilding it from scratch each time. Eventually, if the value of a correspondence in Tabletop drops below a certain threshold (for example, because it has lost a number of competitions), it is (probabilistically) removed from the Workspace and then must be built again.

In Copycat, prior to competitions between structures, this Worldview/Workspace distinction exists implicitly. What one could call Copycat's "Worldview" would consist of those structures represented by *solid* lines. These are structures that have won competitions against rivals and represent the program's current perception of the problem at hand. Structures that have a chance to compete with the various solid-line structures are represented by dashed (weaker) and dotted (weakest) lines. Thus before they compete with solid-line structures, these weaker structures coinhabit the Workspace along with the solid-line (currently perceived) structures. However, after a competition, the losing structures are removed entirely from the Workspace, rather than merely demoted into dashed or dotted status. For example, if a solid-line structure lost a competition to a dashed-line structure, the latter would be promoted to solid-line status, whereas the former would be removed from the Workspace. In Tabletop, by contrast, the losing solid-line structure would simply be demoted to dashed-line status, rather than requiring the program to rebuild it from scratch again. There is thus a pleasing time symmetry in Tabletop: structures come into existence gradually and go out of existence gradually.

This distinction between the Worldview—which is the sole, current interpretation of the table—and the larger Workspace, in which there can be many structures that have been built but are below "conscious threshold," is an important one for two reasons.

First, a system of this sort is psychologically more plausible than a system that irretrievably destroys many items it has already built. Once people have recognized a certain structure, say in doing a Jumble, even if they reject that structure, it is kept intact in the background for a while, even if they are not directly conscious of it. Eventually, of course, it will disappear if it is never reactivated.

Second, there is the old issue of scaling up. For real-world domains, in which the structures that are built up are likely to be very complicated, we do not want each competition to completely destroy all the work previously done in creating the losing structure. This is especially true for structures in which the competition is very close. We want one structure to gradually pull ahead while the other gradually falls behind. A winner-take-all-and-destroy-the-loser philosophy would be very costly, since it would mean, in essence, that a complex structure would have one and only one chance to compete. The only way for that structure ever to compete again would be if it somehow got built up all over again, which is very unlikely if it is complex.

It is important to know how a Worldview is rated. The evaluation of the Worldview is the sum of the following:

The total of the strength ratings of all of the correspondences contained in it.

The degree of coherence of the Worldview This is closely related to the notion of systematicity developed by Gentner (1983) and others. More recently, Spellman and Holyoak (1992), Gentner and Markman (1994), and Clement and Gentner (1991) also elegantly demonstrate subjects' desire for structurally consistent mappings. In the Tabletop domain, this translates into a preference for a "coherent" Worldview in which, basically, correspondences tend to bunch together logically. For example, if there were three groups of objects on the table, the program would penalize a Worldview consisting of four strong correspondences from objects in group 1 to objects in group 2 and one correspondence from an object in group 1 to another object in group 3. The Worldview coherence would be much higher in the above example if *all* of the correspondences went from objects in group 1 to objects in group 2. (See figure 3.12 for an example of an incoherent Worldview.) Consistency is a measure of how close a particular Worldview is to such an ideal arrangement of correspondences.

Degree of parallelism One correspondence is said to be parallel to another if the slippages that support the first have the same labels as the slippages that support the second. For example, if one correspondence in the Worldview is supported by a left-to-right slippage, which has an "opposite" label, then a parallel

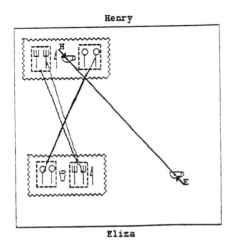

Figure 3.12
An incoherent Worldview

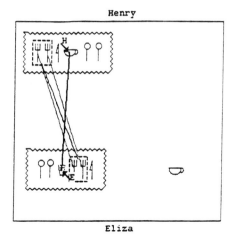

Figure 3.13
A coherent Worldview

correspondence in the same Worldview would have a slippage with the same label (e.g., a right-to-left or an above-to-below slippage). The notion of parallel slippages is more complicated in Tabletop than in Copycat for two reasons:

• There can be two (or more) physically separate groups of correspondences on the table—for example, a set of correspondences between two groups on the left-hand side of the table and another set of correspondences between two groups on the right-hand side of the table—with no interaction between the two. It is as if there are two separate subworlds on the table. If there is a left-to-right slippage in the first set of correspondences, should this affect the second set of correspondences?

• There can be two or more levels of correspondences within correspondences. In other words, when two groups correspond globally to one another, there can be further correspondences between objects inside each of the two groups. Do we require that the kinds of slippages at one level (for example, the level of the group) significantly influence slippages at another (e.g., the level of individual objects)?

These two questions, which constitute what I call the "problem of a single node with multiple activations" (or, alternately, to borrow two terms from computer science, the "problem of context pushing and popping"), are too complicated to be dealt with here, and they will be considered in depth later in this chapter. For the moment, it is sufficient to mention that these issues do enter into the calculation of degree of parallelism of slippages in the Worldview.

3.4.5 Actions of Codelets and "Codelet Sequencing"
A typical codelet generally has a threefold action:

Description-building It notices a particular aspect of the Tableworld—for example, a group of objects, the neighbor of a particular object, the object on the end of a group, a correspondence between two objects, the presence of a particular group of objects, and so on—and attaches an appropriate descriptor to the object concerned.

Sending activation to the Slipnet It sends activation to the Slipnet node that corresponds to the discovery that it has made, allowing the Slipnet to "flex" in reaction to what has been discovered on the table. For example, if a codelet discovers a group of objects, it sends activation to the "group" node in the Slipnet.

Engendering other codelets. This is a crucial part of a codelet's task. A codelet that has just succeeded will put on the Coderack codelets that "follow up" the just-completed action. For example, if a group-finding codelet has just found a group, it will put on the Coderack a number of codelets that will hunt for the end objects of the group just found, others that will hunt for the middle objects of the group, others that will pick elements from the group and determine their immediate neighbors, and so on. This will be discussed in more detail below.

A colleague once asked me why all possible codelet types were not simply put on the Coderack at the beginning of a run of the program. The answer is (again) scaling up. That is, such a brute-force strategy would not allow the program to focus its resources and would lead to combinatorial explosion in a real-world domain. An example will serve to illustrate this.

When a *find-group* codelet finds a group, in addition to sending activation to the "group" node in the Slipnet and updating a short-term record of the number of groups found (a kind of short-term memory), the program puts the following codelets on the Coderack:

- A *find-group* codelet, which will look for more groups
- A *sameness-detector*, which looks to see if that exact configuration of objects appears elsewhere on the table
- A *find-neighbor* codelet, which takes as a parameter an object in the group just found and determines its neighbors
- A *find-end-object* codelet, which will find the end objects of the group
- A *find-middle-object* codelet, which will find objects in the middle of the group
- *Pick-salient-object* codelets, which pick other salient objects on the table

This process of codelet sequencing is essential for allowing the program to focus its resources, essential if the program is to be able to scale up. For example, if there are *no* groups on the table, it makes no sense for there to be any perceptual agents hunting for the neighbors of objects, the end objects of groups, and so on. Such codelets, if present, would run and inevitably fail because, in order for an object to have a neighbor, it must be in a group. If there are no groups, no object has a neighbor and any effort expended by the program in an attempt to find neighbors would be wasted.

The Coderack is the staging area for the codelets. Codelets are hung on the Coderack and wait there until they are selected to run. Each codelet put on the Coderack has an urgency—a number that represents approximately how important the program estimates it is to run that particular codelet. The higher the number, the more important it is to run the codelet.

Each codelet also has an "age" that represents how long it has been on the Coderack. A codelet that has been on the Coderack too long is eliminated, because chances are that it is no longer relevant to the continually evolving representation of the table. In Copycat, codelets are removed from the Coderack based not only on age, but on urgency as well: urgency is divided by age, and if the resulting number is (probabilistically) below a certain threshold, the codelet is removed. This has the effect of removing a number of low-urgency codelets, even if they have not been on the Coderack too long. I chose to leave low-urgency codelets on the Coderack since, at least in theory, this will lead to a greater diversity in representational possibilities.

A typical codelet hung on the Coderack looks like this: (*codelet-name codelet-age codelet-urgency*). Codelets are selected to run based on two factors: their urgency and the current computational temperature. If we ignore computational temperature, the following simplified example will illustrate how probabilistic selection takes place. Assume that the Coderack contains the following codelets:

Codelet name	Urgency
find-group-around (**small-glass$_1$**)	6
find-neighbor (**cup$_1$**)	3
build-object (**fork$_1$**, **fork$_2$**)	1
Total Coderack urgency	10

The program must now select a codelet to run. It will choose the *find-group-around* codelet with a probability of .6, the *find-neighbor* codelet with a probability of .3, and the *build-object* codelet with a probability of .1.

"Urgency Explosion": Difficulties with Codelet Sequencing   Let us return to the issue of codelet sequencing. This proved to be an extremely difficult (and largely unanticipated) problem. There were three problems that had to be overcome—namely:

- Determining which types of codelets should be spawned by a particular codelet
- Determining how a codelet sets the "raw" urgency of the codelets it spawns
- Preventing urgency explosions—somewhat analogous to inflation in economics

The first two difficulties are not surprising and need no explanation. The third problem, however, is less obvious and requires explanation. Assume the program has just begun running and is in the process of hunting for groups. Suppose also that there are four groups on the table, at least three of which are important for the program to find for the purposes of establishing correspondences between objects. But as soon as one group is found, the program will put a number of codelets—*find-group, sameness-detector, find-neighbor, find-end-object, find-middle-object,* and *pick-salient-object*—on the Coderack. For the sake of illustration, assume that before this happens, the entire Coderack consists of only two *find-group* codelets, each of urgency 10. This means that each codelet is of equal importance, accounting for 50 percent of the total urgency of the Coderack. One of these codelets runs, spawning six new codelets, each of which has an urgency of 10. This means that the urgency of the *find-group* codelet sequencing. This proved to be an extremely difficult (and largely unanticipated) problem. There were three problems that had to be overcome—namely: codelet ran. In other words, its importance has been reduced in one instant to approximately one-quarter of its previous value. It is now much more likely that one of the just-spawned codelets will run, engendering a host of child codelets of its own, thereby diminishing the importance of the original *find-group* codelet to the point find-group-1 [urg. = 25]   +   find-group-2 [urg. = 25]

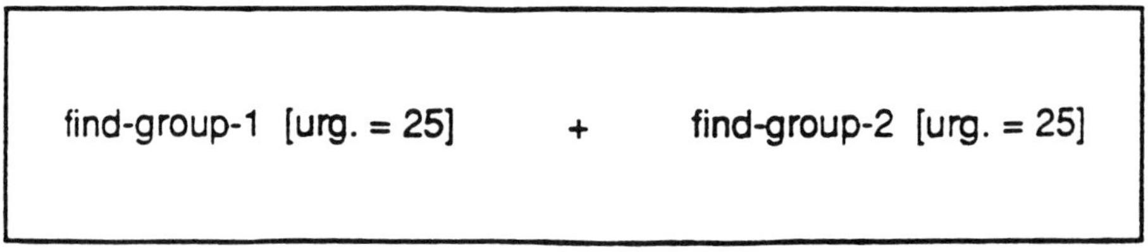

Figure 3.14
Equal importance of two *find-group* codelets on the Coderack.

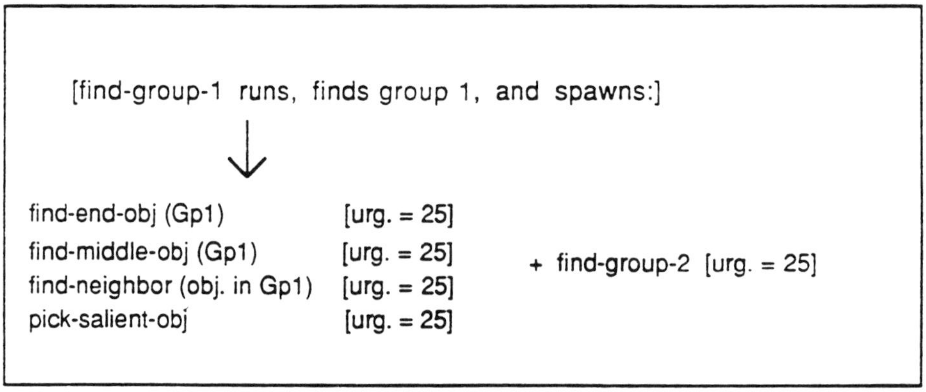

[find-group-1 runs, finds group 1, and spawns:]

↓

find-end-obj (Gp1)   [urg. = 25]
find-middle-obj (Gp1)   [urg. = 25]   + find-group-2 [urg. = 25]
find-neighbor (obj. in Gp1) [urg. = 25]
pick-salient-obj   [urg. = 25]

Figure 3.15
One *find-group* codelet runs, spawning codelets whose combined urgency swamps the urgency of the other *find-group* codelet.

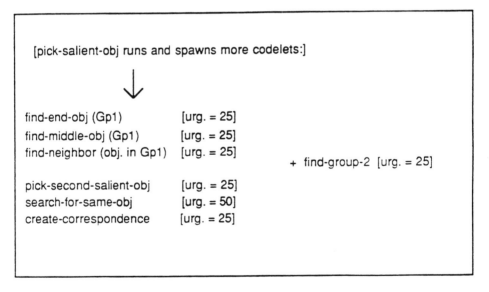

[pick-salient-obj runs and spawns more codelets:]

↓

find-end-obj (Gp1)   [urg. = 25]
find-middle-obj (Gp1)   [urg. = 25]
find-neighbor (obj. in Gp1) [urg. = 25]
                                              + find-group-2 [urg. = 25]
pick-second-salient-obj   [urg. = 25]
search-for-same-obj   [urg. = 50]
create-correspondence   [urg. = 25]

Figure 3.16
One of the spawned codelets runs. The added effect of the combined urgencies of its children now leaves the original *find-group* codelet with little chance of ever running.

where it will probably never get called to run, even though a mere two codelets before it was as important as any codelet on the Coderack. Figures 3.14, 3.15, and 3.16 illustrate this problem.

That this should happen is antithetical to the whole philosophy of codelets. Codelets are small pieces of code that should effect small, gradual changes in the building up (or breaking down) of structure. Only under rare circumstances should a single codelet radically affect the overall course of structure-building. Not only does this problem of urgency explosion lead to the psychologically implausible result of almost completely forgetting past priorities in a very short time (after the execution of two or three codelets), but it wreaks havoc with the program's general ability to focus its resources correctly. If at generation t the program has certain resource priorities, it seems wrong that they would have almost *always* changed completely by generation $t + 2$.

The problem of urgency explosion did not manifest itself in Copycat because that program had the design feature that each codelet engendered at most one follow-up codelet. If no more than one codelet is spawned by each codelet, the relative urgencies of the parent and child will, on average, be the same with respect to the rest of the Coderack. In other words, relative codelet urgencies of both parent and child codelets will, on average, be preserved. Urgency explosion is thereby avoided. As was discussed above, however, in Tabletop one codelet may spawn four or five different codelets, and if there is no adjustment of the urgencies of the spawned codelets with respect to the urgency of the spawning codelet, an urgency explosion will occur. This means that codelets whose importance prior to the running of a competing codelet was relatively high may suddenly find themselves to be of little importance, due to the high total urgency of the newly spawned codelets. The more codelets a single codelet can spawn, the greater the problem.

The crux of the problem is that one codelet of a given urgency can spawn many codelets of the same (average) urgency. A number of possible solutions to this problem have been considered. I discuss below some of these suggested solutions, along with the technique that I finally adopted.

Adopt the Copycat strategy of having any codelet spawn at most one codelet. This produces an unacceptable requirement of sequentiality in running codelets. For example, it is reasonable to assume that once one codelet finds a group, further codelets should be sent out to discover the objects on the ends of that group and others to discover the objects in the middle of the group. In other words, if a *find-group* codelet succeeds in finding a group, it should post at least two codelets to the Coderack, a *find-end-object* codelet and a *find-middle-object* codelet, each of roughly the same urgency. There is no reason for the program to post only one of these codelets—say, the *find-end-object* codelet—and have this codelet, when it finishes running, post the *find-middle-object* codelet. This would be imposing an artificial sequencing of the codelets. Why should *find-end-object* necessarily run before *find-middle-object*? It should not—and this is why the *find-group* codelet should be able to post both *find-end-object* and *find-middle-object* codelets.

Reduce the urgency of the spawned codelets by a constant amount. If it is not possible to restrict the number of codelets spawned to one, then perhaps it is possible to reduce the urgencies of the spawned codelets. For example, if the spawning codelet has an urgency of 10, then it would be possible to insist that the maximum urgency of any spawned codelet be, say, 2 less than 10, in other words, 8. The problem with this is that, although urgency explosion may be a little slower, it will nonetheless occur if the sum of the urgencies of the spawned codelets significantly exceeds the urgency of the spawning codelet. Even if the total urgency of the spawned codelets does not exceed the parent urgency, there would still be a problem with this method. Some codelet types—for example, *find-neighbor* codelets—spawn other codelets of their own type, and it cannot be predicted ahead of time when this chain will stop. If there is a group consisting of **fork₁**, **fork₂**, **knife₁**, **cup₁**, **spoon₁**, and **spoon₂**, the first *find-neighbor* codelet might have as its parameter **fork₁**. It would find **fork₂** and spawn the codelet *find-neighbor*(**fork₂**). If this codelet ran, it would find **knife₁**) and post the codelet *find-neighbor*(**knife₁**), and so on. Since it is impossible to predict ahead of time how long the group might be, it cannot be known how many "generations" of *find-neighbor* codelets there will be. If the urgency of the spawned codelet is decreased linearly at each generation, the situation could arise in which codelets of zero urgency (or even negative urgency!) would be put on the Coderack.

Do not allow the total urgency of the spawned codelets to exceed the urgency of the spawning codelet. This is getting closer to the solution that I feel is the most appropriate, but there is still a problem. In some cases, you *want* it to be possible to post a codelet to the Coderack with an extremely high urgency, far higher than its parent's urgency. If, for example, a codelet discovers an extraordinarily promising avenue of exploration, it should be able to post a codelet to the Coderack whose urgency is high enough to almost *ensure* that it will run. This would not be possible if the present suggestion were adopted to curtail urgency explosion.

Spawn "bundles" of codelets instead of individual codelets. The idea here is that each codelet of a given urgency would post a bundle of codelets to the Coderack, the bundle having approximately the same urgency as the parent codelet. Within this bundle, codelets could have any urgency, but this "internal" urgency would not be felt outside of the bundle. The bundle, and not an individual codelet, would be selected to run. When the bundle was called to run, only one codelet would be selected from the bundle to run, based on the internal urgencies of the codelets within the bundle, and the bundle as a whole would be pruned from the Coderack. This method would indeed eliminate the problem of urgency explosion. It would mean, however, that only one of the codelets in the bundle would get a chance to run and that once that codelet had run, the others in the bundle would never have any chance whatsoever to run. This would pose even more severe problems than the "one-codelet—one-child" philosophy, because there all of the codelets would at least have a chance to run. Under the present suggestion, the competitors within the bundle of the selected codelet would never run.

Use a variation of the bundling strategy whereby the diminished bundle (i.e., after one codelet in the bundle had run) would be returned to the Coderack with its externally visible urgency proportionately reduced. It seems to me that this technique might be able to overcome the problem and should be investigated by researchers implementing this type of codelet-based architecture. I did not explore this method.

Decrease the urgency of spawned codelets as an exponential function of their "generation." This is the solution I have adopted. Each codelet is tagged to indicate the generation to which it belongs. The original codelets on the Coderack are of generation 0, their children are of generation 1, their grandchildren are of generation 2, and so on. The urgency of the spawned codelets put on the Coderack is their "raw urgency" (some number between 1 and 100) divided by the urgency-reduction coefficient raised to their generation number. This solution is discussed in greater detail in the following section.

The problem of urgency explosion plagued the Tabletop architecture from the start, because Tabletop codelets have, in general, always spawned multiple codelets. The various techniques that were originally tried felt very much like ad hoc fixes to a deeper problem. A solution that was Tabletop-specific—that would, for example, dump a lot of *find-neighbor* codelets on the Coderack at a particular time was clearly inappropriate. It is unlikely that solutions of this kind would even have been general enough to apply to a wide range of Tabletop problems, let alone being able to be used for the architecture in general.

The solution that seems to give good results is based on the recognition and use of the notion of the "generation" of a codelet in determining its urgency when it is put on the Coderack. The basic principle is as follows: Each codelet keeps track of the generation to which it belongs. There is an urgency-reduction factor defined as the *urgency-reduction coefficient* (a global variable, ρ, currently set at 3) raised to the power of the codelet's generation (G in the formula below). Each codelet has a *raw urgency*, typically an integer value between 1 and 100, which is the urgency associated with the codelet originally. In other words, within the definition of the *find-group* codelet, there will be an instruction to hang certain codelets on the Coderack, among them *find-end-object* and *find-middle-object*, with certain raw urgencies, say, 10. However, when a codelet is actually put on the Coderack, it is assigned an *adjusted urgency* defined by

$$\frac{raw\ urgency}{\rho^G},$$

where ρ is the urgency reduction coefficient and G is the generation number of the codelet.

Assume, for the purposes of example, that $\rho = 2$ and that there are two second-generation *find-group* codelets on the Coderack, each with an (adjusted) urgency of 4. One of these codelets runs and spawns a *find-end-object* codelet, a *find-middle-object* codelet, and two *find-neighbor* codelets, each with a raw urgency of 8. The adjusted urgency of each of these four spawned codelets when they are put on the Coderack is

$$\frac{8}{2^3} = 1.$$

Thus, the total amount of urgency that the spawned codelets contribute to the Coderack is $1 + 1 + 1 + 1 = 4$, as opposed to 32 in the standard implementation. In the standard implementation, the running of a single *find-group* codelet would have reduced the importance of the competing *find-group* codelet from 50 percent to 12.5 percent. In the approach suggested in this section, the remaining *find-group* codelet would actually *gain* in relative importance. In other words, it would be more likely to run after the other codelets were spawned than before. Of course, relative gains in urgency of this sort are not necessary consequences of this strategy; the gain in this case is simply a result of the specific numbers used in this example. However, I will argue in a moment that it is indeed reasonable to have older codelets sometimes gain in relative importance with respect to more recently spawned ones.

It should be noted first that this technique of exponential reduction of urgency avoids the problem of the third solution proposed in the preceding section—namely, that of not allowing the total urgency of the spawned codelets to exceed the urgency of the spawning codelet. By reducing urgency exponentially, it is possible—even if it is never actually done in Tabletop—to post to the Coderack a codelet whose adjusted urgency is greater than the adjusted urgency of its parent.

Assigning relatively more urgency to older codelets is rather similar to the process of veneration of elders that goes on in a family of several generations. The opinions of grandparents are given more weight than those of parents, whose opinions, in turn, are given more weight than those of their children. But this is not a static process. The older people will eventually die, parents will become grandparents, children will become parents, and the relative importance of everyone's opinions will change accordingly.

Similarly, because the Tabletop Coderack can contain only a certain number of codelets (currently 150), the oldest codelets will eventually be "pushed off" the Coderack in order to make room for the newcomers. Thus, if the "opinions" of the older codelets are not expressed (i.e., they have not yet run) by the time of their demise, they will never be expressed. As child codelets become parent codelets, their importance increases relative to their children, and so on.

This method not only handles the problem of urgency explosion but introduces a parameter, ρ, that can be adjusted to give different weights to the various generations. If ρ is 1, we have the original situation, in which all codelets, when put on the Coderack, are given their raw urgency. If ρ is 1.5 or 2, then we have the situation described above. As the size of ρ increases, the relative importance of parent and grandparent codelets increases with respect to the younger generations of codelets. When this parameter is sufficiently large, the system will run in a completely hierarchical way: parent codelets will invariably run before their children do. This would produce the codelet equivalent of strict breadth-first search (assuming codelets were never pushed off the Coderack when they became too old). On the other hand, if ρ were made very small (less than 1), this would ensure that the most promising of the newly spawned codelets would always run, thus producing strict depth-first search.

The first two issues involving codelet sequencing—namely, determining the codelets that a particular codelet should spawn and assigning raw urgencies to these codelets—continue to pose problems which will have no easy solutions. However, the proposed solution to overcome urgency explosion seems to be both plausible and effective.

3.4.6 The Problem of Single Nodes with Multiple Activations

One other major philosophical and implementational hurdle had to be overcome in building the Tabletop program. This was the so-called problem of single nodes with multiple activations. This problem arises from the fundamental assumption that humans have only one "copy" of each concept in long-term memory. (In short, there is only one set of neurons that correspond to the concept "left.") For example, there is not one concept "left" that is activated when I say "Go left," an entirely different "left" that is activated when I refer to my left pocket, and yet another when I call someone a left fielder. In other words, there is a single *type* "left" stored in long-term memory. (A complementary premise of Tabletop is that there can be any number of *tokens* of a particular type in working memory.) This seemingly straightforward (and reasonable) principle turns out, rather unexpectedly, to pose a very sticky problem.

To see where the problem arises, let us start with the simple observation that concepts in long-term memory, once active, remain active for a certain amount of time, long enough to have some influence on other concepts through spreading activation. This observation dates back at least to the end of the last century (James 1892). Later, in an attempt to bridge the gap between psychology and neurophysiology, Hebb stressed the necessity for groups of neurons to have collective states or modes that remain active for a critical period in order for learning to take place (Hebb 1949). More recently, studies of recall and priming (Meyer and Schvaneveldt 1971) have shown that concepts can apparently maintain low levels of activation for relatively long periods for time.

The difficulty is that, whereas concepts are clearly capable of retaining activation, they also seem capable of suddenly *changing* their level of activation in the presence of a new context and then *reverting* to their former state when the new context is no longer present. A host of problems arise, most notably, how this rapid activation-switching might be possible. Put another way, how is the former level of activation stored so that it can be restored when the second context disappears? Can the mind maintain something like a stack of activation values for each concept, or must it reconstruct the earlier activation level "from scratch" when the second context disappears? And why does there seem to be so little influence of one level of activation in one context on the level of activation of the same concept in the other context? I think answering these questions poses a serious challenge to researchers engaged in cognitive modeling. In what follows, I first indicate a few examples of where the problem of multiply active concepts manifests itself in everyday life and language. I then illustrate how the problem arises in Tabletop, indicate the results of a small series of experiments carried out on subjects, and discuss my preliminary solution to this problem.

The first example of the problem was given in chapter 2. In that example, I considered the case of a friend giving directions to Ann Arbor, Michigan, from Detroit ("Go west on I-94"). Even with our friend's directions still fresh in our minds—presumably causing the concept "west" to become highly active—we do not necessarily choose the west exit over the east exit as we leave the parking structure of the apartment complex, heading for Ann Arbor. While in the parking structure, we seem not to be under the influence of the activation of the concept "west." Our choice of exit is (largely, if not completely) independent of the concepts activated in the prior instruction from our friend. However, the moment we exit, "west" regains its central status as the main goal to accomplish now. It is as if there are three distinct worlds: the first, our friend's apartment, in which our concept "west" was activated when we heard the instruction "Go west on I-94"; the second, the parking structure; and the third, the freeway itself.

Here is another example, related to me by a friend who has two close friends named David. A few years ago, he drove across the country with one of them—

David M.—and so, at least for the duration of the trip, any reference to David would naturally have bound itself in his mind to the concept "David M." Two days into their trip, my friend called his father in California, thereby mentally displacing himself from a New Mexico gift shop to his parents' California residence. During the phone conversation, his father asked, "How's David?" referring to the friend with whom he was crossing the country. However, "David" in past discussions with his father in California had always meant a *different* David—David P.—a close and longtime friend of the family. Consequently, my friend assumed his father was referring to David P., rather than his current traveling companion, David M. His telephonic self-teleport to California had effectively "erased" all (or most) of the "David" activation associated with "David M." and caused it instead to be bound to his "David P." concept, which less than a minute before in the New Mexico context had been totally dormant. And yet, when my friend popped out of the mental California—whether by hanging up the phone or by being reminded of the New Mexico context by seeing Navajo trinkets on the gift rack of the shop he was standing in—the level of activation of his "David" node associated with the concept "David M." instantly returned to its pre-telephone-call level.

A final example in this vein involves renting a car and driving in England. Looking through the windshield of your rented car puts you in a rules-of-the-road context. In this context, "left" is very active, since you continually have to remind yourself to drive on the left-hand side of the road. Left turns are done differently, the shoulder of the road is on the left, you turn left into traffic circles, the curb is to your left, and so on. However, when you enter the inside-the-car subworld, the activation of "left" from the rules-of-the-road context seems to vanish almost entirely, at least in the sense that your actions in the new context are not significantly influenced by the prior activation of "left" in the former rules-of-the-road context. For example, the prior activation of "left" does not cause you to look for the accelerator with your left foot, or to turn the radio knob to the left to turn it on, and so on. The outside-the-car, rules-of-the-road activation slate is wiped clean. In the new context inside the car, a new activation level will be established for "left." Of course, in the inside-the-passenger-compartment context, some things *will* be different, but other things will not be. You will shift gears with your left hand, for example, but the shifting pattern is unchanged from that of American cars. The same sorts of questions arise within the car: Does the fact that you turn the radio on with your left hand mean that you are more likely to turn the volume knob to the left? Probably not. Again, you enter a new context (the radio context), wiping the former activation slate clean and proceeding afresh. Of course, as you "pop" out of these levels, the former activation of "left" returns in each case instantly.

These problems are somewhat reminiscent of the variable-binding problem discussed in connectionist modeling (Clossman 1987; Smolensky 1988; Ajjanagadde and Shastri 1990).

The problem of a single node with multiple activations does arise in Tabletop. Consider the table configuration in figure 3.17. Suppose the program has built two correspondences, one from the upper left-hand to the lower left-hand corner of the table, the other from the upper right-hand to the lower right-hand corner of the table.

The correspondence between the silverware groups ($\mathbf{cp_1}$) is supported by a "left"-to-"left" identity slippage, and the correspondence between the cups ($\mathbf{cp_2}$) is sup-

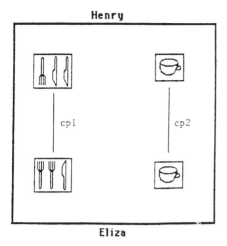

Figure 3.17

ported by a "right"-to-"right" identity slippage, where the terms "left" and "right" refer to the sides of the table *as a whole*. Both of these identity slippages will cause activation to be sent to the "mirror symmetry" concept node in the Slipnet. The concept "mirror symmetry" will therefore become very active.

Let us assume that the program has built the fork-fork sameness groups on both sides of the table (figure 3.18). When the correspondence cp_1 was built, a number of *examine-cp*($\mathbf{cp_1}$) codelets were posted to the Coderack. The role of these codelets is to take the group-level correspondence and whether there are any correspondences to be built between the *objects* making up the connected groups. Now comes the crucial point: in some sense, it is as if when *examine-cp*($\mathbf{cp_1}$) runs, it enters a subset of the full Tableworld, a smaller world consisting of just the two groups in question (figure 3.19).

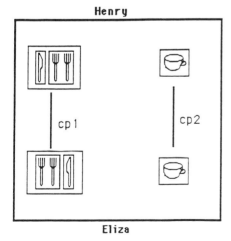

Figure 3.18

There is a problem. On the one hand, one wants Tabletop to go for the very obvious and attractive diagonal mapping; on the other hand, there is a strong prior activation of "mirror symmetry" from the previous, higher-level context. So what happens? Humans seem to treat the two contexts as esssentially independent, meaning that they would ignore the prior activation of "mirror symmetry" and go for the diagonal mapping, and that is therefore how they are treated by Tabletop.

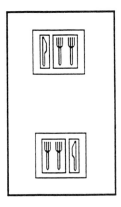

Figure 3.19

Consider a slightly more complicated example (figure 3.20). As before, at the top level, mirror-symmetric correspondences (again, we will use the names cp_1 and cp_2) are built. But now when the *examine-cp*(cp_1) codelet enters the silverware-correspondence subworld of the full Tableworld, there are two competing pressures:

- A *size* pressure, pushing for the program to map pairs of objects to pairs of objects, and single objects to single objects (insofar as their object types, although possibly different, are not radically different)
- An *object-type* pressure, pushing for the program to map entities with identical object types onto each other (in this case, a single fork to a pair of forks, and a pair of knives to a single knife)

A small, preliminary survey indicated that for humans, in the absence of any other influences, object-type pressure is favored over size pressure (62 percent vs. 38 percent). In other words, without the presence of the cup-cup mapping in the configuration given in figure 3.20, 62 percent of subjects would have mapped Henry's knife group onto Eliza's knife, and Henry's fork onto Eliza's fork group. The additional pressure of the mirror-symmetric cup-cup mapping in figure 3.4 did not increase the percentage of subjects who chose the mirror-symmetric mappings within cp_1 (i.e., Henry's knife-group to Eliza's knife, Henry's fork to Eliza's fork-group). With the cups present, 56 percent of subjects opted for the mirror-symmetic mapping *within* cp_1 (i.e., the object-type mapping). Thus, the activation of "mirror symmetry" produced by the two *top-level* mappings cp_1 and cp_2 apparently has only a slight influence on the lower-level mappings *within* cp_1.

The moral of the story is clear: Activation of a concept (in this case, "mirror symmetry") in one context may have no significant influence on choices made in a

Henry

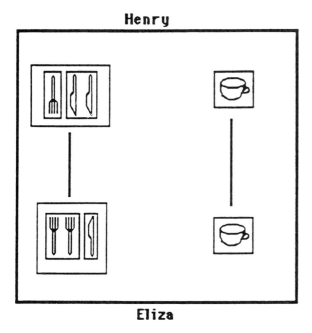

Eliza

Figure 3.20

different context. In sum, it is as if a single concept—a single node in the Slipnet—could have two different activation levels, one for the "main world" and one for the "subworld."

Returning to the configuration in figure 3.18, let us suppose that when the *examine-cp*($\mathbf{cp_1}$) codelet runs, the Slipnet activation for the concept "mirror symmetry" is wiped clean, or nearly so. Suppose that the obvious diagonal correspondences are now built between Henry's forks and Eliza's forks and between Henry's knife and Eliza's knife. This would send considerable activation to the concept "diagonal symmetry." But what happens when the program "pops" back to the top level? Does "diagonal symmetry" retain its activation, or is the former activation of "mirror symmetry" restored while "diagonal symmetry" effectively dies—and if so, how?

As can be seen, two questions need to be answered:

- What happens to the old activation level of a concept when the agents of the program enter a new level (in computer sciences jargon, this might be called a "context push")?
- How are the former activation levels restored when the program leaves the new level (a "context pop")?

The answer to the first question is that the activation level is set to its initial value (in this case, 1). So, in Tabletop, the activation slate really is wiped clean. But a central question remains—namely, *which* concepts have their activation thus reinitialized? Clearly, not *all* concepts in the Slipnet should have their activations reinitialized. In the "Go west on I-94" example, that would be equivalent to saying that when you enter the parking structure, *everything* in your mind becomes inactive. This is certainly not right. The following two proposals, however, do seem reasonable:

• Only concepts whose activation is above a certain threshold level are re-initialized.

• Only concepts that participate in the supporting slippages of the correspondence under investigation are reinitialized.

The solution adopted by Tabletop was essentially the latter. In reality, however, only the "mirror-symmetry" and "diagonal-symmetry" nodes are reinitialized, these being the only concepts that would have had a significant influence on the subsequent formation of "sub-correspondences".

The problem of which activation levels should be reinitialized, to what degree, and under what contextual circumstances definitely deserves to be studied more carefully. The most fruitful path of research would seem to be along the lines of the second proposal above.

Let us now consider the second of the two questions—namely, how are the former activations *restored* when the program returns to a former context? There are numerous possible solutions to this question, including the following:

• The program maintains an "activation stack" for each node, pushing that node's activation value onto the stack each time the program enters a new level and popping that value off the stack whenever it leaves the level.

• A "self-watching" mechanism keeps a "notebook" in some region of short-term memory (i.e., the Workspace) containing the activation values of very active nodes in the Slipnet. Different "pages" of this notebook would correspond to different worlds and subworlds. As the program moved in and out of various contexts, it would consult the notebook to restore the activation values that it had kept. This amounts to a weak form of the stack architecture above.

The notion of maintaining explicit stacks, like those by computer operating systems, in either long-term memory or short-term memory is unappealing, because, in some sense, stacks are too "clean." The whole idea of a stack is that the items saved on them really *are* saved, in order to be recovered intact at some later time. But brains are not so clean. We know that activation spreads between related concepts. How could it be, then, that we could have a stack of extremely related concepts (in fact, just different copies of the same concept) and yet have no activation spreading between them? Another problem is that stacks can be arbitrarily deep, and certainly brains do not keep track of large numbers of levels correctly. Perhaps the brain does, in fact, maintain some sort of activation stack, but it is not clear how it would work. An alternative notion seems more reasonable: the program inspects the structures present in the Workspace and then *reconstructs* the old activations on the basis of what it has observed.

This is the solution adopted in Tabletop. When the program leaves one context, it reinitializes the activation values of the concepts associated with the correspondences in that context. When it then reenters a former context (i.e., "pops" to a previous context), it reconstructs the activation values at that level by looking around in the Workspace and finding the correspondences in that context. It then reactivates concepts—in Tabletop, only "mirror symmetry" and "diagonal symmetry" are affected—on the basis of the slippages that support the correspondences it finds. For example, for each "right"-to-"left" slippage, it puts a fixed amount of activation into the concepts "right," "left," and "diagonal symmetry." Similarly, for each "right"-to-

"right" slippage it finds, it puts a fixed amount of activation into "right" (twice) and into "mirror symmetry." In this way, it roughly rebuilds the activation profile of that level.

This solution bypasses the apparent psychological implausibility of having the program maintain an explicit stack. On the other hand, it means that once the program leaves a particular context, it will no longer be able to retrieve the *precise* original activation values when it returns to that context. In other words, when the program returns to an old context, the reconstructed activation values will necessarily be approximate. At first glance, this might be considered a serious flaw of the architecture, but on reflection, this loss of information is probably not psychologically implausible, as long as not too much information is lost. There is, after all, no a priori reason that the activation values should be restored with complete accuracy when moving back into a particular context. In fact, one would expect there to be a certain amount of information lost.

A more complex reconstruction technique than the one implemented in Tabletop is needed, however. It is not enough merely to put a fixed amount of activation into the Slipnet for each concept encountered in the structures present at a particular level of the Worldview. Although this certainly captures some of the information stored in the prior patterns of activation, too much is lost. For example, all of the (possibly considerable) activation that might have *spread* to these concepts from other concepts is lost. More refined reconstruction techniques, perhaps taking into account the activation levels of the nodes connected to the reinitialized nodes, might permit a greater amount of the information to be recovered in the activation-reconstruction process. In any event, I believe that reconstruction techniques, rather than any resort to an "activation stack," will provide the ultimate resolution to this difficulty.

3.4.7 Computational Temperature in Tabletop
The final area that must be considered before concluding this chapter on Tabletop's architecture is the all-important notion of computational temperature and how it is used to determine when the program has found an answer. The underlying mechanisms as well as the justifications for computational temperature have been discussed at length by Hofstadter and Mitchell (1991) and Mitchell (1993).

Computational temperature is a measure of the program's "belief" that it has found all the perceptual structures (groupings, correspondences, etc.) necessary for a good answer. In other words, the lower the temperature, the more the program considers that it has spent enough time and resources in its attempt to structure the Tableworld perceptually.

The philosophy behind temperature is much the same as the philosophy behind the local manner of finding groups on the table. Recall that the program is continually attempting to find new, high-quality correspondences. Typically, this will proceed as follows: Initially, a lot of new correspondences will be found and put into the Worldview. Whenever, by chance, a new high-quality correspondence is found, it will compete with, and usually replace, weaker competitors in the Worldview. In this way, a process akin to natural selection among correspondences gradually improves the quality of the Worldview. Ultimately, the correspondences in the Worldview will cease to be replaced by new ones, simply because the ones already in the Worldview are stronger than any competitors that come along.

This does not imply, of course, that the program will infallibly discover a route to an optimal solution. Sometimes it may never even notice a very good correspondence. Or it may do so so late that it makes no difference. It should be recalled that each time the Worldview emerges victorious from a competition with a rival interpretation of the table, all of its correspondences are strengthened. Thus, the longer a particular Worldview dominates the scene, the harder it is for new correspondences, however good, to force themselves into it.

How does this relate to computational temperature? The idea is that just as a decline in the rate of group finding tells Tabletop there may not be many more groups to be found (and, consequently, to expend fewer of its resources looking for new groups), a drop in the rate of good correspondences being added to the Worldview tells Tabletop there may not be many more good correspondences to be found. In this case, the temperature drops and the program expends fewer resources to discover new correspondences.

Temperature reflects the program's assessment that it has developed a good representation of the table. In Tabletop, the program uses a more indirect method than in Copycat of ascertaining when it has achieved such a state. Four factors determine temperature in Tabletop:

Quality of the Worldview The quality of the Worldview is based on the average quality of the correspondences comprising it. In the formula for temperature, this is measured as a fraction of an optimally good correspondence.

Average rate of change of the quality of the Worldview This is the heart of this particular means of computing temperature. The idea is that if very few changes are occurring in the quality of the Worldview, the program has probably found a good representation of the table, and the temperature drops. The rate of change of Worldview quality is determined by the difference between the quality rating of the current Worldview and the rating of the previous Worldview. This rate of change of the quality of the Worldview is averaged in with a certain number of past rates of change (generally averaged over the last six). This defines the average rate of change of the quality of the Worldview.

Number of changes of the correspondences in the Worldview There is a problem with calculating only the quality and the change in quality of the Worldview over time—namely, it is conceivable that the following scenario could occur. Suppose that two rival correspondences are almost equally good. In other words, both are of high quality and both fit well into the current Worldview. Further, assume that because they are equally good, they more or less alternately win the competition. They take turns moving in and out of the Worldview. Thus the variable containing the quality ratings of the Worldview would look, for example, like this: 274 (with the first correspondence), 267 (with the second), 280 (with the first), 273 (with the second again), 285 (with the first). In this scenario, the change in quality between alternate Worldviews is very small, even though there is a considerable amount of change in the identity of the correspondences.

Should the temperature drop or not under these circumstances? This can be argued both ways. One could maintain that it does not matter that the physical composition of the Worldview (i.e., the correspondences) is oscillating. Since the rivals are of equal quality and produce equally good Worldviews, it makes no difference which of them is picked. According to this reasoning, the temperature *should* fall, just as it would if the correspondences were not changing. In other words, this side of the argument maintains that the only important factor is the *quality* of the Worldview, not its precise composition.

On the other hand, one could argue that the lowering of temperature should reflect a growing certainty that *one* good representation is being settled on and that this will lead to an answer to the problem. This, after all, is the ultimate *raison d'être* of computational temperature. According to this view, then, continual oscillation between two different choices should prevent the temperature from falling, since the system is not settling on a single representation.

The latter alternative was the one implemented in Tabletop, because it seems that temperature should represent one's degree of satisfaction with one particular representation or solution to a problem. For temperature to fall quickly, one representation should stand out head and shoulders above the others. But this does not occur when there are two equally plausible solutions. Each time one solution seems better, there is the nagging doubt that there are still a lot of good reasons to pick the other one. For this reason, the number of actual physical changes in the correspondences in the Worldview is also taken into consideration. In short, the more often the Worldview changes, the higher the temperature.

Number of competitions Since the program considers picking an answer only when the temperature is sufficiently low, a Buridan's-ass type of paralytic indecision could be created by the presence of two equally good correspondences (see previous point). This is psychologically unrealistic because, of course, people *do* decide, if only because they get sick of trying to make up their mind.

The presence of two equally good choices will keep the temperature fairly high and this could mean that the program might simply go on forever, oscillating back and forth between them. The program, like people, must eventually tire of trying to decide, and that is why temperature slowly falls as a function of the number of competitions.

The equation incorporating these four factors to calculate temperature is as follows:

$$T = \alpha \frac{\Delta Q}{Q} + \beta \Delta_{WV} - \gamma T_{cp}$$

where:

Q is the average quality of the Worldview ($0 < Q \leq 1$);
ΔQ is the change in quality of the Worldview;
α, β, and γ are positive constants;
Δ_{WV} is the number of changes in the Worldview in the last ten competitons;
T_{cp} is the total number of competitions.

Note that the values of the coefficients β and γ are chosen to ensure that the latter two terms determining temperature play a less significant role than $\Delta Q/Q$, which is the dominant factor in the calculation of temperature. It can be justified as follows:

- If ΔQ is small (few recent changes in the Worldview) and Q is large (good quality of the structures), then $\Delta Q/Q$ is small. Consequently, the temperature is low.

• If ΔQ is large (many of recent changes in the Worldview), the temperature will remain relatively high, because Q would have to be very high to compensate for this. Since Q can be at most 1, a large ΔQ will necessarily produce a high temperature.

• If Q is small (the quality of the Worldview is poor), the temperature will remain high unless no better structure is found. If no additional structure is found, even if Q is high, the value of ΔQ will decrease over time, thus causing $\Delta Q/Q$ to become small as well. The temperature will then decrease.

One metaphor for temperature involves the amount of effort one is willing to expend looking for a mate. Consider the case of Joe, a typical college freshman, who has no girlfriend when he starts college. Initially his "mate-finding" temperature is high: he expends an inordinate amount of energy looking for a girlfriend, going to parties and other social events designed explicitly to bring single people together. Once a small number of potential candidates have been found, the temperature drops a bit, and Joe concentrates on the smaller group of women. By the end of his sophomore year, the temperature has dropped significantly: His relationship with one of the women has become solid, and he is no longer actively looking, although certainly if a woman comes along whom he finds very attractive, he may well attempt to initiate something with her, in spite of his relationship with his girlfriend. At about that time, a senior with broad shoulders and blue eyes sweeps Joe's girlfriend off her feet and, within the space of a month, Joe is without a girlfriend. The temperature then soars. Joe starts going to parties he would not have dreamed of going to before. He unearths long-forgotten phone numbers and makes conversation with women in his classes and even on the sidewalk, on the flimsiest of pretexts. He may even put an ad in the personals column in the student newspaper. His attempts to meet women take on a much more random "look-anywhere" character. The strategy eventually works and, as before, he meets someone and gradually settles into a relationship and, once again, the temperature drops. Finally, when the temperature is low enough, he and his girlfriend decide to get married and the dating game is over. (However, extra-marital flirtation can still take place, potentially leading to …)

Temperature has roughly the same effect on Tabletop, affecting all of its decision making. For instance, consider codelet selection. Each codelet has an assigned urgency that determines its probability of being executed, but urgency varies as a function of temperature. The higher the temperature, the more random (i.e., the less biased) the selection of codelets; the lower the temperature, the less random (i.e., the more biased). In the limit of very low temperatures, this strong bias turns into determinism. The example below will serve to illustrate exactly how temperature affects the urgency of codelets (a is the "temperature exponent").

Codelet name	Assigned urgency	Temp.-dependent urgency
find-group-around (**small-glass$_1$**)	6	6^a
find-neighbor (**cup$_1$**)	3	3^a
build-object (**fork$_1$ fork$_2$**)	1	1^a
Total Coderack urgency	10	$6^a + 3^a + 1^a$

The value of a varies linearly between 6 (when the temperature is 0) and 0.1 (when the temperature is 100). When the temperature is 100, the temperature-dependent urgency for all codelets, for all intents and purposes, is 1. In other words, at this temperature, codelet execution is an almost completely random process, with any codelet being as likely to run as any other. At the other end of the scale, when the temperature is 0, the fact that we are raising each of the assigned urgencies to the sixth power means that even small differences in assigned urgency will be greatly amplified. In our example above, with a equal to 6, we get these results:

Codelet name	Assigned urgency	Temp.-dependent urgency
find-group-around (**small-glass$_1$**)	6	46,656
find-neighbor (**cup$_1$**)	3	729
build-object (**fork$_1$, fork$_2$**)	1	1
Total Coderack urgency	10	47,386

Clearly, codelet selection here will be essentially deterministic. The probability that *find-group-around* will be chosen is 46,656/47,386, that is, 0.985 (compared to 0.6 when $a = 1$); that *find-neighbor* will be picked is 729/47,386, i.e., 0.015 (compared to 0.4 when $a = 1$); and that *build-object* will be picked is infinitesimally small (less than 0.001, compared to 0.1 when $a = 1$). The "amplifying" effect of raising the assigned urgencies of codelets to a high power ensures that those with higher assigned urgencies will almost certainly be picked before those with lower assigned urgencies. (If two codelets have the same assigned urgency, the selection between them remains, of course, random.)

As might be expected, temperature affects not only codelet urgencies but *all* of the probabilistic processes of the program. A simple example is the action taken by a *pick-salient-object* codelet. One of the factors in determining the salience of an object is its location on the table with respect to the touched object. When the temperature is very low, the program deterministically respects the priorities of the regions that human subjects were shown to choose preferentially with respect to the touched object. In other words, an area diagonally opposite the touched object is most preferred, an area directly opposite the touched object is next, and so on. However, if the temperature goes up, the chances decrease that the program will rigorously respect this order. If the temperature should ever happen to reach 100, the program is as likely to choose any region as any other.

The selection of objects or correspondences based on their salience works in the same way. The selection process approaches determinism as the temperature approaches 0, is completely unbiased (i.e., uniformly distributed random) at 100, and has varying degrees of bias at intermediate temperatures.

Copycat and Tabletop do not calculate temperature in exactly the same way. In essence, the Tabletop calculation is much more local and therefore, at least theoretically, would be more amenable to being scaled up to larger domains. In Copycat's temperature calculation, the *quality* of the structures in the Workspace is of paramount importance. Temperature is inversely proportional to the quality of inter- and intrastring relationships, and it falls when good high-quality relationships are found. In Tabletop, the emphasis is much less on *good* structure than on *changes* in structure in the Worldview. The quality of the structures in the Worldview does play a role, but it is much less significant and, especially, less direct than in Copycat. The assumption is that the process of "natural selection" among correspondences competing for a place in the Worldview will eventually result in the best correspondences finding their way into the Worldview.

What happens, though, if there is very little good structure to be found? In Copycat, under these circumstances the temperature will remain high. In Tabletop, by contrast, the temperature will nonetheless fall, because what is important is the *change* in the quality of the Worldview. When quality stops changing over a significantly long time, the program effectively concludes that it has done its best, and temperature falls. The Worldview is continually being bombarded with correspondences trying to get in. If, under these circumstances, the Worldview remains unchanged for a period of time in the face of this bombardment, the conclusion must be that the correspondences in the Worldview are probably pretty good and temperature falls.

Finally, how does Tabletop use temperature to decide that it has found an answer? In other words, how does it decide that its representation of a particular situation is good enough, and pick an answer based on the representation it has developed? The answer is, when the temperature is sufficiently low, the program concludes that the representation it has built is as good as it is going to get, and it selects the answer that is consistent with the structure it has built up.

There is, of course, no sharp temperature threshold below which the program decides on an answer and above which it continues to build up its representation of the problem. Rather, on each cycle of the program, a certain number of *find-answer* codelets are put on the Coderack. The lower the temperature, the more such codelets are hung on the Coderack. When a *find-answer* codelet runs, an answer to the "Do this!" challenge is picked, and the program stops.

Chapter 4

Tabletop's Performance Up Close

The purpose of this chapter is to give insight into Tabletop by following a specific run of the program from the time the table configuration is presented until an answer is finally produced. The run that was chosen, which is presented in a series of nine screen dumps, demonstrates many central features of the architecture, including the interaction between the Workspace and the Slipnet, activation levels of concepts in the Slipnet, when and where various structures are built, the varying state of the Coderack, and the competitions between various structures.

After this detailed look at one run, there is another set of partial screen dumps (the Slipnet and Coderack have been omitted), which show that the program can arrive at the same answer as in the run in a variety of ways and how the program can arrive at a different answer. Finally, there is a screen dump that illustrates the strange correspondences that the program can make when the computational temperature is high. This behavior, which might at first glance appear to be aberrant and undesirable, is argued to be necessary for fluidity. The flip side of the ability to discover novel, interesting analogies is the occasional "ridiculous" answer.

The series of screen dumps in this chapter was taken from a nonideal run—that is, a run in which not all of the good structure was found by the program. This choice was intentional, made in order to illustrate the fact that, although Tabletop usually does find most of the good structure in any given problem, it, like people, sometimes decides on an answer before finding all of the good structure. If a run of Tabletop is cut short, its answer will, in general, be based more on object category than on relational structure. The longer the program runs, the more likely it will be to find relational structure. This is similar to the relational shift—"a shift from early attention to common object properties to later attention to common relational structure" (Gentner, Ratterman, and Campbell, 1993)—that has been observed in comparing how children do analogies to how adults do them.

Figure 4.1 shows the configuration of objects presented to Tabletop. To the left of the table is the palette used to select objects for the table. These objects are forks, knives, and spoons, (in four possible orientations); cups; saucers; plates; big glasses; small glasses; pepper shakers; saltshakers; and soup bowls.

Immediately to the right of the table is the thermometer. This will indicate the computational temperature, which falls in the range from 0 to 100.

To the right of the thermometer, the Slipnet is represented. The various nodes of the Slipnet are represented by the square boxes forming the grid. The activation of a node is indicated by the number in the upper right-hand corner of the corresponding box. This activation is also represented graphically by the black square within the box. Activation values range from 1 to 150.

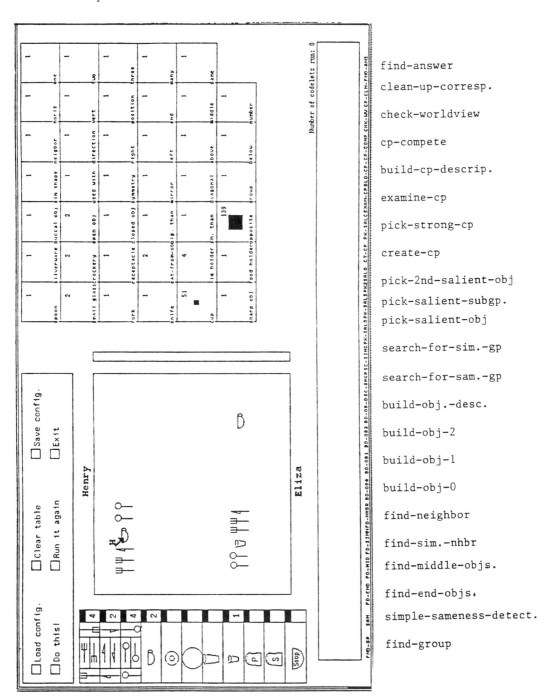

Figure 4.1

Below the table is a representation of the Coderack, indicating the percentage of particular codelet types waiting to run. The total number of codelets run so far is also indicated. The number of codelets of a particular type on the Coderack is indicated (as a percentage of the total number of codelets on the Coderack) by the height of the bars of the bar graph. In general, the types of codelets that run early in the program are to the left of the bar graph; those that run later are to the right.

Henry has just touched an object on his side of the table. In a moment, this will cause the Coderack to be loaded up with its standard set of starting codelets, but things are already happening in the Slipnet. For instance, the node "opposite" in the Slipnet has been given a large amount of activation. The reason for this is that Eliza is sitting *opposite* Henry at the table. In addition, since it was a cup that Henry touched, the concept "cup" is active. Even though no codelets have yet run, some activation has already begun to spread from "cup" to "liquid holder," "crockery," and so on.

The Coderack having been loaded up, the run has started in earnest, as shown in figure 4.2. At this point only two codelets—one of them a *find-group* codelet—have run. The *find-group* codelet discovered that the touched cup is part of a group of objects. For the moment, though, the program knows next to nothing about this group, other than that it is a bunch of objects that are physically close together. This is a gestalt view of the group: It involves top-down visual chunking of several undifferentiated things solely on the basis of physical proximity, *before* any individual details of the chunk are analyzed. In other words, it amounts to recognizing the group *qua* group from afar and then focusing on its details.

Other codelets will now focus on this group and try to discover something about its internal structure. To this end, the *find-group* codelet, on finding the group, posted a number of other codelets to the coderack, among which are: codelets that look for *sameness groups* (i.e., groups of neighboring objects all having the same object type— for example, a group consisting of two adjacent forks) within the group just found, others whose job it is to determine the objects at the ends and in the middle of the new group, and others that pick objects inside the group and "look" to the right and left of those objects to determine their immediate neighbors. In addition, the *find-group* codelet, having just run successfully (i.e., having just found a group), has sent a standard jolt of activation to the "group" node in the Slipnet.

The situation, as shown in figure 4.3, has evolved significantly. Probably the most conspicuous change is that the program has just made a tentative (i.e., dashed) correspondence between the touched cup and the isolated cup in the lower right-hand corner of the table. This correspondence was attractive because the cup in the lower right-hand corner is one of the most salient objects on the table. Its salience is due to two facts: it shares object type ("cup") with the touched object, and it is in a very good position on the table with respect to the touched object (i.e., roughly diagonally opposite from it).

The group discussed in figure 4.2 has become an important focus of attention. For instance, the program has discovered that the objects in it seem to be arranged horizontally, thus activating the concept "horizontal." The program has further discovered many of the neighbors of objects inside this group, and therefore the concept "neighbor" is active, causing more "find-neighbor" codelets to be posted on the Coderack. The concept "group" is fairly active, since a *find-group* codelet was successful (a group was found); the Slipnet node "group" has thus spawned a fair number of similar *find-group* codelets. This is clearly visible in the representation of the

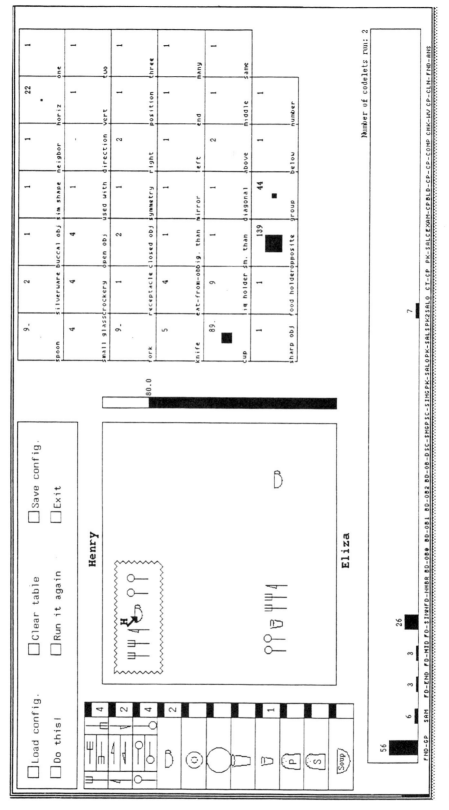

Figure 4.2

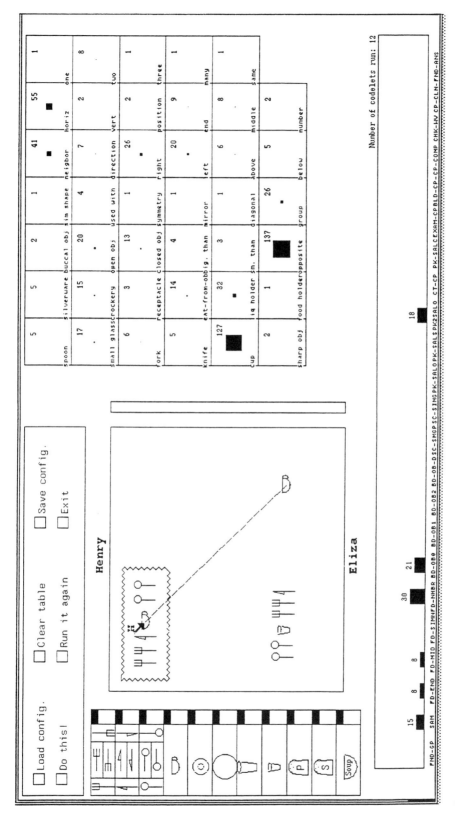

Figure 4.3

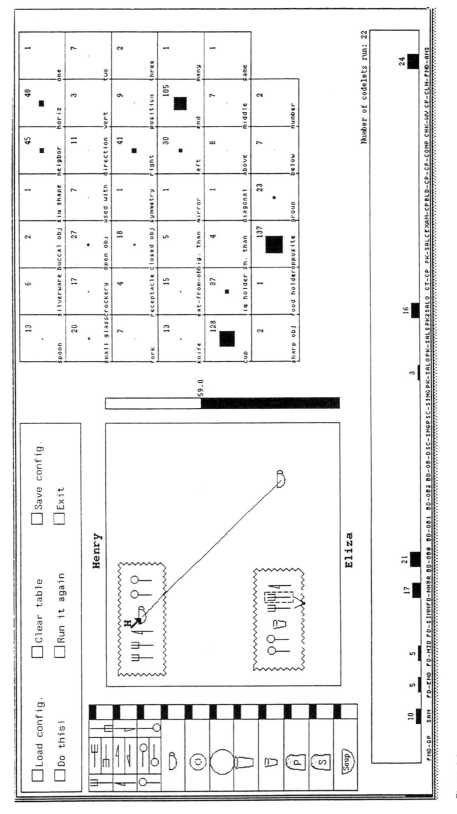

Figure 4.4

Coderack at the bottom, which shows that 21 percent of the codelets are ones whose job it is to find (and possibly build) new groups of objects.

Note also that a considerable amount of activation has spread in the Slipnet. After "cup," the concept "small glass" is the most active table-object concept, having received its activation from "cup."

Figure 4.4 shows that the tentative (dashed) cup-cup correspondence has now been solidified and is thus now officially part of the Worldview. A large group of objects on Eliza's side of the table has also recently been discovered, and the program has (probabilistically, of course) focused its resources on finding the neighbors of the various objects in the group. For instance, it has just discovered that the two forks in that group are neighbors.

In the meantime, back in the big group on Henry's side, the program has also discovered the fork-fork subgroup and the spoon-spoon subgroup. (These subgroups cannot be seen in the picture, because a subgroup is visible only when the program first discovers it, and thereafter only if it forms the end point of a correspondence in the Worldview.) The program has noticed that these subgroups are on the ends of the group, which is why the concept "end" is highly active in the Slipnet. It has also discovered that they are on the left- and right-hand ends of the group, respectively, which explains why "left" and "right" (and not "above" and "below") are active.

In figure 4.5, the program has just built a spoon-spoon subgroup in the group around the small glass, and that subgroup is therefore briefly visible. As soon as this subgroup was built, a large number of *search-for-same-group* codelets were posted to the Coderack (shown by the tall bar in the middle, with "70" above it). The program is therefore very likely to go and search for other occurrences of spoon-spoon groups.

Notice that the temperature has fallen. This is because the correspondences in the Worldview (only one, in this case, running from the touched cup to the isolated cup) have changed very little. This lack of change starts to suggest to the program that perhaps the structure is getting pretty good, and thus the temperature decreases.

A while back, the program spotted a spoon-spoon subgroup at the right end of the group surrounding Henry's cup. Figure 4.6 shows that it has now made a tentative correspondence between the two spoon-spoon groups and is testing its quality. (Incidentally, when a correspondence is first discovered, it is highlighted by flashing boxes at both ends. This screen dump happens to have recorded the reverse-video part of the flashing.) The quality of this correspondence is very high, since the two subgroups not only are identical in terms of category membership but also are in very good positions with respect to one another (i.e., they more or less directly face each other across the table). Since this correspondence is not a rival to any correspondence already in the Worldview, it is put in the Worldview without a fight.

Notice that this act makes the Worldview *incoherent*—that is, one correspondence goes from an object inside one group to an object inside another group, and the second correspondence (between the two cups) starts inside one group and ends on an isolated object. Although incoherence of this sort is permitted, it is "discouraged"— that is, the program greatly prefers all Worldview correspondences to start and finish "together." There is strong pressure for all Worldview correspondences to originate in a single group and to end in a single group.

For two correspondences to be incoherent should not be confused with their being *rivals*. Rival correspondences start or finish at the same end point, and for this reason

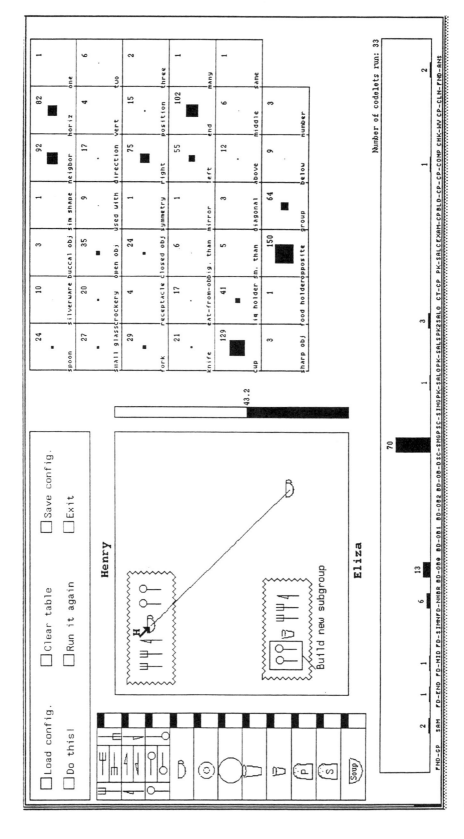

Figure 4.5

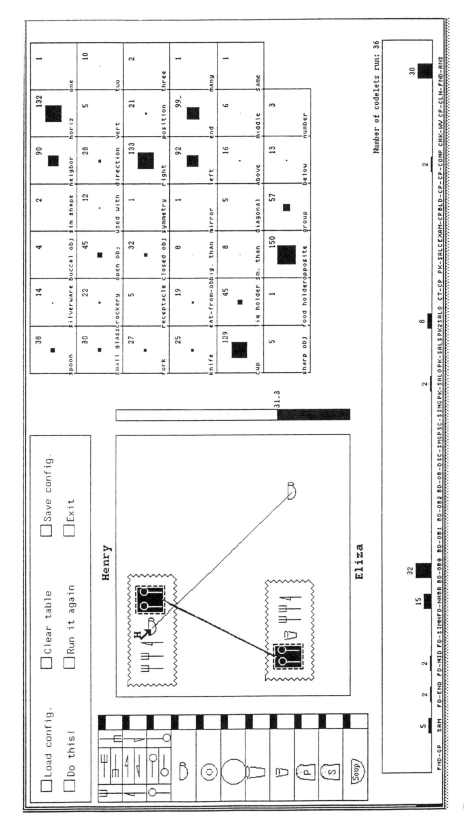

Figure 4.6

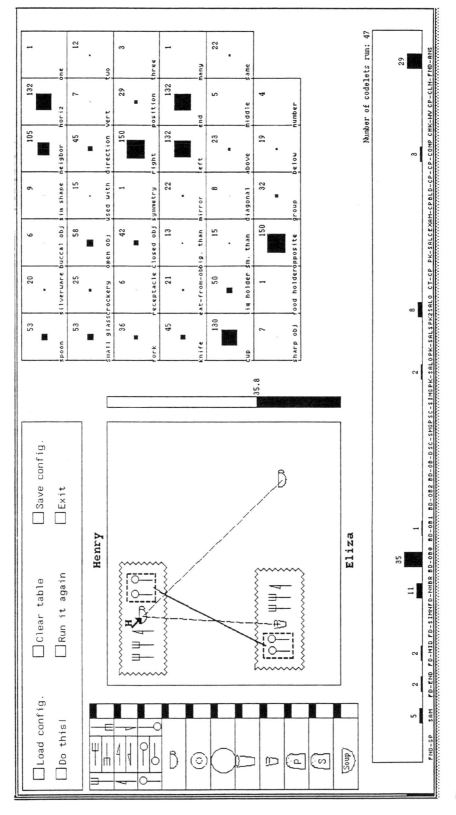

Figure 4.7

they are forbidden to belong to the Worldview at the same time. In other words, rival correspondences are like Necker-cube interpretations: they are mutually exclusive and must therefore fight each other for primacy. On the other hand, incoherent correspondences are like local aspects of an impossible figure (such as the "impossible triangle"): globally, they add up to something bad, but they can nonetheless coexist.

In figure 4.7, a tentative correspondence from Henry's cup to Eliza's glass has been suggested. This correspondence is a rival to the already-existing one from Henry's cup to Eliza's cup, so there is a fight to enter (or remain in) the Worldview. (The winner will be revealed in the next screen dump, figure 4.8.) Also, the correspondence from the touched cup to the isolated cup is indicated during the competition with the new rival correspondence with a dashed line (actually a flashing dashed line on the computer screen). This is merely to indicate that it is competing with the newcomer.

Notice that the temperature has gone up relative to figure 4.6. This is because the building of the new Worldview correspondence between the two spoon groups sent mixed signals to the program. On the one hand, adding a very strong correspondence to the Worldview pushes for the temperature to decrease somewhat. On the other hand, adding the new correspondence is taken by the program as a hint that there may be still more such correspondences. This pushes for increasing the temperature, because the program does not want to stop with some stones left unturned. The result of these opposing pressures is a slight increase in the temperature, slightly reducing the probability for the program to run a *find-answer* codelet (whose function is to announce the current object corresponding to the touched object and to stop the program).

It should be noted that the default object corresponding to the touched object is the touched object itself. Thus, if a *find-answer* program runs very early on before any significant structure is built (unlikely, but theoretically possible), Eliza will elect to touch the touched object.

Figure 4.8 shows that the cup/small-glass correspondence has won the fight, because the structure rating of a *coherent* Worldview containing a cup-glass correspondence is higher than that of an *incoherent* Worldview containing a cup-cup correspondence, even though a cup-cup correspondence is a priori stronger than a cup-glass correspondence. (Of course, this probabilistically determined victory given that Tabletop is a nondeterministic program.)

The fact that the Worldview has just changed (the cup-cup correspondence has been removed, and the cup-glass correspondence has been added) would tend to increase the temperature. On the other hand, when structure improves, this tends to cause the temperature to decrease. These constitute opposing pressures. In this case, the overall Worldview rating has improved so much (the program is quite heavily biased against incoherent Worldviews) that this fact by far dominates the pressure to increase the temperature. The temperature therefore drops. This is not yet the end of the run, however. The run ends only when a *find-answer* codelet is run.

The correspondences in the Worldview in figure 4.9 are no longer changing. This lack of change is by definition what makes the temperature fall, so the temperature does fall. As a result, the program "concludes" that it has probably found all the good structure that it is going to find—even though it has missed all the correspondences between the silverware to the left of Henry's cup and to the right of Eliza's glass. A *find-answer* codelet finally runs, Eliza touches the small glass (her choice is always shown by a short arrow with an *E* at its back end), and the program comes to a halt.

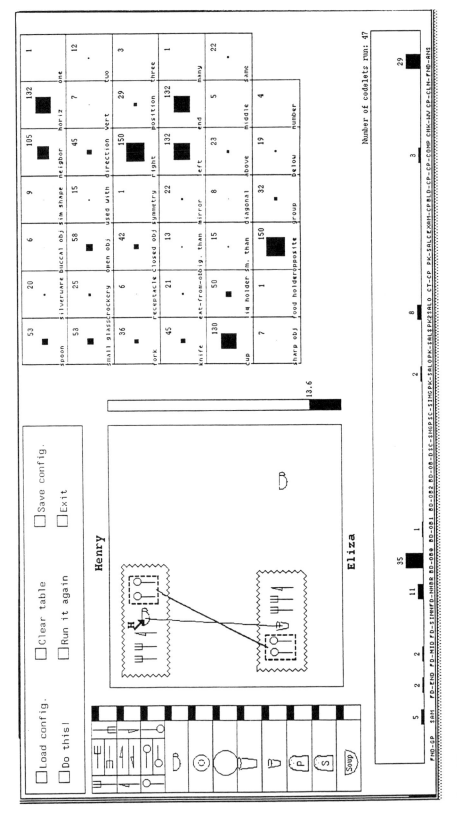

Figure 4.8

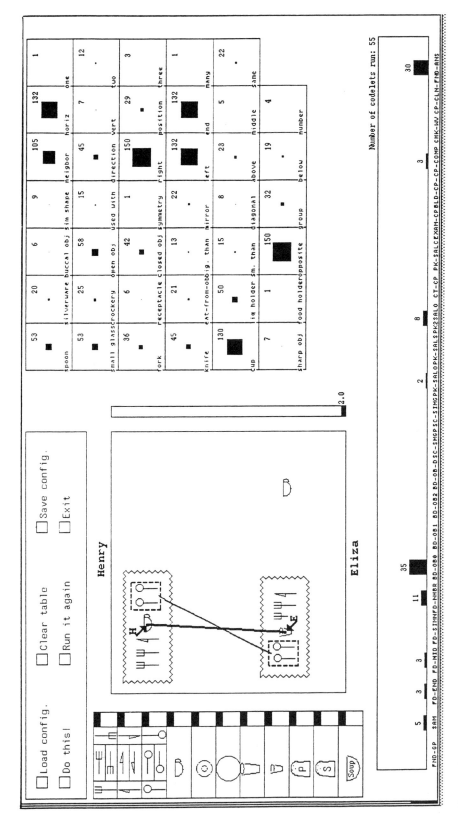

Figure 4.9

It is extremely important to note that, because of its probabilistic architecture, Tabletop does not follow a fixed sequence of steps to arrive at its answer to a given challenge; rather, on different runs it follows different pathways, sometimes leading to different answers, sometimes leading to the same answer, but even in the case of many runs all leading to a single answer, the pathways will all differ—sometimes in big ways, sometimes merely in small ways.

Figures 4.10 through 4.14 show a number of other Worldview structures that, on different runs, led the program to choose the small glass over the isolated cup.

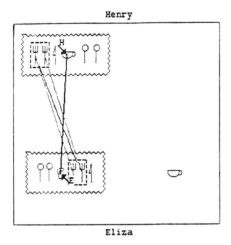

Figure 4.10

In the run shown in figure 4.10, the program developed quite-detailed mappings between the two fork-fork groups. It built correspondences from both of the forks of the upper group to corresponding forks in the lower fork-fork group, as well as a correspondence between the two subgroups themselves. It did not, however, notice that there were two spoon-spoon groups that could similarly be put into correspondence. Nonetheless, the support provided by the mapping between the two fork groups was enough to convince Eliza to touch the small glass instead of the isolated cup.

In the run depicted in figure 4.11, the program has discovered the structure seen in the previous figure and in addition has realized that Henry's cup and Eliza's small glass are both flanked by spoons. These spoons are put into correspondence. Although this new spoon-spoon correspondence is not as strong as the spoon-spoon/spoon-spoon correspondence found in the earlier-described run, it nonetheless strongly bolsters the program's confidence in picking the small glass as the best object for Eliza to touch.

The run in figure 4.12 involves a very typical set of Worldview mappings, one of the most frequently found by the program. Notice that the program did not take the trouble to look for correspondences *inside* the subgroup-to-subgroup correspondences. It does not need the additional "within-correspondence" mappings to decide that the set of Worldview correspondences it has found are good enough to justify Eliza's touching the small glass.

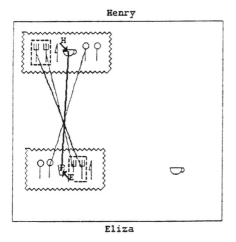

Figure 4.11

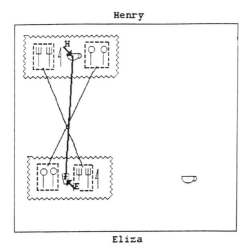

Figure 4.12

Notice also that the program did not find the knife-knife correspondence, even though this correspondence is extremely obvious to humans, especially once the neighboring correspondence between the two fork groups has been found. This seemingly glaring oversight is due to the fact that, when there are groups of objects on the table, the program is strongly biased to hunt for group-level correspondences in preference to object-level correspondences. Thus, this bias is clearly a bit too strong.

Figure 4.13 illustrates that, on rare occasions, Tabletop is capable of finding a great deal of very good structure between the two main groups of objects on the table but still deciding to pick the isolated cup. The program does not do this often, but it does occur.

The structure value for such a run is, perhaps surprisingly, quite good—after all, the program *has* found a large number of excellent mappings between the two large groups of objects. The only thing that this Worldview has going against it is that it is

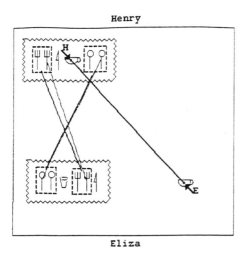

Figure 4.13

incoherent (i.e., lacks "systematicity" [Gentner 1983]), since the cup-cup correspondence is off by itself. However, if the program were ever to put the cup-glass
correspondence in competition with the cup-cup correspondence, the former would
almost certainly win, because that correspondence would make the Worldview become coherent, a state of affairs to which the program is extremely attracted. One
of two things apparently happened in this rather strange case: either the program
never even noticed the potential of a cup-glass correspondence, or else it did do so,
but when that correspondence was suggested, it was defeated by the rival cup-cup
correspondence.

Figure 4.14 includes the current temperature. It clearly shows the effect of high
temperature. It is rare for a cup-spoon grouping, as shown here, to survive. The program is, in general, highly unlikely to group together objects of such disparate
categories.

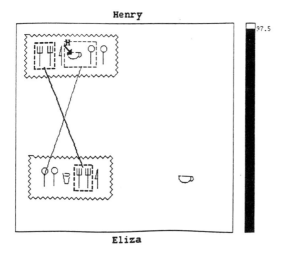

Figure 4.14

However, if the temperature is high, the program is relatively willing to try such things out. Similarly, it strongly resists mapping groups onto individual objects, although under some circumstances it might be happy mapping a spoon-spoon group to an individual spoon. Here, however, it suggests, tests, and even winds up putting into the Worldview, at least for a short time, a correspondence from a cup-spoon group to a single spoon. At lower temperatures, such a correspondence would almost certainly never have been given the time of day.

At first blush, the building of such strange structures as shown in figure 4.14 might be regarded as a mistake on the part of the program (or worse, on the part of the programmer). I believe, however, that it would be wrong to consider the presence, on rare occasions, of such structures to be a mistake. After all, Tabletop is intended as a psychological model, and the fact is that, under some circumstances, people do, at least fleetingly, entertain many very strange notions (remember the space aliens who I thought might have taken my chisel)—every bit as strange as making an implausible mapping of an implausible cup-spoon group to a single spoon. Furthermore, it would be wrong if the program were incapable of *ever* making such mappings, even fleetingly. This would mean that some pathways of exploration were theoretically completely closed, which would violate one of the major tenets of the philosophy behind the architecture—namely, that all pathways should always be, at least theoretically, open to exploration (although not with equal probabilities).

The reply to those who would criticize the fact that the program occasionally tries out strange structures is that, even though strange structures are usually bad, on rare occasions, they can be good—even extraordinarily good—and, for that reason alone, you do not want to close off those avenues of exploration completely. It is just that you do not want such structures to be built too often or to be given overly strong ratings. The fact that Tabletop was run thousands of times on some forty to fifty different problems and virtually never produced any truly weird answers, even though it has certainly flirted with strange structures at intermediate stages of many runs, is a testimony to its robustness.

Chapter 5

Tabletop's Personality Profile

In this chapter, I present statistics summarizing some two thousand runs of Tabletop on four families of problems, called Surround, Blockage, Buridan, and Figure/Ground. For most of the forty or so problems, the program was kept constant, and the objects and their disposition on the table were varied, to examine the influence of these changing pressures. For a small number of problems, the program's parameter settings were varied, and the resulting statistical changes were studied. And in the last section of the chapter, the results of experiments with human subjects are presented. It turned out that Tabletop's appreciation of relational structure was greater, in general, than that of most subjects, who frequently—and sometimes, surprisingly—chose responses based on object category, even when a clearly more "relational" answer was available. By decreasing the relative importance that the program attaches to relational structure compared to object-category similarity matching, the performance of Tabletop can be brought quite closely in line with that of human subjects.

Varying the table configurations presented to the program will show how changes in various pressures, such as the position of various objects, the grouping of objects, the mutual proximity of salient objects, the presence or absence of corresponding objects, and so on, subtly affect the answers given by the program. Because Tabletop is a stochastic program, no run will be exactly the same as any other, but over a large number of runs, statistical regularities emerge, and, in a metaphorical sense, these large-scale statistical tendencies reveal—or constitute—the program's "personality." In that sense, they are very important, because they afford the highest-level overview of what this program really is.

It must be emphasized that until beginning testing of Tabletop on a relatively wide range of problems, I had no clear sense of the high-level, statistically emergent traits of the program. It was therefore with a certain amount of trepidation that I began the series of experiments described in this chapter. Simply put, for all I knew, the program might give extremely stupid answers for some of the problems. But to my delight, when it ran, very gratifying preferences started emerging gradually, and a coherent and perfectly reasonable personality came into view.

When discussing the answers the program gave to each of the problems, I will consider three variables:

> *The frequencies with which the program gets each different answer* This is the most important statistic, revealing the relative "popularities" of the diverse answers to a given problem, and is indicated by the bar graph to the right of the table configuration. These bar graphs give a clear indication of how the program responds to various changes of the pressures in different table configurations.

The average quality of the structure built for each answer This expresses how "good" each of the answers is, measured in terms of the quantity and quality of the structures ultimately constituting the Worldview. In most problems, rank order by popularity agrees with rank order in terms of quality of structure. Particular attention is paid to those cases in which the structurally best answer is not the most popular answer.

The average number of codelets required to produce an answer This represents the average amount of effort required by the program to find a particular answer and is an important measure of the program's ability to focus its resources. Certain analogy-making programs, most notably ACME (Thagard and Holyoak 1989), start by considering *all* theoretically possible mappings and then choose an appropriate one. In the Tabletop domain, this would mean an exponential growth of computing resources as the number of objects on the table increased. Even though Tabletop does generally take longer to solve more complex problems, as might be expected, there is no *explosive* growth in computing resources as more objects are put on the table. In fact, one problem (Surround 5.10) is devoted expressly to showing how the "progressive alignment" (Kotovsky and Gentner 1994) focusing mechanisms of Tabletop allow the program to largely avoid combinatorial explosion. It should also be noted that, in general, the better the structure built by the program, the more codelets will be needed.

Almost all of the configurations were run fifty times. No configuration was ever run fewer than forty times. An experiment consisting of fifty runs of the program usually took about three hours on a Sun IV workstation.

The program was run on four key families of problems:

Surround This family is so named because various assortments of objects are placed around two of the key objects in order to manipulate the pressures on Eliza, specifically pushing against the natural tendency to touch whatever object on her side of the table has the closest conceptual resemblance to the touched object.

Blockage A specific pressure, not explicitly anticipated, causes a particularly natural answer to be blocked.

Buridan This family is named after the legendary Buridan's ass, who supposedly starved from indecision: when placed exactly halfway between two bales of hay, it was not able to make up its mind which one to feed on. I adjusted the program to produce an exactly balanced response to one particular configuration; then I varied the configuration in several ways to see how the adjusted program would react.

Figure/Ground The standard version of the program was not able to get a certain, very "structural" answer. In this section, the reasons for this are examined.

In all of the problems presented below, the object touched by Henry is designated by an arrow marked *H*. Depending on the problem, in different runs Eliza might give one, two or sometimes even three different answers. These various answers are labeled *E1*, *E2*, and so on.

The statistics for each of these problems were based on approximately fifty runs of the program per problem. The bar graph next to the depiction of the table configuration indicates the frequencies of Eliza's responses. Finally, there are two additional statistics: the average structure value at the end of the runs and the average number of codelets run in runs giving the answer in question. In other words,

Object Eliza touches	Average structure	No. of codelets run
E1	128	88

means that the average final structure value over fifty runs of the program on the problem at hand was 128 when Eliza made the choice designated by *E1*. In addition, it took the program an average of 88 codelets to come up with this particular answer.

5.1 Runs of the Program

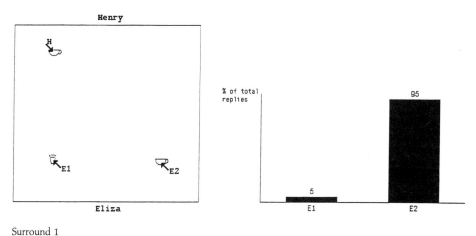

Surround 1

Object Eliza touches	Average structure	No. of codelets run
E1	58	52
E2	89	50

The first and simplest of the ten-member Surround family is shown in Surround 1. An experiment with human subjects showed that when an object is put in the upper left-hand corner of the table and they are asked where they think the most likely place to find a corresponding object might be, their first choice is the diagonally opposite corner of the table (in this case, the lower right-hand corner), then the directly opposite corner (the lower left-hand corner). In this configuration, the presence of an object of the same category as the touched object, combined with the fact that this object is in an optimal location with respect to the touched object, means that the program should very strongly favor touching the cup in the lower right-hand corner of the program. This is, in fact, what the program does: 95 percent of the time Eliza opts to touch the cup.

Because of Tabletop's inherent nondeterminism, the program will on occasion choose the glass over the cup, even though the cup is certainly the better answer. It is, nonetheless, important to allow the program to explore—sometimes, but not too often—unlikely pathways like this.

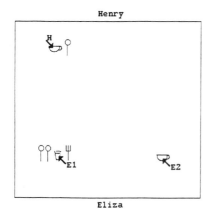

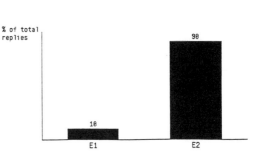

Surround 2

Object Eliza touches	Average structure	No. of codelets run
E1	98	68
E2	83	50

In Surround 2, the pressure of belonging to a group is added. There are two groups on the table: one group around the touched cup and another around the small glass. Notice, however, that the group of objects around the touched cup has very little in common with the group around the touched cup. The two groups are not the same size, and the objects comprising each group differ considerably. The only thing they share is the presence of a spoon. Nonetheless, the touched cup and the small glass are both members of groups, however disparate those groups may be. This fact should slightly increase the pressure to touch the small glass instead of the isolated cup.

This effect does in fact occur. The percentage of times that the program touches the small glass increases from 5 percent in the preceding configuration to 10 percent here. Notice also that when the program does choose the small glass, it rates this answer as having a higher structural quality than when it chooses the isolated cup.

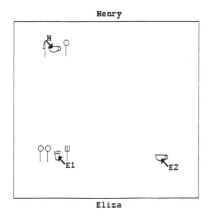

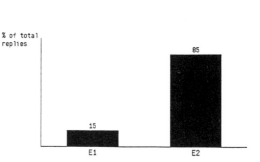

Surround 3

Object Eliza touches	Average structure	No. of codelets run
E1	112	89
E2	84	64

In Surround 3, the groups around the touched cup and the small glass are now more similar than in the previous configuration. For one thing, they are closer in size; for another, there is silverware on either side of both the cup and the small glass. In addition, knives and forks are considered by the program to be conceptually fairly close, since they are both items of silverware and are used together. This increases the likelihood of a correspondence from the knife to the left of the cup to the fork to the right of the small glass. Since there is a reasonable chance that the spoon immediately to the right of the cup and the spoon to the left of the small glass may also be put into correspondence, this will further improve the quality of a solution in which the touched cup is mapped to the small glass. (Notice that there is a much more appealing mapping of the single spoon next to the cup to the *pair* of spoons to the left of the small glass. The program will rarely make this mapping—even though humans would almost certainly be attracted by it—because it has a strong a priori bias against mapping single objects onto pairs of objects or onto groups in general.)

The small glass is, in fact, touched more frequently than in the previous problem. In addition, as might be expected, when the program does choose this mapping, it "likes" this answer better: the average quality of the structure developed when touching the small glass is 112 as opposed to 84 for the cup.

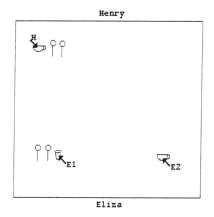

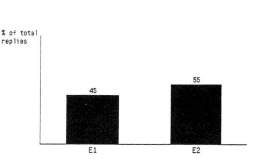

Surround 4

Object Eliza touches	Average structure	No. of codelets run
E1	186	64
E2	107	56

In Surround 4, the subgroups next to the touched cup (i.e., a pair of spoons) and next to the small glass (another pair of spoons) are identical. There is thus a very strong mapping of the two spoon groups onto one another, which should greatly strengthen the cup-to-glass mapping. This is indeed what occurs: Eliza now touches the small glass 45 percent of the time. As might be expected, the average quality of the structure when she touches the small glass (186) is significantly higher than when she decides to touch the cup (107).

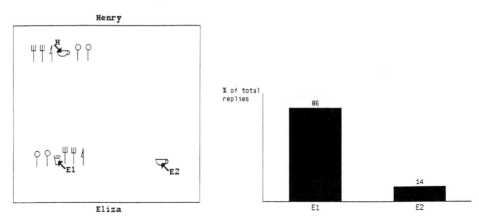

Surround 5

Object Eliza touches	Average structure	No. of codelets run
E1	248	101
E2	146	94

In Surround 5, the groups around both the touched cup and the small glass are very similar. There are exactly the same number of objects in each group, and the subgroups are identical. In this table configuration, the cup in the lower right-hand corner is seen as a "loner," and so there is a good deal of pressure to touch the small glass. As the results show, not only does Eliza touch the small glass far more frequently than the isolated cup, but the average quality of the structure associated with the first choice is far higher than for the rival choice. Notice, though, that it tends to take the program about 10 percent longer to produce the better structure associated with the small-glass answer.

One might ask why, if the structure of the small-glass answer is so much better than that of the rival answer, the program would *ever* pick the isolated-cup answer. The reason it sometimes picks the isolated cup over the small glass is that in those cases, it either has not noticed the good structure or, more rarely, has noticed it, but has chosen—probabilistically, that is—to ignore it and go for the isolated-cup answer. As the results of experiments will show, many people react in a similar fashion. Even though they may be aware of the relational structure, they will decide that the salience of the object-type match (i.e., mapping a "cup" to a "cup") overwhelms the relational structure. In an initial, informal survey, experimental subjects were asked to draw in all of the relevant correspondences and, although they often drew in the mapping between the two spoon groups, the one between the two fork groups, and the one between the two knives, they nevertheless rejected the relational structure and chose to touch the isolated cup in more than half of the cases. These initial results were borne out in the experiment presented in this chapter in which over two-thirds of subjects touched the cup in this situation. Tabletop's "personality," it would seem, is more attuned to noticing relational structure than most subjects.

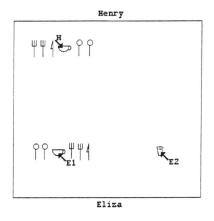

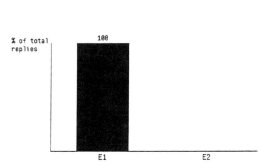

Surround 6

Object Eliza touches	Average structure	No. of codelets run
E1	237	62
E2	—	—

In Surround 6, the isolated cup and the small glass are switched. It would have been very strange, and somewhat unsettling, had the program done anything but touch the cup in the lower left-hand corner. This is not to say that the program would never (for example, once in a hundred thousand runs) go for the isolated glass; it simply does not do it very often.

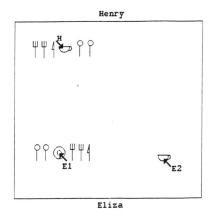

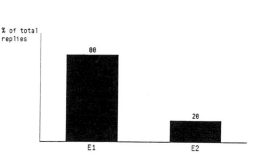

Surround 7

Object Eliza touches	Average structure	No. of codelets run
E1	231	109
E2	127	107

In the Slipnet, the conceptual distance between "cup" and "saucer" is small. This is so for a variety of reasons; for example, a cup and a saucer are both types of crockery and are used together. For the Tabletop program, these two concepts are almost as close together, albeit for different reasons, as the concepts "cup" and "small glass."

For this reason, we would expect that when the small glass in Surround 5 is re-placed by a saucer, approximately the same distribution of answers should result. This is indeed what was observed. In Surround 5, Eliza touched the small glass 86 percent of the time, whereas in Surround 7 she touches the saucer 80 percent of the time. Notice that the relative difference in structure between the two answers in this problem is virtually the same as that in Surround 5.

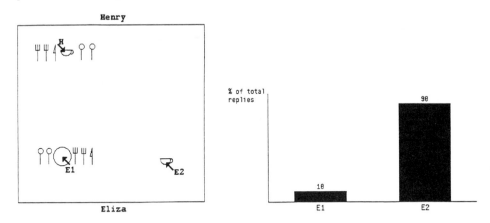

Surround 8

Object Eliza touches	Average structure	No. of codelets run
E1	214	204
E2	151	102

The saucer in Surround 7 has been replaced in Surround 8 by a plate. Now because plates are conceptually quite far removed from cups, we would expect this to shift the pressure significantly back to the isolated cup. This does indeed happen.

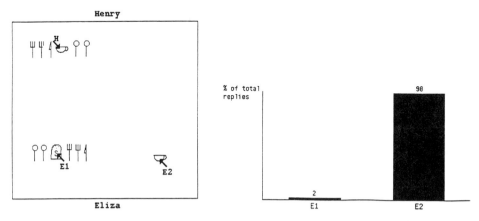

Surround 9

Object Eliza touches	Average structure	No. of codelets run
E1	266	445
E2	150	99

The plate in Surround 8 has now been replaced by a saltshaker, which conceptually is completely dissimilar to the touched object. This should shift the pressures even more back to the isolated cup. This is what occurs: in fifty runs of the program, Eliza touches the saltshaker only once. Nonetheless, we notice that the quality of the structure for this rarely chosen answer was still very high.

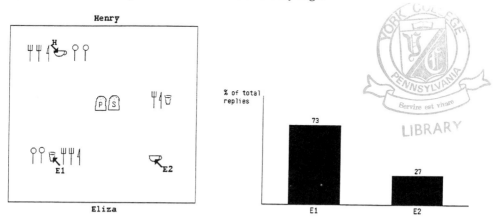

Surround 10

Object Eliza touches	Average structure	No. of codelets run
E1	259	88
E2	141	78

The specific purpose of Surround 10 is to examine the effect of adding superfluous "junk" to a particular table configuration, in this case to Surround 5. If the focusing mechanisms built into Tabletop are operating as they should, the junk should not make a significant difference, either to the amount of processing required to find an answer or to the distribution of answers found.

We observe that Eliza touches the small glass only 13 percent less often than in the Surround 5 configuration (the quality of the structure is essentially the same). The reason for this is that, because of occasional interference from the "junk," the program is slightly less likely to notice the important correspondences between the groups around the touched cup and the small glass and therefore will choose the isolated cup somewhat more often. It is important to note that the program took approximately the same amount of time to decide on an answer here as it did in Surround 5, an identical configuration but with no distractor objects on the table.

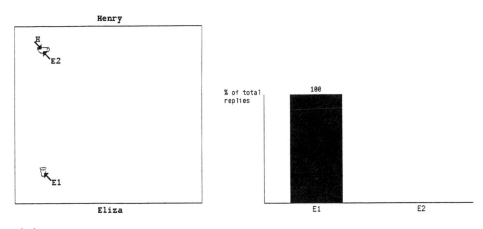

Blockage 1

Object Eliza touches	Average structure	No. of codelets run
E1	66	67
E2	—	—

We now embark on a new family—the Blockage configurations—of which Blockage 1 is the first and simplest. Even though the touched cup and the small glass do not belong to exactly the same category, the concepts "cup" and "small glass" are very close in the Slipnet. In addition, the small glass is in a very salient position with respect to the touched cup. There is thus a great deal of pressure to touch the small glass, and Eliza always does so.

It turns out that when human subjects were presented with this simple problem, a significant percentage of them (33 percent) touched the touched cup instead of the glass on the opposite side of the table. This indicates that people seem to be more strongly influenced by object-type matching than Tabletop is.

In the series that follows, I introduce certain specific pressures that encourage Eliza to move away from choosing the small glass on her side of the table, touching the touched cup.

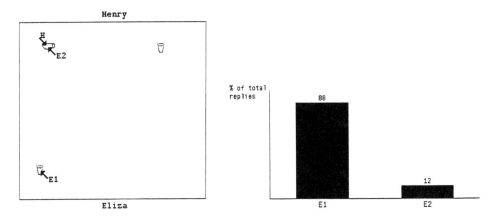

Blockage 2

Object Eliza touches	Average structure	No. of codelets run
E1	71	106
E2	94	158

A small glass has been added to the table in the upper right-hand corner, in Blockage 2. In contrast to the additions to the Surround series, the addition of the small glass to Blockage 1 does not create a new group; moreover, the small glass is not in a salient position on the table with respect to the touched object. We might therefore initially suspect that this addition would have very little effect, in much the same way as adding "junk" to the Surround 5 configuration had little effect (see Surround 10).

However, there is another, rather subtle kind of effect—namely, the additional small glass gives rise to a pressure to build a correspondence between the two small glasses. When this is done, these two objects are then viewed as part of a single, albeit relatively weak, structure, even though they are located at opposite corners of the table. The effect is similar to, although weaker than, the one achieved by placing one object next to another, thus causing the two objects to be seen as a single structure—namely, a group. Eliza decides, 12 percent of the time, to preserve this glass-glass correspondence and to touch the cup.

Notice that even though Eliza touches the cup in front of Henry 12 percent of the time, the average quality of this answer is rated 30 percent higher than that of the alternate choice of the small glass. In addition, when Eliza touches the touched cup, it takes her approximately 50 percent longer than for the small glass. Once again, this is not surprising: answers with more structure almost always take longer to build than those with less.

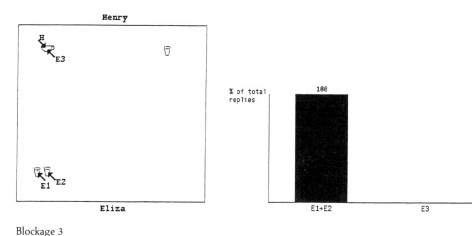

Blockage 3

Object Eliza touches	Average structure	No. of codelets run
E1 or E2	78	101
E3	—	—

In Blockage 3, one more small glass was added in the lower left-hand corner. Now there is a group in the lower left-hand corner, which the program invariably finds. Being loath to map a group of objects onto a single object, Tabletop systematically refuses the mapping of the group of two glasses onto the isolated glass. Not only is there less pressure to build a diagonal correspondence than in the previous problem, but even if this correspondence is built, it will not be as strong. This significantly decreases the pressure for Eliza to touch the cup in front of Henry. In addition, a significant percentage of the time the program will map one of the two grouped glasses to the glass in the upper right-hand corner of the table and then, in spite of the pressure to maintain coherence, will map the other glass in the group to the touched cup (figure 5.1).

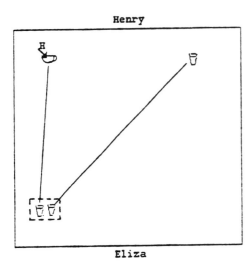

Figure 5.1

This will provide two strong correspondences, offset only by the incoherence of the Worldview they create. As a result, Eliza *never* touches the cup. Tabletop could undoubtedly be refined to allow the glass-group/isolated-glass correspondence to be built more frequently, thus causing Eliza to touch the cup a small percentage of the time.

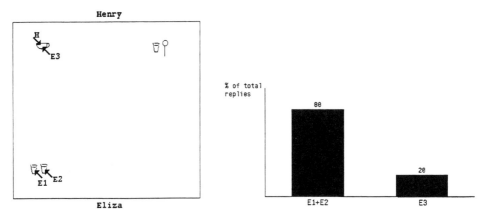

Blockage 4

Object Eliza touches	Average structure	No. of codelets run
E1 or E2	64	125
E3	88	179

A spoon has been placed next to the small glass in the upper right-hand corner. The program will almost always spot this group qua collection of unidentified items but, because a spoon is conceptually very far from a glass, it may not always group these objects in a bottom-up manner (i.e., forming a much more solid structure in which each of the elements knows about its neighbors).

As in the previous configuration, it often happens that a correspondence is made between one of the glasses in the lower left-hand corner and the glass in the upper right-hand corner. A correspondence is also made between the cup and the remaining glass in the glass-glass group. The fact that these mappings are incoherent is usually not enough to force Eliza to abandon the cup-glass mapping and choose the cup as her answer.

However, sometimes the bottom-up glass-spoon group does form and is mapped onto the diagonally opposite glass-glass group. This does create a strong enough mapping—even though it is not an exceptionally good one—to prevent Eliza from touching either of the glasses in the glass-glass group. She then goes for the touched cup.

It should be noted that Tabletop favors group-to-group mappings and abhors group-to-isolated-object mappings. Therefore, even though the diagonal mapping in the Blockage 3 configuration might seem cleaner (because it involves only glasses), the program does not make it (or only very rarely), whereas in Blockage 4 it does make the (somewhat forced) diagonal mapping between the glass-glass group and the glass-spoon group. This strong bias against group-to-isolated-object mappings should probably be relaxed.

The average structure value associated with the "cup" answer is about 40 percent higher than when the program picks one of the small glasses in front of Eliza, and this structure takes about 45 percent longer to build.

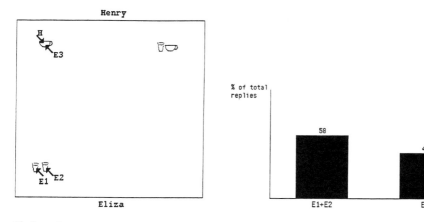

Blockage 5

Object Eliza touches	Average structure	No. of codelets run
E1 or E2	58	95
E3	144	190

The spoon in the upper right-hand group has been replaced by a cup. Unlike a spoon, a cup is conceptually very close to a glass. For this reason, not only will the program discover the group in the upper right-hand corner as "a collection of objects," but also it will make it into a bottom-up cup-glass group (kind of a "diluted-sameness group"). This group will be mapped to the glass-glass group, and the mapping will be a good one, much stronger than the diagonal group-group mapping in Blockage 4. Because of the improved quality of this diagonal mapping, Eliza now chooses the cup in front of Henry more than twice as often as she did in the previous configuration.

When the group-group mapping is made and remains in the Worldview, Eliza will touch the touched cup. When this diagonal mapping is not made, the most common occurrence is that the touched cup maps to one of the small glasses in the glass-glass group, while the other glass in this group is not mapped to anything. Sometimes, in this situation, the program will map the other glass to the glass in the upper right-hand corner. This will lead to an incoherent Worldview but one that is nonetheless acceptable.

Notice that when Eliza does choose the cup, the structure that has generally been built to give rise to this answer is much better than when one of the glasses in front of Eliza is chosen. Again, it is to be noted that it takes the program significantly longer to build the structure that gives rise to the better answer.

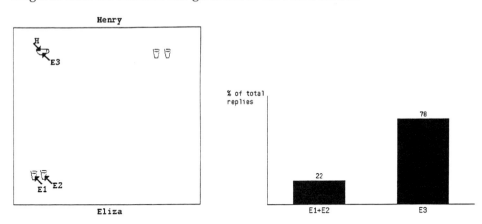

Blockage 6

Object Eliza touches	Average structure	No. of codelets run
E1 or E2	57	66
E3	177	94

Blockage 6 constitutes a turning point in this series. Now there are two glasses in the upper right-hand corner of the table. Since both of the diagonally opposite groups are sameness groups, and since they share a single unifying object type ("small glass"), the correspondence between them is very strong. It turns out to be strong enough to make Eliza very reluctant to break it by touching one of the glasses on her side of the table. As a result, she touches the cup in front of Henry 78 percent of the time. As might be expected, the average structure-rating for this answer is approximately three times better than for the answers involving touching one of the glasses on Eliza's side of the table. As usual, it tends to take Eliza longer (in this case, about 40 percent longer) to get the answer with the better structure.

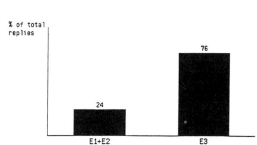

Blockage 7

Object Eliza touches	Average structure	No. of codelets run
E1 or E2	59	59
E3	196	119

Does strengthening the intuitive "pull" of the diagonal mapping in Blockage 7 further increase the frequency with which Eliza touched the cup in front of Henry? It turns out it does not. Even though the new diagonal correspondence is, technically speaking, stronger because there are more objects that are the same in both groups, it is also reasonable to suppose that there is some asymptotic upper bound to the amount of pressure that would block the building of a cup-to-small-glass correspondence. In this case, the addition of the silverware has virtually no effect on the frequency with which Eliza touches the cup.

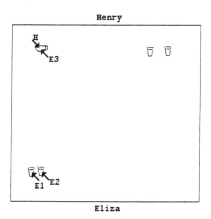
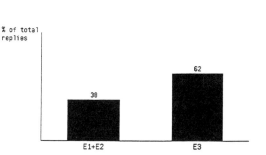

Blockage 8

Object Eliza touches	Average structure	No. of codelets run
E1 or E2	73	142
E3	153	124

In this subfamily consisting of three problems, I wish to examine what happens when the two objects in the upper right-hand corner of Blockage 6 are gradually pulled further apart. The greater the separation, the less the pressure to view those glasses as forming a group. If the glasses are *not* viewed as forming a group, no group-group correspondence can, of course, be built. It is possible, however, to have two parallel glass-glass correspondences from the glass group in the lower left-hand corner to the two now-isolated glasses, but there is considerable pressure against this, because it would produce an incoherent Worldview. (The program prefers that a set of correspondences starting in a single group all end in another single group, instead of being "scattered" all over the table.)

The frequency with which Eliza touched the cup in front of Henry did, in fact, drop—from 78 percent (Blockage 6) to 62 percent (Blockage 8) where the gap is one glass-width wide.

In the next two problems, the distance between the glasses is increased, each time by the width of one glass more than in the preceding problem. In other words, in Blockage 8, a third glass could be placed between the two glasses; in Blockage 9, two glasses could be placed between the original two glasses; and in Blockage 10, three glasses would fit in the gap.

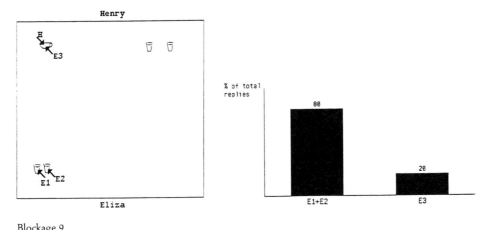

Blockage 9

Object Eliza touches	Average structure	No. of codelets run
E1 or E2	81	130
E3	165	124

The gap in Blockage 9 is two glasses wide, and so the diagonal correspondence is built much less frequently. In the present configuration, Eliza touches Henry's cup only 20 percent of the time.

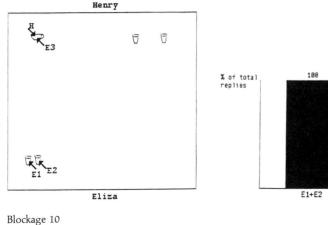

Blockage 10

Object Eliza touches	Average structure	No. of codelets run
E1 or E2	83	106
E3	—	—

The gap in Blockage 10 is so wide that the program no longer perceives the glasses as forming a group. Curiously, the program now acts as if the glasses in the upper right-hand corner have *no* effect on the choice of the object to be touched. As in Blockage 3, where there was a single glass in the upper right-hand corner, Eliza always chooses one of the glasses on her side of the table. The two glasses on Henry's side become something like the "junk" in the Surround series; that is, for all intents and purposes, the program ignores them.

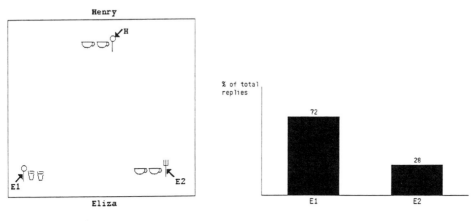

Buridan 1 (original program)

Object Eliza touches	Average structure	No. of codelets run
E1	170	88
E2	201	78

This is the first of the so-called Buridan family. To understand the motivation for this series, imagine this picture with no cups or glasses (Buridan 9). Presumably, Eliza would invariably touch her spoon. A set of pressures was required that would cause her response to be balanced exactly between the fork and the spoon on her side of the table. I added two new identical objects (cups, say)—one next to Henry's spoon, the other next to Eliza's fork. This would clearly swing the pressure toward the fork (see Buridan 10). To counterbalance this, I then put an object next to Eliza's spoon that was *similar* but not identical to the cup next to Henry's spoon—a glass, say. This would swing Eliza's response back to the spoon (see Buridan 2). The only weakness in this idea is that these "sidekick" objects are much less important than the touched object itself and the candidate answers. To strengthen the pressures engendered by the sidekicks, I converted the cups and the glass into *doubled* objects—small sameness groups. The hope was that the pressures might now be roughly balanced.

I began with the same Tabletop parameter settings as for the "Surround" and "Blockage" families. As can be seen, Eliza touched the spoon (*E1*) approximately two and a half times as often as the fork (*E2*). My prediction that adding the cup groups and the glass group would significantly increase the pressure on her to touch her fork was correct. But in the absolute, a spoon-spoon correspondence *is* significantly better than a spoon-fork mapping. Thus, the program, like many people, frequently builds both the correspondence between the two cup groups *and* the correspondence between the two spoons—an incoherent mapping. Of course, there is a penalty for incoherent mappings, but it is not severe enough to prevent the program from making them. With the standard penalty value, the program goes for the spoon on Eliza's side of the table about 72 percent of the time.

When the penalty for incoherent mappings was increased—in short, when the value place on good, coherent structure is increased—I was able to adjust the program so that Eliza's choice was precisely poised, like Buridan's ass between two equidistant bales of hay, between the spoon and the fork on her side. All the subsequent configurations in this family were run with this modified version of the program, which is more strongly resistant to incoherent mappings.

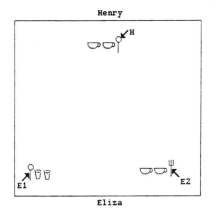

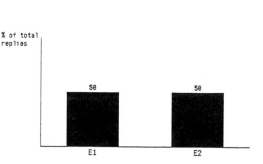

Buridan 1 (modified program)

Object Eliza touches	Average structure	No. of codelets run
E1	246	86
E2	280	75

This configuration, identical to the previous one, is the critical configuration of this series, but the statistics given here are for the modified program. As can be seen, Tabletop's new internal parameters are such that Eliza now goes for the spoon and the fork on her side of the table with exactly the same frequency. The problems in the remainder of this family systematically modify various pressures; we shall see the effects on Eliza's responses.

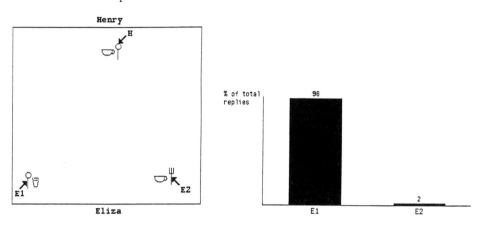

Buridan 2

Object Eliza touches	Average structure	No. of codelets run
E1	96	62
E2	192	105

The purpose of the Buridan 2 variant was to determine the importance of doubling the "sidekick objects." As can be seen, if they are not doubled, her reaction is not too different from what it would be if they were totally absent—that is, she goes for her spoon overwhelmingly more often than her fork. The message is thus clear: in this type of configuration, weak sidekicks (i.e., single objects as opposed to small sameness groups) are not sufficient to persuade Eliza to touch her fork very often.

Notice, however, that when she does pick her fork, she considers it to be a much stronger answer (in terms of structure value) than her spoon. Although counterintuitive at first, this makes good sense. The explanation is that although in coming up with answer *E1*, Eliza *sometimes* builds two coherent correspondences (namely, from spoon to spoon and from cup to glass), she more often gets by with far less support. In particular, answer *E1* is usually produced either with just a single correspondence (spoon-spoon) underlying it or, worse yet, with incoherent correspondences (spoon-spoon and cup-cup) underlying it. On the other hand, there is no way for *E2* to be selected unless two coherent correspondences are built (cup-cup and spoon-fork). Obviously, a coherent mapping of this latter sort rates much more highly than an incoherent mapping, such as usually gives rise to *E1*. Thus the fork, although hardly ever chosen, is a well-justified "structural" answer, which is not always the case for the spoon.

This type of discrepancy between frequency and structure value crops up in some problems that follow—especially Buridans 9 and 11.

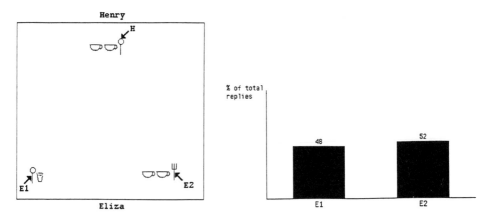

Buridan 3

Object Eliza touches	Average structure	No. of codelets run
E1	95	74
E2	272	77

In Buridan 3, I reestablish the possibility of the program's building a strong mapping between two paired-cup groups. Compared to Buridan 2, this should pull Eliza back to the fork. We can see that it very clearly does do this. As might be expected, the quality of the structure built when the fork is touched is significantly higher than in the rival answer.

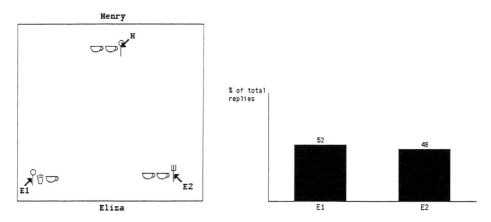

Buridan 4

Object Eliza touches	Average structure	No. of codelets run
E1	122	89
E2	279	113

In this variant of Buridan 1, one of the glasses in the lower left-hand corner has been replaced by a cup. Does this change enhance or diminish the appeal of the spoon? If one thinks solely in terms of conceptual distance between objects, it would appear that the group containing the spoon has become more attractive (relative to Buridan 1); after all, a cup is more similar to a cup than a glass is. One would thus conclude that *E1* ought to have a higher frequency here than it did in Buridan 1.

But there is an interesting alternative point of view: one can look at the level of groups rather than objects. (Recall that Tabletop has an intrinsic drive toward perceiving situations on an abstract level whenever possible, so a group-level point of view should, in general, exert more appeal than an object-level point of view.) The cup and glass next to the spoon form a "shared-ISA" group (both are "hold-liquid" objects; both are "crockery") and, as such, can map *as a group* onto the sameness group consisting of the two cups on Henry's side. However, this group-to-group correspondence will be rather weak for two reasons: first, shared-ISA groups are intrinsically weaker entities than sameness groups, so the cup-glass group itself is not extremely appealing; second, the two groups are not of the same type, which makes for a relatively weak correspondence. Thus from a group-level point of view, *E1* appears to be a *less* appealing answer in Buridan 4 than in Buridan 1.

Which point of view has more force with Tabletop? In ordinary situations, the abstract, higher-level point of view ought to dominate the more concrete point of view, but the interesting conflict here is that the abstract point of view is flawed (it involves both a weak group and a weak correspondence), whereas the concrete point of view has no such defect. Thus there is both a pro and a con to the abstract point of view. Tabletop ran on this problem many times, and sometimes the abstract point of view won out, sometimes the concrete one did. As the statistics show, the two arguments were almost perfectly balanced.

In effect, the fight between ways of mapping the lower left-hand cluster onto Henry's cluster (in chunked or unchunked form) presents a *second-order* Buridan's-ass problem, in which Tabletop is forced to choose between a high-level but weak point of view and a low-level but strong point of view.

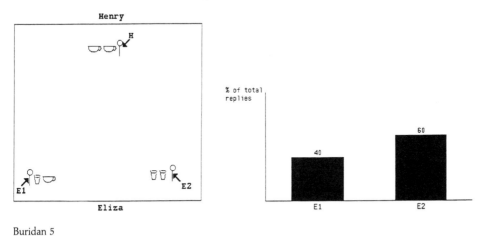

Buridan 5

Object Eliza touches	Average structure	No. of codelets run
E1	138	96
E2	237	83

Buridan 5 features spoons as the sole type of silverware; in so doing, it eliminates the previous imbalance of pressures that was due to the conceptual disparity of a spoon-spoon mapping and a spoon-fork mapping. The only question now being examined is whether the program will prefer a mapping betweeen sameness groups or a mapping between groups that are further apart at the conceptual level (i.e., not both sameness groups) but closer together at the level of their component objects (i.e., the cup-cup and cup-glass groups differ by only one item, instead of two in the case of the cup-cup and glass-glass groups). It can be seen that the program clearly favors the more abstract mapping, causing Eliza to touch the spoon to her right—the spoon associated with the sameness group—60 percent of the time.

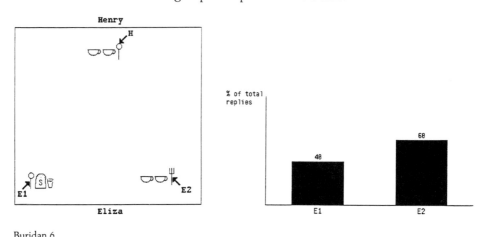

Buridan 6

Object Eliza touches	Average structure	No. of codelets run
E1	75	77
E2	277	88

In the Buridan 6 variant of the base Buridan configuration, one of the two glasses in the group around the spoon on Eliza's side of the table has been replaced by a saltshaker. As expected, Eliza will now touch the fork considerably more often than the spoon on her side of the table (60/40 percent as opposed to 50/50 percent in the base Buridan configuration). In addition, since on average the objects around Eliza's spoon are now conceptually quite distant from the two cups around Henry's spoon, it is not surprising that the quality of the structure accompanying the "spoon" answer is much lower than the quality of the structure for the "fork" answer.

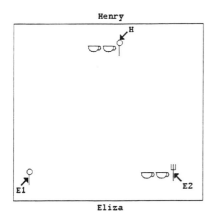

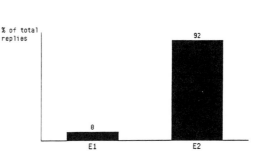

Buridan 7

Object Eliza touches	Average structure	No. of codelets run
E1	74	113
E2	285	95

There is nothing particularly surprising about the distribution of Eliza's responses for Buridan 7. The two pairs of cups map strongly onto each other, significantly enhancing the spoon-fork mapping. Since there are now no objects at all next to the rival spoon, the spoon-spoon mapping no longer has any additional support, even weak support, from neighboring correspondences. Thus, the facts that (1) there is a very strong mapping between the two cup groups; (2) both the group on Henry's side and the fork group on Eliza's side of the table have the same number of elements; and (3) forks and spoons are conceptually relatively close, add up to a very strong pressure for Eliza to touch the fork.

It is interesting to note that the mappings that give rise to the fork answer are so salient that the program builds them relatively quickly. Therefore, unlike most of the problems, in which better structure requires more time to develop, in this problem the program actually chooses the fork (with its excellent accompanying structure) about 20 percent faster than the spoon.

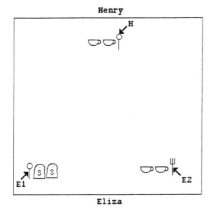

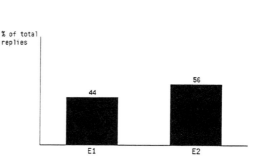

Buridan 8

Object Eliza touches	Average structure	No. of codelets run
E1	74	80
E2	283	91

It might seem surprising at first that Eliza chooses the spoon more frequently for Buridan 8 than in Buridan 6, in which the glass-glass group was replaced by a glass-saltshaker group. One might think, "A cup is conceptually much closer to a glass than to a saltshaker, therefore a cup-cup group would be conceptually *farther* from a saltshaker-saltshaker group than from a glass-saltshaker group. Therefore, the spoon-spoon mapping should be *weaker* when it is supported by a cup-cup/saltshaker-saltshaker mapping."

But of course this reasoning overlooks the obvious fact that Henry's pair of cups and Eliza's pair of saltshakers are both *sameness groups*, which fact adds to the strength of their correspondence. Although this is not a very strong pressure, here it is nonetheless strong enough to make it somewhat more likely (44 percent as opposed to 40 percent) for Eliza to touch her spoon than in Buridan 6, in which there were a saltshaker and a small glass, instead of two saltshakers, next to her spoon.

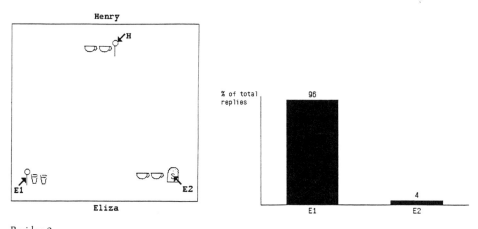

Buridan 9

Object Eliza touches	Average structure	No. of codelets run
E1	187	98
E2	248	139

Buridan 9 is a fairly straightforward configuration. Since a spoon is conceptually very distant from a saltshaker, there is little pressure to touch the saltshaker. Even the strong cup-cup/cup-cup correspondence is not enough to overcome this a priori tendency to avoid building a correspondence between such conceptually disparate objects. In addition, the cup-cup/glass-glass mapping supporting the spoon-spoon correspondence is a strong one. Consequently, Eliza almost always touches the spoon in front of her.

Notice, however, that *E2* still gets a higher structure rating than *E1*. This is essentially for the same reasons as were given in Buridan 2—selection of *E2* necessitates a coherent mapping and hence a high structure value, whereas selection of *E1* can be made under conditions of an incoherent or sparse mapping, either of which entails a low structure value.

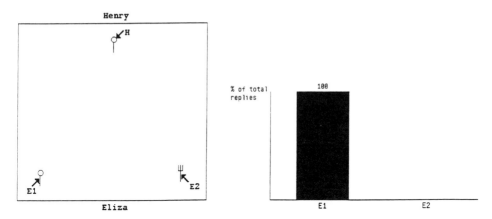

Buridan 10

Object Eliza touches	Average structure	No. of codelets run
E1	65	85
E2	—	—

The complete lack of any positional or grouping factors in Buridan 10 means that Eliza will do the obvious: she always chooses the spoon in front of her. Of course, "always" must be read with a grain of salt. The program was run only fifty times on this problem. Had it been run, say, ten thousand times, the inherent nondeterminism of the architecture would amost certainly have produced the spoon-fork answer at least once or twice. The point, though, is that this answer would be (and should be) extremely rare.

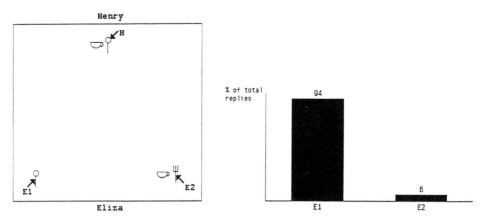

Buridan 11

Object Eliza touches	Average structure	No. of codelets run
E1	57	84
E2	199	93

The addition of cups next to the touched spoon and the fork in Buridan 11 increases the pressure for Eliza to touch the fork. Most of the time, though, she still goes for the spoon. However, when Eliza does touch the fork, the quality of this answer is far higher than for the rival answer. The reason for this is similar to the explanation given in Buridans 2 and 9.

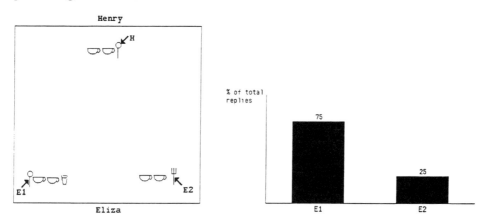

Buridan 12

Object Eliza touches	Average structure	No. of codelets run
E1	311	81
E2	264	105

In Buridan 10, in which there were no glasses or cups on the table, Eliza invariably chooses her spoon. When pairs of cups are added next to each piece of silverware, as in Buridan 12, cup-cup/cup-cup correspondences will be built. These are very strong, compared to the spoon-spoon and spoon-fork correspondences in isolation—so strong, in fact, that they tend to "swamp out" the single-object-to-single-object correspondences; so strong that they make the presence of the small glass in the lower left-hand group irrelevant. In Buridans 2, 9, and 11, the spoon-spoon mapping is frequently supported by an incoherent mapping from the touched spoon's sidekick object(s) to the fork's sidekick objects. However, in the present problem the cup-cup/cup-cup correspondence alongside the spoon-spoon mapping is considerably stronger (because it is next to a strong correspondence, which improves its rating) than the rival cup-cup/cup-cup mapping alongside the spoon-fork correspondence. As a result, the structures inducing Eliza to touch her spoon will almost always include the cup-cup/cup-cup mapping alongside the spoon-spoon correspondence, rather than the rival cup-cup/cup-cup mapping. This explains why this structure is considerably better than the structure associated with the answer in which Eliza touches her fork.

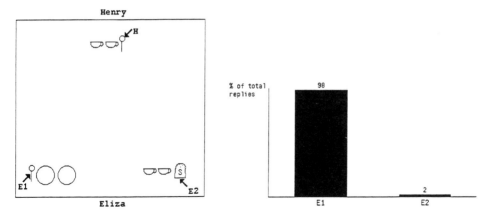

Buridan 13

Object Eliza touches	Average structure	No. of codelets run
E1	173	98
E2	161	155

Again, there are no major surprises in the outcome of Buridan 13. Saltshakers are conceptually very far from spoons, and even the cup-cup/cup-cup mapping cannot overcome that handicap. In addition, cups and plates are at least weakly related conceptually, and the cup-cup and plate-plate groups share the abstract feature of each having a single object type for their members. For this reason, Eliza opts overwhelmingly to touch the spoon.

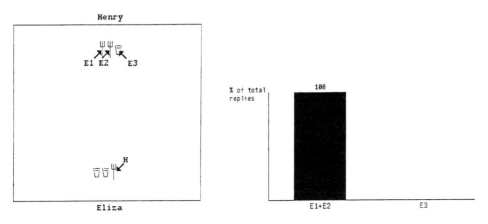

Figure/ground 1

Object Eliza touches	Average structure	No. of codelets run
E1 or E2	92	57
E3	—	—

In Figure/Ground, Henry reaches across the table and touches the "figure" object on Eliza's side of the table that echoes the "background material" on his side of the table—namely, the fork. It was hoped that, at least on occasion, the program would map the group of "background objects" (forks) on Henry's side of the table to the group of background objects (glasses) on Eliza's side of the table, even though the object types of these two sameness groups were very different. The hope was that this would then force the touched-fork/glass mapping. This certainly reflects the thinking of a good number of people. The effect is, of course, much stronger if one imagines that, instead of two forks on Henry's side and two glasses on Eliza's, there were ten of each.

Eliza's fork—the touched object—and Henry's glass tend to map onto one another for at least three reasons:

1. Because each one, when seen only in the context of the side it is on, is an *exceptional object*—a "figure object" standing out against a dull background

2. Because each one echoes, in object type, a larger group on the other side of the table

3. Because when Henry's group of forks gets "equated" with Eliza's group of glasses, there is a temporary rapprochement of the *concepts* "fork" and "glass," which then encourages the isolated fork and the isolated glass to be "equated" as well—in other words, there is a kind of temporary conceptual symmetry, in which just during this problem, forks and glasses are seen as "opposites"

Thus, in an exaggerated version of this configuration (for example, in which there were ten forks on Henry's side of the table and ten glasses on Eliza's side), a human Eliza would be strongly induced to touch the isolated glass on Henry's side. Even in this scaled-down version with just two objects acting as background, many people can see the appeal of choosing the isolated glass on Henry's side, even if they did not necessarily prefer it. However, the tabletop program did not initially get that answer *at all*. It is quite revelatory to analyze why this is so.

To begin with, aside from the desire to use only "real" table configurations (even at the Tour d'Argent in Paris, you don't get *ten* forks and glasses), as opposed to artificial patterns, the problem as presented to Tabletop contains only two forks and two glasses as background. This is because the process by which Tabletop builds large groups of identical objects (by progressively adding adjacent objects to already-existing groups) is flawed. To build a group of four identical objects—say, a sequence of six cups numbered 1 through 6—the program would end up making many of the possible groupings of cups (e.g., cup_1-cup_2, cup_2-cup_3, cup_3-cup_4, etc., and then cup_1-cup_2-cup_3, cup_3-cup_4-cup_5, etc., gradually working its way up to the entire group of cup_1-cup_2-cup_3- ... cup_6). It keeps all of the intermediate subgroups around, considering each of them important in its own right and trying to establish mappings with other "similar" groups. However, when we humans view a group of six adjacent cups, we tend to see them simply as a group of cups, and only under the most exceptional of circumstances as, say, a group of two cups next to a group of four cups. Unlike humans, however, Tabletop retains all of the subgroups, which means that it gets hopelessly confused whenever it is given a problem containing groups made up of more than three identical objects. This is a problem with Tabletop that needs to be fixed.

As can be seen in the Figure/Ground statistics the program never selected Henry's glass. The pressure against mapping two conceptually very different groups onto each other was too great. Eliza always chose to touch one of the two forks on Henry's side of the table (*E1* or *E2*).

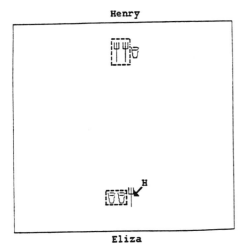

Figure 5.2
The glass-glass and fork-fork groups are built

In addition, a surprising mapping, one that humans would be very unlikely to make, was often made by the program to produce its answer. Soon after Henry touches the fork, the program builds the very salient glass-glass group on Eliza's side of the table and fork-fork group on Henry's side (see figure 5.2). Whenever any group is created, there is a top-down pressure to hunt for more groups that look exactly the same. Of course, in the case of these two groups, the program finds no more of them.

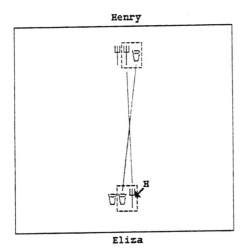

Figure 5.3
The two implausible fork-glass groups and the "natural" correspondences they suggest

Now for the rather unhumanlike action: The program will often also create a fork-glass group containing the touched fork (see figure 5.3). This may seem somewhat strange, since forks and glasses have very little in common. However, the most salient object on the table is always the object touched by Henry. Because of the high degree of salience of the touched fork, the program "reasons" that if it creates a group out of the touched fork and the neighboring glass, the new group will be, if not a great one, at least not too bad. Indeed, without the presence of the touched object, such a group would probably never be made in the first place.

Once this fork-glass group has been created, there is again a top-down pressure to find groups like it on the table. In this case, the program does indeed find an exact copy of this group on the other side of the table (see figure 5.3). Quite naturally, then, the program puts these two groups into correspondence. Of course, the objects inside them map perfectly onto one another. And as it happens, one of the mappings is from the *touched* fork to the fork on Henry's side of the table. The program ranks this as a very strong mapping and puts it in the Worldview. But this mapping constitutes an answer! And in fact it is the answer generally given by the program.

5.2 Synthesis of Results

Perhaps the most striking result of this long series of runs is the clear evidence that Tabletop gives reasonable answers on virtually all of the problems given to it. Over the course of these several thousand runs, certain trends were observed:

- At least qualitatively, over a large number of runs and over a relatively diverse set of problems, the program almost always seems to give psychologically plausible answers.
- The program is able to focus on promising areas of the table and ignore irrelevant objects. Adding extraneous objects to the table when there are good answers to the problem does not diminish the program's ability to home in on an answer.
- The program does not always pick the most obvious reasonable answer. Sometimes it eschews the paths to an obvious answer in favor of a structurally better answer (e.g., Surrounds 3, 4, 8, and 9; Blockages 2 and 5). The capability of Tabletop to do the nonobvious occasionally and arrive nonetheless at a high-quality answer is a very important consequence of its underlying stochastic design.
- Answers involving better structure generally take more time before they are selected.

5.3 Experimental Results

I asked subjects (thirty-four students in an introductory experimental psychology class at Willamette University) to do these problems and, in general, found that they were far more influenced by object-type matches than Tabletop, which usually weighted structural relations more heavily in its determination of the best counterpart of the touched object. For example, if the touched object was a cup and there was a cup on the opposite side of the table (e.g., the Surround series), the students frequently touched the cup, in spite of the presence of (sometimes considerable) relational structure that pulled Tabletop toward a different answer.

Tabletop was then run on a sample of twenty-three problems from the original forty. Because pilot studies had shown Tabletop to be more "structurally oriented" than most subjects, I slightly increased the relative importance that the program attached to object-type matches compared to relational structure in the evaluation of good correspondences. The entire Buridan series was tested, and five representative problems were chosen from each of the Surround and the Blockage series (Surrounds 1, 2, 3, 4, and 5 and Blockages 1, 2, 5, 6, and 7).

The performance of Tabletop (TT) and subjects on these problems are shown in tables 5.1, 5.2, and 5.3. The figures indicate the percentage of subjects who chose a particular answer compared to the percentage of times (out of fifty runs) that the program chose the same answer. These results are summarized in the graph in figure 5.4. In this graph the percentages for the answer most frequently chosen by subjects are compared to how often the program got the same answer in fifty runs. The problems are arranged in decreasing order of goodness of fit.

It can be seen that only on a few problems does the program perform very poorly compared to human subjects. In particular, when the touched object is inside a group of objects and there is an isolated object of the same type elsewhere, subjects seem to

Table 5.1
Buridan series

	E1		E2	
Buridan no.	Subjects	TT	Subjects	TT
1	75	75	25	25*
2	66	100	31	0
3	66	84	34	16
4	66	72	34	25*
5	22	47	78	53
6	53	59	47	41
7	62	72	38	28
8	62	75	38	25
9	100	100	0	0
10	97	100	3	0
11	75	100	25	0
12	56	84	44	16
13	97	100	3	0

*TT also touched the cup close to E1: 3%

Table 5.2
Surround series

	E1		E2	
Surround no.	Subjects	TT	Subjects	TT
1	0	0	100	100
2	0	3	100	97
3	16	16	81	84
4	22	75	73	25
5	33	81	72	19

*3% touched the touched cup

Table 5.3
Blockage series

Blockage no.	Either small glass		Originally touched cup	
	Subjects	TT	Subjects	TT
1	67	100	33	0
2	38	47	62	53
5	16	28	34	47
6	26	19	72	81
7	22	28	78	72

*The other cup on Henry's side of the table

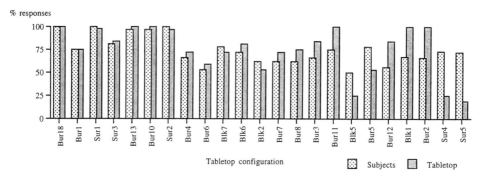

Figure 5.4
Comparison of Tabletop and subject performance on twenty-three problems from three different families of Tabletop configurations

be very prone to make a literal object-object match, rather than choosing answers based on relational structure. Perhaps the very isolation of the object adds to its salience. That, combined with the fact that there is an exact object-type match, could be why subjects pick the isolated counterpart more than what would seem to be structurally more coherent answers. This problem is particularly evident in Tabletop's performance on Surrounds 4 and 5.

On the other hand, on over half of these problems, Tabletop's answers differ from those of subjects by no more than 10 percentage points, and, as can be seen in figure 5.4, even when the difference is greater than this the general trend of Tabletop's responses is quite similar to that given by subjects.

5.4 The "Turing-Test" Approach to Testing Models of Analogy-Making

In this section, I wish to introduce the notion of a "Turing-test" approach to testing models of analogy-making. In a seminal article written in 1950, Alan Turing (Turing 1950) proposed a novel way of determining whether a machine was actually thinking. He suggested that in one room be placed the putative thinking machine, in another room a person. An interrogator, unaware of which room contained the machine and which the person, would then attempt to find out by means of questions asked over a teletype. Any and all questions were fair game. If the interrogator remained fooled by the machine after intense questioning, the machine would be declared to be thinking. French (1990) has shown just how difficult it would actually be for a machine to imitate a human in the face of the interrogator's no-holds-barred probing.

We probed Tabletop in a way based loosely on the Turing test. The essence of the Turing-test approach is to start with a core problem (or a small number of such problems) and to "probe" the program by giving it a large number of variations on the original problem, systematically exploring diverse combinations of pressures. The idea that this method of probing resembles the Turing test was first suggested to me by Douglas Hofstadter.

One difficulty with the common practice of using a wide range of isolated and unrelated problems chosen from different domains to test analogy-making programs is that in each case the programmer, and not the program, sculpts the representation of the individual problem, so that all that remains for the program to do is to find the appropriate set of mappings and then cry victory. Although finding an appropriate set of correspondences is certainly a nontrivial task, it is immeasurably facilitated by having the "right" (or almost "right") representations of the situations to be mapped onto one another. (The "representation problem"—the problem of relying on hand-coded representations—is discussed in detail by Chalmers, French, and Hofstadter [1992].)

Relying on a wide range of isolated and unrelated problems to demonstrate the validity of a model, in contrast to the Turing-test approach, lacks the crucial feature of using systematic variations on input to observe and quantify the corresponding variations on output. The Turing-test approach is about systematic probes and not isolated problems. Probes, much like the questions in a Turing test, involve systematic and gradual variations with respect to a core problem.

By systematically and gradually varying the pressures and studying how this affected the program's performance, I was able to probe Tabletop's "personality" quite extensively. In doing so, a "performance landscape" of Tabletop emerged. In other words, this technique reveals the "ridges" in this abstract space where the program switches from one preference to another. I will argue for the utility—possibility even the necessity—of this kind of Turing-test-like methodology for other cognitive models.

The Turing-test approach can be made to probe beneath the surface of the program by either (1) bombarding the program—with all of its parameters frozen—with many variations of a core problem, or (2) giving the program a single problem and systematically varying the program's parameters. In both instances, one gets a systematic and detailed look at the program's behavior. Tabletop's behavior was, to a large extent, examined by the first of these two techniques. At the end of each run, Tabletop indicates the object touched by Eliza, the sequence of structures that led to that answer, the amount of resources expended, and the type and quality of structures present at the end of the run.

Each problem given to the program was run approximately fifty times, and statistics for each series of runs were computed. It was thus possible to study not only the range of answers given by the program but also *why* the program gave those answers. The resemblance to the Turing test is clear: the problem variants correspond to a systematic series of deeply probing questions in a Turing test; the responses and associated data correspond to the answers to these questions.

Other analogy-making programs have generally not been subjected to careful and systematic statistical analysis. This applies to all of the programs using (supposedly) real-world examples, especially examples drawn from science. These programs are not typically studied by submitting to them a host of variations on a single problem, nor are systematic statistics gathered about *how* the program produced its answer. I strongly advocate that other researchers in cognitive modeling adopt this type of behavior-oriented Turing-test methodology to test their programs.

The key philosophical notion underlying this method of testing is that if we probe two entities that purport to be doing "the same thing" deeply and carefully enough, then if any differences exist in their underlying operant mechanisms, these differences will eventually become apparent (French 1990; Hofstadter 1985e). The decision about whether the underlying mechanisms of the two entities are indistinguishable will be made purely on a *behavioral* basis.

Consider the following analogy. Assume we are attempting to build a machine that will simulate seagull flight and someone comes along with a Boeing 747. Now, although it is true that the Boeing 747 can, in fact, fly, it does not do so in a "seagul-logically plausible" way. A few tests will quickly demonstrate this—for example, can it land on the top of a tree? If, on the other hand, someone brings us a one-foot long, two-pound, radio-operated helicopter and asserts that it shares with seagulls under-lying mechanisms of flight, it will probably take us a bit longer than in the first case to debunk the claim. The simple probes (e.g., "Can it land on the top of a tree?" "Does its air speed ever exceed one hundred miles an hour?" "Can it effect a ninety-degree turn in less than ten yards?") that allowed us to determine that the underlying flight mechanisms of a Boeing 747 and a seagull were, most probably, not the same will no longer suffice. The probing will now have to be deeper, and, presumably, the new probes will suffice to distinguish the miniature helicopter from a seagull. How-ever, as the models get better and better—as flapping wings, feathers, and symmetric eyes one and a half inches apart are added, as well as myriad other mechanisms that allow all of the flight patterns of a seagull to be imitated in the minutest of detail—it will take extremely subtle probing to tell them apart.

The key issue is this: At what level do "mechanisms of flight" actually exist? If we go down far enough (say, to the level of chemistry), we will always find differences between any model simulating a seagull and any other, even if the latter is another seagull.

One unambiguous way of defining levels of mechanisms is in terms of the probes capable of detecting them. So, if a certain set of probes cannot distinguish between two models, I wish to say that, *with respect to those probes*, the mechanisms underlying the two models are indistinguishable. Thus, in our example, with respect to the coarsest possible probe, "Can it move through the air on its own power?" both sea-gulls and Boeing 747s have indistinguishable underlying mechanisms of flight. This is not, however, the case when our set of probes becomes more refined. Thus, with re-spect to air speed, weight, and turning radius, the flight mechanisms of a Boeing 747 and a seagull are distinctly different.

In Tabletop, the level of the probes is determined by the set of variants of a prob-lem given to the program and the statistical distribution of responses to repeated runs of the program on each of those problems. This distribution includes not only the frequency of occurrence of various answers, but also the associated quality of structure, the length of time required to produce those answers, and occasionally other features. The psychological mechanisms of the program are determined with respect to these probes.

It is quite conceivable that someone might fully agree that Tabletop does indeed act like a human at the level of my probing, but maintain that the degree of psychological plausibility conferred by my probes is insufficient to establish that Tabletop is a genuine cognitive model (as opposed to, say, an engineering feat). There is, in my opinion, no response to this criticism, any more than there is to the criticism that we must compare seagulls and flying machines at the molecular level in order to establish the appropriate mechanisms of flight. The only thing to do is to convince the skeptic that your level of probing is appropriate. If this can be agreed on, then the degree of validity of the mechanisms of a particular model will depend on how well the model performs at the agreed-on level of probing.

Let us now return to the more concrete question of why it would be hard to apply a Turing-test methodology to programs purported to make scientific analogies. In the first place, "tweaking" the world of science is harder to do than tweaking problems in a microworld. It was relatively easy in Tabletop to study, for example, the effects of varying many types of pressures (e.g., the presence of groups of objects or the separation between objects) on the structures built and the answers given by Eliza. But how would one go about doing this with a scientific-analogy problem? It is much harder to come up with convincing and meaningful "variations" of scientific phenomena. Consider the classic analogy between the solar system and the Rutherford atom. Do we tweak facts about gravity? For example, do we ever assume that gravity *increases* as the square of the distance, or that it does not decrease at all out to a radius of ten thousand miles and then just stops altogether, and so on. Such alternatives to reality seem so far-fetched as to make us want to reject any analogy based on them—not because a priori there would be anything wrong with such an analogy but because, at a visceral level, people balk at tampering with immutable laws in such a cavalier manner. The scenarios suggested are simply very hard to imagine.

I maintain, however, that in order to carry out any systematic investigation of any cognitive model (including one for analogy-making), it is necessary to be able to make many, many such small variations and study their effects. This is not to say that many of the current researchers in the field of computer modeling of analogy-making could not do such systematic tweaks on their test problems, but doing so would unfortunately be much less natural than in Tabletop. For example, Tabletop's reaction to a variety of situations can be examined by simply adjusting the various pressures involved: by replacing the small glass in Surround 5 first by a saucer, then by a plate, and, finally, by a saltshaker; by replacing the glass-glass pair in Buridan 1 by a single glass, by a glass and a cup, and by a glass and a saltshaker; or by gradually increasing the separation between two of the glasses in the Blockage series. The Tabletop microworld is perfectly suited to this kind of manipulation, which is one reason it is such an ideal domain to study.

Pressures could also be tweaked in real-world domains, and this is what I suggest that researchers engaged in testing their analogy-making programs on real-world domains should do. First, the "classic" examples of scientific analogies—for example, analogies between the Rutherford atom and the solar system—should be avoided. This is for two related reasons:

1. There is assumed to be only one correct answer. Even if it might be possible to "tweak" aspects of either the source or the target situations, the prior knowledge by people of the standard analogy will make the whole exercise of probing through variations seem ridiculous and implausible.

2. Variations of these well-known situations will be viewed not as tweaks but as introducing *errors*. Counterfactuals in science do not sit well with people, because they are viewed as tampering with the (immutable) laws of physics. One of the basic assumptions that people make about objects on a table is that they *can* be moved around, whereas it is not one of people's basic assumptions about physics that electrons could follow square orbits, or that they could have negative masses, or that gravity might obey anything but an inverse-square law, and so on. This reluctance to accept tweaks of a scientific situation has effectively ruled out the possibility of using Turing-test-like probing in such domains.

Even though it is true that certain scientific facts are *somewhat* slippable in most people's minds (e.g., the gravitational constant could be altered slightly, the speed of light could be slipped to 175,000 miles per second, the moon could be 500,000 miles away, and so on), it is nonetheless very hard to concoct reasonable variations of a classic analogy. For example, I spent a considerable amount of time trying to find reasonable "tweaks" on the Rutherford-atom/solar-system analogy and was unable to find any variations that were in any way comparable to the easily obtained variations of a particular problem in Tabletop.

This does not, however, imply that there are no real-world domains in which tweaks of the desired sort would be relatively easy to come up with. Three reasonable real-world domains that might serve the purposes of those investigators who do not wish to use microworlds are interpersonal, political, and legal analogies.

An example of an interpersonal analogy might be "President Kennedy's relationship to Marilyn Monroe in the early sixties was analogous to Gary Hart's relationship to Donna Rice in the late eighties." People are quite comfortable counterfactualizing about situations involving people and, in the above example, this could easily give rise to a host of reasonable variants of the core analogy. It should be noted that sometimes *real* (as opposed to counterfactual) tweaks are available as well. For example, we might tweak the above situation as follows: "Bobby Kennedy's relationship to Marilyn Monroe in the early sixties was analogous to Gary Hart's relationship to Donna Rice in the late eighties."

An example from politics involves Greece's siding with Britain in the Falklands conflict. Third-world, small-country, anti-imperialism concerns certainly constituted a very strong pressure on Greece, as on many small, poor countries, to side with Argentina. However, the key pressure constituted by the fact that Cyprus is much closer to Turkey than to Greece made Greece the obvious analogue of Britain. Siding with Argentina not only would have been hypocritical but would have been a dangerous political precedent for Greece. Aside from the amusing and possibly fascinating counterfactual tweaks on such a situation (e.g., "What if Cyprus had been poised midway between Turkey and Greece? Right next to Greece?"), a virtually unlimited number of new, related analogy problems, each with its own unique constellation of pressures, can be generated by viewing the Falklands conflict from various other countries' perspectives (e.g., "Which country did Chile align itself with? What about China? What about Spain?"). Although the psychological plausibility of answers to the counterfactual tweaks could be checked by comparing them with the responses of human subjects, in the case of the real situations, the psychological plausibility of an answer could be ascertained by checking how the country in question actually behaved.

5.5 Conclusion

By running Tabletop on a wide spectrum of interconnected problems, I have tried to illustrate its major capabilities. It is interesting to note that, even in configurations that feature many different table objects in a wide variety of groupings and positions on the table, Tabletop generally quickly homes in on two or three reasonable answers and almost always avoids fringe answers, even though they of course remain theoretically accessible. However, if the program were to be adjusted so that *only* completely obvious answers could be given, there would be a serious risk of eliminating rare but potentially excellent answers. The trick is to find a middle pathway that seldom, if ever, produces bizarre answers to ordinary problems, yet which under unusual circumstances will be able to come up with subtle and insightful viewpoints, when they exist. To my gratification, Tabletop seems to have been able to walk this tightrope fairly effectively.

Chapter 6

Comparisons with Other Work

In this chapter I consider the work of a number of other researchers in analogy-making. However, since a good deal of the research in analogy-making involves either learning or retrieval—issues not addressed in this book—these models will be touched on only briefly.

It is also important, I believe, to discuss how Tabletop fits into current research paradigms in artificial intelligence, based purely on architectural considerations, irrespective of the domain or facet of cognition being modeled. Therefore, at the end of this chapter, I attempt to situate Tabletop along the continuum of models running from purely bottom-up connectionist models to purely top-down symbolic models.

6.1 "Standard" Analogy-Making and Prosaic Analogy-Making

One overall comment is in order about the nature of the analogy-making that Tabletop does. Virtually all researchers in the field of analogy-making are concerned with "standard" analogies—that is, situations that are *clearly* perceived as "doing analogies." Thomas Evans (1968), who in the sixties wrote the first analogy-making program, was concerned with classic, "proportional" analogies, of the IQ-test, geometric sort. Dedre Gentner's work (Gentner 1983) relates the hydrogen atom to the solar system, heat flow to water flow, balls falling from a tower and from the mast of a ship, and so on. These are quite sophisticated scientific analogies. Mark Burstein (1986a, 1986b) focuses on "analogies explaining the behavior of physical devices [and] physical explanations of natural phenomena," thus exploring analogies in high-level pedagogy. Patrick Winston (1980) considers analogies between Cinderella and Juliet, Macbeth and Hamlet—sophisticated literary analogies. Smadar Kedar-Cabelli (1984) chose to model legal reasoning from precedents. Keith Holyoak and Paul Thagard (1989) are concerned not only with the same scientific analogies as Gentner and her colleagues but also with a sophisticated metaphor linking Socrates' teaching to the role of a midwife. Mitchell and Hofstadter's Copycat, like Evans's ANALOGY, also does something that is clearly perceived, at least by people who draw up IQ tests and college entrance examinations, as analogy-making—in fact, quite creative analogy-making. Marsha Meredith (1986, 1991), Daniel Defays (1986), and Kok-Wee Gan (1994), even though they are not modeling analogy-making per se, are modeling high-level cognitive processes that involve generalization and problem-solving skills closely related to analogy-making.

Tabletop, on the other hand, is modeling something much more prosaic than these other programs model: most people do not even recognize that analogy-making is involved when they respond to the "Do this!" challenge (see, for example, the me-too examples in the first chapter). Tabletop thus makes a subtle, and in my opinion, important point: it highlights the *everyday* aspect of analogy-making. It emphasizes the fact that we humans are doing analogy-making not only when we recognize that the hydrogen atom is like the solar system, but also when a friend across the table from us touches her cheek and says, "You've got a bit of spaghetti sauce right here" or when we are shopping in a grocery store we have never been in before and she remarks, "They usually keep the sugar around here." It is a fundamental tenet of this research that the same analogy-making mechanisms are at work both in such prosaic situations and in the more exalted cases of IQ-test, scientific, literary, and legal analogies, as well as pedagogical and philosophical metaphors.

6.2 The Earliest Program: ANALOGY

The first significant attempt to write an analogy-making program was made by Thomas Evans in the mid sixties (Evans 1968). His program, ANALOGY, was designed to solve analogy problems involving combinations of simple geometric shapes, such as circles, triangles, squares, rectangles, and dots. Many of the geometric-analogy problems that Evans's program attempted to solve were taken from standardized IQ tests given to high-school students (figure 6.1). These are classic "ratio" analogies of the form $A:B::C:D$. In other words, there is a relation between the pattern in box A and the one in box B, which the student (or program) must discover and then apply "the same" relationship to the pattern in box C in order to select the correct answer from among the five solution figures given.

Evans's program had two functional parts or modules: a representation-builder and a rule-builder. In the first module, "the input figures are decomposed into subfigures and various properties of and relations between these subfigures are computed." In the second module, the program attempts "to construct a rule which transforms Figure A into Figure B and Figure C into exactly one of the five answer figures" (Evans 1968).

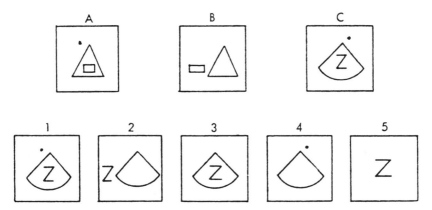

Figure 6.1
A geometric analogy problem

The representation-building module analyzes the input figures in figure 6.1 and provides descriptions of the following sort:

For figure *A*:   (inside *P2* *P3*)
                   (above *P1* *P3*)
                   (above *P1* *P2*)

where *P1* is the dot, *P2* is the small rectangle inside the triangle, and *P3* is the triangle.

For figure *B*:   (left *P4* *P5*)

where *P4* is the small rectangle and *P5* is the triangle.

For figure *C*:   (inside *P7* *P6*)
                   (above *P8* *P6*)
                   (above *P8* *P7*)

where *P6* is the triangle with the bowl-shaped bottom, *P7* is the *Z*, and *P8* is the dot. The program computes similar descriptions for all five of the possible solution patterns.

The descriptions have been transcribed as they are in Evans's article for more than reasons of historical authenticity. For example, to have written for figure *A* "(inside rectangle triangle)" instead of "(inside *P2* *P3*)" might have given the impression that ANALOGY actually knew about triangles and rectangles in a way resembling how we humans know about these concepts. This would have been misleading, since the program's knowledge of these geometrical figures bears no resemblance whatsoever to our own. It has no notion of conceptual distances—for example, the fact that "rectangle" is closer in most people's mental metric space to "square" than to "circle" or "dot." The same goes for the relational concepts it uses, such as "above," "below," and "inside."

This is in contrast to a Slipnet, one of whose main purposes is to establish conceptual distances. Were there to be a Slipnet for the kinds of analogy problems that ANALOGY was designed to solve, "square" and "rectangle" would by default be closer together than "square" and "dot," so that a priori "square" would be more likely to slip to "rectangle" than to "dot." Now, clearly, Tabletop's Slipnet does not contain the same wealth of knowledge about, say, cups as people do, but at least theoretically such an architecture could accommodate an extremely rich set of concepts.

The fact that Evans's program was concerned not only with finding correspondences between situations but also with building up representations for those situations sets it apart from most current analogy-making programs. Chalmers, French, and Hofstadter (1992) argue at length for the necessity of interleaving the representation-building and -mapping processes. Although Evans views these two processes as sequential, his program at least has the merit of attempting to develop a representation of the input. Most current programs (Burstein and Adelson 1987; Falkenhainer, Forbus, and Gentner 1989; Kedar-Cabelli 1988b; Thagard et al. 1990) essentially ignore the representation problem and handle only the question of discovering and selecting mappings. And although some programs, most notably MAC/ FAC (Gentner and Forbus 1991; Gentner, Ratterman, and Forbus 1993), do tackle the representation problem, representation-building is still apparently regarded as a separate function, distinct from the process of finding correspondences. This tends to make analogy-making appear to be a special-purpose faculty, divorced from the rest of cognition, brought out only to resolve conceptual crises or to bring about deep scientific or literary insight. Most current analogy research fails to recognize the absolute ubiquity of analogy in thinking.

Let us return to ANALOGY. Once the program has decided on a representation for each of the eight boxes, it attempts to describe the set of transformations that would convert the pattern in figure *A* into the one in figure *B*. The program has a limited set of transformations to choose from: horizontal and vertical reflection, rotation, uniform scaling, and removal and addition of objects.

Having constructed its rule (i.e., set of transformations) mapping the objects in figure *A* to those in figure *B* (referred to here as the "template mapping"), the program then maps figure *C* onto each of the five solution boxes. If the number of objects in an answer box differs from the number in figure *B*, or if the number of objects removed or added with respect to figure *C* is not the same as in the template mapping, then that candidate answer is immediately eliminated. This type of rigid pruning is far too black-and-white. It could well be that *everything else* matched perfectly, but that, say, five objects were added as opposed to just four in the template mapping. This would cause ANALOGY to reject the answer instantly, even though from a human point of view it might have made a far better analogy than all the other answers, which might nonetheless have made it past the first cut simply because they did not violate the constraint involving the number of objects added or removed. It is not hard to construct examples in which this rigid pruning technique would eliminate excellent answers.

In any event, after this initial pruning, the program does an exhaustive search, guided by the original rule transforming *A* to *B*, of all possible combinations of transformations that would map *C* onto each of the candidate answers. The *C*-to-answer rules are then scored according to how closely they match the original rule transforming *A* to *B*. The rule with the highest score is then chosen and the answer corresponding to this rule is selected.

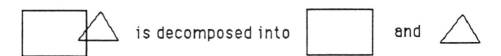

Figure 6.2
Overlapping figures

Evans was aware that context might play a role in the representations developed by his program. For example, the program would decompose the drawing on the left side of figure 6.2 into a rectangle and a triangle "on the basis that these figures are present in several of the answer figures" (Evans 1968, p. 296). In other words, the context generated by the presence of triangles and rectangles in the other figures is sufficient for the program to correctly parse the drawing on the left side of figure 6.2.

The importance of Evans's work lies in

- Its being the first attempt to model analogy-making
- Its recognition of the importance of both representation-building and mapping to the modeling of analogy-making
- Its use of an extremely rich microdomain in which the analogies are abstract—that is, are not tied directly to the real world and are not driven by a specific purpose

• Its recognition, albeit minimal, of the role played by context

ANALOGY, even though a very interesting and advanced program for its time, suffers from a number of shortcomings:

The use of brute-force techniques ANALOGY computes all possible C-to-answer transformations and all possible rules for all the answer figures. This is a direct route to combinatorial explosion in scaled-up domains.

Absence of a Slipnet I have discussed elsewhere the need for a Slipnet and the problems that arise in architectures lacking this type of structure. Thus, for example, ANALOGY has no sense that a square ought to be perceived as more similar to a rectangle than to a dot.

No systematic notion of conceptual slippage This of course comes from the absence of a Slipnet. For all intents and purposes, words in the A-to-B rule must map to identical words in the C-to-answer rule. (There was a special case in which conceptual slippage did occur, but it was done in an ad hoc manner. Slippage was not in any fundamental way part of ANALOGY's architecture.)

Essentially serial architecture The program's analogy-discovery strategy is completely serial. Representations are built first, then mappings are constructed based on those representations. Further, representations are built box by box, with no interleaving and no reciprocal influences.

Deterministic control mechanisms ANALOGY operates in a completely deterministic manner. Even in problems in which from a human point of view there may be two very strong answers, it will always choose the one that has the higher rating, regardless of how slight this difference is. Not only is it psychologically implausible for the program always to go for the slightly better answer, but the deterministic control structure means that the program will never explore, even on rare occasions, unpromising pathways that ultimately could lead to a very good answer.

In conclusion, ANALOGY was the first attempt to mechanize analogy-making. Even though Evans's problems were chosen from IQ-test-like geometric-analogy problems, there was no attempt to model how humans actually solve these problems, as, for example, Newell, Simon, and Shaw had attempted to do with GPS (Newell, Shaw, and Simon 1959). Moreover, ANALOGY's architecture includes many design decisions that would clearly prevent it from being scaled up.

6.3 Reitman's Argus

Walter Reitman's Argus (Reitman 1965) was, like ANALOGY, written in the sixties, partly in reaction to problems Reitman saw in GPS. The analogy problems that Argus could solve were extremely limited, almost trivially so. Here is an example of a problem Argus could solve: bear:pig::chair:{foot, table, coffee, strawberry} (i.e., "bear" is to "pig" as "chair" is to "foot," "table," "coffee," or "strawberry" [choose one]). The answer, "table," is astoundingly simple-minded. The justification for this answer is merely that, just as both "bear" and "pig" share a superordinate ("animal"), so do "chair" and "table" (namely, "furniture"). The only other example Reitman gives of an analogy Argus solved was: hot:cold::tall:{wall, short, wet, hold}. Clearly, Argus must be judged not on the basis of its performance on actual problems but on the farsighted basis of its architecture.

Some of the major principles of Argus anticipated some of the features of Tabletop, among them the following:

- Existence of a conceptual network in which activation spreads around in parallel, Hebbian fashion.
- Reliance on a mutual interaction between a semantic network and a serial process trying to perform a certain task (an analogy problem, for example). This amounts to recognizing the necessity of top-down/bottom-up interaction.
- Rejection of the notion of using hand-coded, context-independent representations that would be fed into a mapping module.

These three central ideas of Argus are also of critical importance to Tabletop. It is regrettable that Argus was not developed to the point where its performance was more impressive and that some of the ideas underlying Argus did not have a greater influence on subsequent research in artificial intelligence.

6.4 Gentner's Structure-Mapping Theory and Its Implementation

The work on analogy by Dedre Gentner and her associates (Gentner 1983; Falkenhainer, Forbus, and Gentner 1989) is probably better known than any other at the present time. It is important to note that, unlike Winston and Evans, Gentner is interested in developing a psychological model of human analogy-making, and this brings her concerns far more in line with those of this book.

More than a decade ago, Dedre Gentner developed a theory of analogy-making (Gentner 1983) that was subsequently implemented in a computer model called the Structure-Mapping Engine (SME) (Falkenhainer, Forbus, and Gentner 1989). Since that time her theory and its computer implementation have been expanded and refined by a number of researchers (Falkenhainer 1992; Gentner, Ratterman, and Forbus 1992; Markman and Gentner 1992; Kotovsky and Gentner 1992; and others).

SME takes as input representations of the two situations to be compared (called the *base situation* and the *target situation*). It maps objects and relations in the base situation to objects and relations in the target situation and then makes certain inferences about the latter situation, on the basis of the mapping. It is important to note that, in contrast to the work presented in this book, Gentner's work is largely, if not entirely, unconcerned with the problem of building representations of the base and target situations. For her, the process of analogy-making is more involved with finding appropriate correspondences between already-supplied, fixed representations of the base and target situations than it is with actually building the representations of the situations. In distinct contrast to this point of view, one of the major themes of this book is that the two processes are inseparable.

There are at least two major principles of Gentner's theory of analogy-making:

The relation-mapping principle Analogies are determined not by mapping the attributes of the objects in one situation to the attributes of the objects in another situation, but by mapping the relations among objects in one situation to the relations among objects in the second situation. Although the discovery of these relations may be influenced by attribute similarity, good analogies are determined by mappings of relations rather than attributes.

The systematicity principle Mappings involving relations that form part of a coherent whole are preferred over mappings of isolated relations.

For Gentner, these principles can be used to distinguish among several types of comparisons between two situations. She distinguishes at least three different types of comparisons:

- "Surface similarity," in which only attributes are mapped.
- "Literal similarity," in which both attributes and relations are mapped.
- "Analogy," in which only relations are mapped. The quality of an analogy is determined by the systematicity of its mappings. The greater the systematicity, the better the analogy.

These distinctions seem to be too black-and-white. To begin with, the notion that analogies involve mapping relations only is certainly incorrect in many cases. As Holyoak and Thagard (1989) have pointed out, "attributes sometimes seem to be more important than relations in analogical transfer, both in solving problems ... and in interpreting simple metaphors (e.g., 'Tom is a giraffe')."

Subjects' responses to Surround 5 from the Tabletop domain would also seem to pose a problems for the notion that people prefer relational structure in making analogies. In this configuration, there is a very clear, highly structural answer (the small glass on Eliza's side of the table) competing with an answer in which only surface similarity is important (the cup on Eliza's side of the table). Henry touches the cup on his side of the table, and subjects are asked to "Touch the object that, in your opinion, is the best counterpart to the object (Henry) just touched." There were no limits placed on time and in one case I had the subjects pencil in all of the relations they saw, and they invariably mapped the two-spoon subgroup on Henry's side to the corresponding one on Eliza's side of the table, ditto for the two-fork group and the two knives. Clearly, these relations do not go unnoticed. And yet subjects overwhelming chose the surface-similarity answer (72 percent chose the cup on Eliza's side of the table, 33 percent chose the small glass, 3 percent chose the same cup that Henry touched.) This finding has been repeated on at least three separate occasions. The point is that subjects are clearly aware of the strong relational mappings, are told that they are being asked to make an analogy and to find the "counterpart" of the object Henry touched, but nevertheless reject the relational answer in favor of one based solely on one salient attribute, namely, the object type.

Another problem with Gentner's two principles of analogy-making (and the three types of comparisons that derive from these principles) is an implicit assumption that the presumed distinction between objects, attributes, and relations is relatively clear-cut and objective. The problems with this assumption have been discussed in detail by Mitchell (1990) and by Chalmers, French, and Hofstadter (1992). A clear statement of the argument against this assumption is presented in the latter paper:

> A related problem arises when we consider the distinction that Gentner makes between *objects, attributes,* and *relations.* This distinction is fundamental to the operations of SME, which works by mapping objects exclusively to objects and relations to relations, while paying little attention to attributes. In the atom/solar-system analogy ... such things as the nucleus, the sun, and the electrons are labeled as "objects," while mass and charge, for instance, are considered to be "attributes." However, it seems most unclear that this representational division is so clean in human thought. Many concepts, psychologically, seem to float back and forth between being objects and attributes, for example. Consider a

model of economics: should we regard "wealth" as an object that flows from one agent, or as an attribute of the agents that changes with each transaction? There does not appear to be any obvious *a priori* way to make the decision. A similar problem arises with the SME treatment of relations, which are treated as *n*-place predicates. A 3-place predicate can be mapped only to a 3-place predicate, and never to a 4-place predicate, no matter how semantically close the predicates might be. So it is vitally important that every relation be represented by precisely the right kind of predicate structure in every representation. It seems unlikely that the human mind makes a rigid demarcation between 3-place and 4-place predicates—rather, this kind of thing is probably very blurry.

The need to differentiate objects, attributes, and relations is part of a larger problem referred to by Chalmers, French, and Hofstadter (1992) as the "representation problem." There, the authors argue that it is impossible to separate analogy-making into two distinct phases—namely, a representation phase followed by a mapping phase. Rather, they claim, these operations are intimately interdependent and cannot be temporally separated. As I have already pointed out, Evans separates the two processes and treats them serially. Gentner, on the other hand, ignores the representation process entirely, treating only the mapping phase. SME is simply handed fixed, human-coded representations of the situations. Its job is then to find the appropriate mappings. But Chalmers, French, and Hofstadter's contention is that, once one has the data represented in an appropriate form, discovering the "correct" mappings is, comparatively speaking, a piece of cake.

In order to discuss this problem, let us consider one of the standard examples from Gentner's research, where SME is said to discover an analogy between an atom—the Rutherford atom, in particular—and the solar system. Here, the program is given representations of the two situations, as shown in figure 6.3.

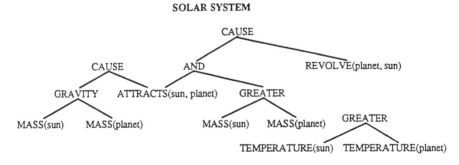

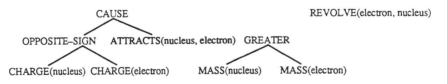

Figure 6.3
Representations given to SME to find an analogy between the solar system and the Rutherford atom

Again quoting from Chalmers, French, and Hofstadter (1992):

> Starting with these representations, SME examines many possible correspondences between elements of the first representation and elements of the second. These correspondences are evaluated according to how well they preserve the structure apparent in the representations. The correspondence with the highest score is selected as the best analogical mapping between the two situations.
>
> A brief examination of (figure 6.3) shows that the discovery of the similar structure in these representations is not a difficult task. The representations have been set up in such a way that the common structure is immediately apparent. Even for a computer program, the extraction of such common structure is relatively straightforward.
>
> We are in broad sympathy with Gentner's notion that the mappings in an analogy should preserve high-level structure.... But when the program's discovery of the correspondences between the two situations is a direct result of its being explicitly given the appropriate structures to work with, its victory in finding the analogy becomes somewhat hollow. Since the representations are tailored (perhaps unconsciously) to the problem at hand, it is hardly surprising that the correct structural correspondences are not difficult to find. A few pieces of irrelevant information are sometimes thrown in as decoys, but this makes the task of the mapping process only slightly more complicated. The point is that if appropriate representations come pre-supplied, the hard part of the analogy-making task has already been accomplished.
>
> Imagine what it would take to devise a representation of the solar system or an atom independent of any context provided by a particular problem. There are so many data available: one might, for instance, include information about the moons around the planets, about the opposite electric charges on the proton and the electron, about relative velocities, about proximities to other bodies, about the composition of the sun or the composition of the nucleus, about the fact that the planets lie in one plane and that each planet rotates on its axis, and so on. It comes as no surprise, in view of the analogy sought, that the only relations present in the representations that SME uses for these situations are the following: "attracts," "revolves around," "gravity," "opposite-sign," and "greater" (as well as the fundamental relation "cause"). These, for the most part, are precisely the relations that are the relevant factors in this analogy.

In short, the use of hand-coded representations is a significant problem with SME. Whereas in Tabletop building representations goes hand in hand with building and testing mappings between objects, in SME the representation problem is, in essence, peeled away and solved in advance by the programmer/researchers. More recently, the MAC/FAC architecture (Gentner and Forbus 1991), which subsumes SME, does indeed address the problem of representation building, but the procedure is nonetheless a *serial* one in which there is a first phase, in which lots of different representations are proposed ("Many (representations) are called" [MAC]), followed by a second phase, in which SME is used to find the best matches from the first stage ("Few are chosen" [FAC]). This again assumes that, when making analogies, representation-building goes on in the absence of correspondence building. This is in direct contrast to the Tabletop philosophy, in which representation-building and correspondence-discovery are mutually interactive, dynamic processes.

As Chalmers, French, and Hofstadter argue (1992), this technique lacks the dynamic focusing mechanisms of an architecture like Tabletop's. Spotting two matching objects on opposite sides of the table suggests a possible correspondence, which in turn suggests that it might be worthwhile examining the structure around those objects, which in turn suggests other possible correspondences between those objects, and so on. In other words, finding correspondences is *part of* the representation-building process and vice versa. Certain aspects of a representation consciously come to light only *after* certain correspondences have been noticed. It is precisely this manner of representation-building via correspondence-discovery that makes jokes of the "Why is an X like a Y?" genre funny. It is usually only when the comedian explicitly tells you what the correspondence between X and Y is that certain features of X that *were not originally* part of your initial representation of X become part of your explicit representation of X. If they had been there to begin with, then chances are you would not have found the joke funny. It would seem unlikely that there would be an a priori way to represent both X and Y that include in working memory all possible features that would allow us to make the appropriate correspondences required by the joke. And if we could do this, wouldn't the joke cease to be funny?

A joke I once heard on a late-night talk show illustrates this point: "Why is marriage like flies on a windowpane?" As you try to figure out the punchline ahead of the comedian, you align parts of a rapidly constructed, working-memory representation of marriage with an equally rapidly constructed representation of flies on a windowpane. Flies are little, black, buzz, crawl, have wings, are annoying, in some cases disgusting, and so on. Nothing in that representation seems to correspond even remotely to your representation of marriage, which includes concepts like "love," "spouse," "children," "evenings at home," "sex," and "joint checking accounts." Then comes the punchline: "Because those on the outside want to get in, and those on the inside want to get out." You laugh, or at least find the answer clever, precisely because your working-memory representations of marriage and flies on a windowpane did not initially include this outside-in, inside-out feature that constitutes the punchline of the joke. And, while this is an appropriate feature in the context of this joke, you would not ordinarily include this feature when the concept "marriage" is introduced into working memory.

Now let us consider the mapping phase—the phase that apparently constitutes, for Gentner, the lion's share of analogy-making. To discover which relations in one situation map to relations in the other situation, SME relies on "match rules." These are rules that look for matches in the *names* of relations, the *number* of predicates of relations, the *degree of systematicity* in a set of relations, and so on. (Such a match is also called a "pairing.") The program then rates each set of pairings—mappings between situations are defined by *sets* of pairings—in terms of the four criteria below. The better the match, the higher the score of a particular mapping. The mapping with the highest score is chosen as the analogical mapping from the base situation to the target situation. The four domain-independent criteria that determine the quality of the mappings from the base domain to the target domain are the following:

> *Clarity* This is a measure of how obvious the mappings are of items in the base domain to items in the target domain.
> *Richness* This is a measure of the *quantity* of mapped attributes and relations (all of which can be expressed as predicates). The more mapped predicates, the better.

Abstraction Gentner proposes a hierarchy of the kinds of predicates mapped. At the bottom of the hierarchy are the attributes of the objects involved in the mapping; next come first-order relations (i.e., relations between the objects' attributes); then come second-order relations (i.e., relations between first-order relations), and so on. The higher the mapped predicates are in this hierarchy, the better the analogy.

Systematicity *Causal* systems of relations (i.e., hierarchical systems that include relations that constrain lower-order relations) are preferred over *isolated* relations for mapping from the base domain to the target.

In order to satisfy the clarity criterion, SME considers only sets of one-to-one mappings of objects and relation. Many-to-one mappings from a set of objects to a single object, for example, are not permitted in SME, but are handled in PHINEAS (Falkenhainer 1990). Richness is ensured by making each set of pairings as large as possible while maintaining a kind of syntactic consistency. Abstractness comes from mapping relations to relations and ignoring attribute mappings. The degree of systematicity is determined by the extent to which a set of pairings maps a "systematic" set of relations in the base situation to a systematic set of relations in the target situation.

In addition, in SME predicates used in the representation of the base domain must be mapped on *identical* predicates in the target domain. There is no sense in which, in the tabletop idiom, one predicate in one domain can be "slipped" to a conceptually close predicate in the other domain. Recognizing the shortcomings of this requirement, Falkenhainer (1990) developed a technique called context structure-mapping (employed by his program, PHINEAS), which allows functionally analogous predicates to be mapped onto one another. This is much closer to what happens in Tabletop, in which conceptual slippages mediate mappings.

In her critique of Gentner's work, Mitchell (1990, 1993) has pointed out a number of difficulties with the policy of always favoring more abstract, more systematic mappings over less abstract, less systematic ones. These criticisms notwithstanding, I think that systematicity is in general a good heuristic for gauging the depth of an analogy.

Given that Gentner's four criteria are indeed very useful in judging the quality of a particular mapping, any computational model of analogy-making must be largely consistent with them, even if they are not *explicitly* included in the system's design. See Hofstadter and Mitchell's work (1991) for a discussion of ways in which a drive toward systematicity *emerges* from more fundamental principles in the Copycat (or in this case, the Tabletop) architecture.

The only input to SME is the "syntactic" structural features (i.e., the "graphs" of the relations among the objects) of the two situations under consideration. SME does not have access to semantic knowledge, at least not in the way that Tabletop does. In particular, it has no knowledge about the conceptual proximity of the concepts associated with the objects in the base and target domain. In the example in figure 6.3, SME might be said to "know" that the mass of the sun is greater than the mass of a planet. But the sum total of SME's knowledge about mass, gravity, suns, and planets is expressed in the predicate $\text{GREATER}(\text{mass}_{\text{sun}}, \text{mass}_{\text{planet}})$. But this is a funny, isolated kind of knowledge, uncoupled, as it were, from all other knowledge about planets, celestial bodies, and gravity, to say nothing of concepts like "mass," "gravity," and "greater than." It is as if, in the model of the Rutherford atom, all of the English words for concepts were replaced by mere letters of the alphabet. This would bring into focus the dearth of content—there would be only a tree structure with letters for nodes of the tree.

Even if one ignores the fact that SME needs hand-coded representations, there is still a serious problem with SME's attempt to make analogies on the basis of structure-mapping alone. Matching of structures (and in Gentner's case, identical matching) alone is not sufficient to determine which mappings should be preferred over others. A recourse to concepts and to their associations—in a word, a recourse to meaning—is necessary. To see this, let us again consider the analogy between the Rutherford atom and the solar system. In the representations of the base and target situations provided to SME, many facts and relationships are simply ignored. For example, there is no a priori reason that the representation of the atom would not also include facts about the gravitational attractions between its constituent particles (figure 6.4).

Even though gravity, compared to the electromagnetic and nuclear forces, is extremely weak, it nonetheless generates an attraction between the nucleus and the electron. Thus, there would be an additional set of relations in the target domain, with "charge" replaced by "mass" and "opposite sign" replaced by "gravity."

The matching rules of the program would *invariably* cause the program to pick the set of relations in the target domain in which "opposite sign" was replaced by "gravity." Among the candidate inferences—undoubtedly, the strongest candidate inference—that SME would draw would be that the electron revolved around the nucleus of an atom because of the gravitational attraction between the nucleus and the electron.

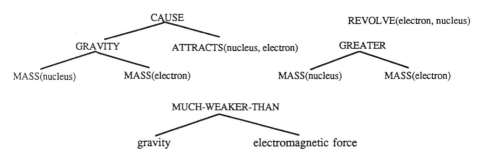

RUTHERFORD ATOM

Figure 6.4
The representation of the Rutherford atom, including the "much weaker than" relation

To SME—and no doubt to people who did not know anything about nuclear physics—this would be an entirely plausible candidate inference, since the program does not know that in the world of subatomic particles gravity is a much, much weaker force than the electromagnetic force. How could SME be "told" that the correspondence between "gravity" (in the sun-planet domain) and "opposite sign" (in the Rutherford-atom domain) is a much better mapping than the identical match between "gravity" in the sun-planet domain and "gravity" in the Rutherford-atom domain? In other words, how could the program be made to evaluate the (apparently good, because identical) gravity-gravity match as weaker than the gravity-opposite-sign match? Would it help to throw in the relationship MUCH-WEAKER-THAN(gravity, electromagnetic force)? To a human, this would seem to tell the program quite directly that the whole gravity story is a red herring and ought to be ignored. Unfortunately, however, this conclusion, so obvious to a human, relies on one simple fact: understanding the *meaning* of the phrase "much weaker than." But meanings are not part of an approach that relies entirely on structure mapping. The only way a relation can affect the program is by having a "match." Otherwise, it is ignored (after all, the program has no idea what to do with relations other than to match them with other ones). This new relation, "much weaker than," does not match anything else in the presented data; it is simply trying to give SME some good advice about how to go about the mapping process. Thus it is, in some sense, "meta-level" information. But for SME this information might as well be in Chinese. It is not understood and is therefore ignored, leading to a preference for gravity in the analogy.

The (recurring) moral of the story: Relational structure mapping may serve to flush out candidate analogical inferences, but a conceptual network (in some form or another) is needed to determine which of the candidate inferences is the best one. As we have seen, a set of relations used to produce one candidate inference might consist entirely of identity matches and still be weaker than another one in which not all of the matches are identical.

The proper approach to such a problem is understanding the meaning of the word "weak"—and understanding does not merely mean knowing that "weak" is a synonym of "feeble" or an antonym of "strong." There must be a mediation between the concept network and the processing, which explicitly tells the system that when a force is very weak (with respect to another one), less attention can be paid to facts about the much weaker force. This is what understanding "weak" really means; it involves an interconvertibility between the *declarative* forms of information stored in the system's concept network and *procedural* forms of information.

Further, the lack of a Slipnet means that SME has no notion of conceptual distance and thus no counterpart to conceptual slippage. Relations that map to one another do so either because the structures have been so tailored that an *identity* mapping will be produced or because, like pieces in a jigsaw puzzle, they fit into a larger scheme defined by *higher-level* identity mappings. Ultimately, therefore, identity mappings (rather than conceptual closeness) determine everything in SME's analogies.

Consider, for example, the predicate "revolve" chosen by Falkenhainer, Forbus, and Gentner for both the solar system and the Rutherford atom. In the classical Rutherford model of the atom, electrons move in circular paths around the nucleus, whereas in the solar system, planets move in elliptical orbits around the sun. If the predicate for the solar system had been "ellipse" (meaning, in this case, "moves in an ellipse around") instead of the more general "revolve," and if for the Rutherford atom it had been "circle" (meaning "moves in a circle around"), the two predicates would not have matched exactly. As a result, there would have been no more reason a priori for SME to map CIRCLE (electron, nucleus) to ELLIPSE (planet, sun) than to any other relation between a planet and the sun—for example, HEATED-BY (planet, sun). This unfortunate situation is created by the fact that SME has no idea that "circle" and "ellipse" are conceptually closer than "circle" and "heated."

On the other hand, one might claim that "ellipse" and "circle" are not the correct predicates to use—that Gentner and her colleagues were right, and we *should* have REVOLVE (planet, sun, ellipse) and REVOLVE (electron, atom, circle), because, in some sense, "revolve" is a more natural concept than "circle" or "ellipse." But ever since antiquity, circles have been considered the perfect form. That circles and ellipses are today considered similar is, historically speaking, a rather recent development; it is not an a priori obvious fact. The fact that the two notions were far apart in the minds of sixteenth-century European astronomers was why it took Kepler so long to realize that the planets actually moved in elliptical rather than circular orbits about the sun. It was also why his conclusion was considered so radical.

But assume the representations chosen are REVOLVE (planet, sun, ellipse) and RE-VOLVE (electron, atom, circle), where the shape of the orbit is now just one more argument to the predicate "revolve." In this case, it is true that the predicates now match, but it looks like this particular representation was chosen precisely so that the predicates *would* match. If not, one should at least be able to provide a clear reason why this representation would be better than one that used "ellipse" and "circle" as predicates. But if one were asked to construct one of these representations in one circumstance and the other in a completely different, unrelated circumstance (as would presumably happen in real life), it would be a remarkable coincidence if both of them chanced to use the orbit shape as a parameter—in fact, the *third* parameter in a list of precisely three parameters.

This problem has been recognized and addressed in Falkenhainer's work (Falkenhainer 1990). Even though the original problem of a priori representations remains in Falkenhainer's work, his program PHINEAS has a scheme of re-representation of nonidentical predicates based on context information that then allows SME's identicality matching to be used as before.

To summarize, the philosophies of Tabletop and SME share certain points of agreement but also differ on a number of scores. Both approaches share a concern for cognitive plausibility and recognize the importance of the four criteria outlined by Gentner in her structure-mapping theory—namely, clarity, richness, abstractness, and systematicity—even though the realization of these criteria is implicit in Tabletop. On the other hand, there are a number of major differences between the two approaches:

- SME essentially ignores the problem of how to get a machine to represent the base and target situations and concentrates on the mapping problem, whereas Tabletop perceives the situation it is faced with and builds up all of its representations dynamically. The belief underlying Tabletop is that the representation and mapping phases are completely intertwined and cannot be separated. Although extensions of the basic SME architecture, such as MAC/FAC do address the representation issue, it is still done in a serial, "represent first, then find correspondences" manner.
- SME relies on predicate logic for its representations; Tabletop does not.
- SME's lack of a Slipnet means that it cannot appreciate the conceptual proximity of concepts.
- Predicate matching alone is not sufficient to evaluate the quality of candidate inferences. In the "gravity is far weaker than the electromagnetic force" example above, it is impossible for SME to understand—that is, make use of—the (crucially important) fact about the weakness of gravity with respect to electromagnetic force. Adding a predicate that said: IGNORABLE-BECAUSE-WEAK (gravity) would be of no use to the program either, since the predicate IGNO-RABLE-BECAUSE-WEAK would not map onto anything. There must be the possibility of converting this type of declarative knowledge into procedural knowledge usable in the program's processing.

• SME critically relies on the existence of a distinction, especially when it is run in literal-similarity mode, between objects, attributes, and relations. Although that distinction exists de facto in Tabletop, it is in no way a necessary or critical feature of the Tabletop architecture.

• According to Gentner, good analogies ignore attributes and map only objects and relations. Although there is certainly a significant bias in Tabletop to favor the mapping of more abstract structures over less abstract ones, no mapping is absolutely decided in advance. In particular, there is no hard-and-fast rule that dictates that "more abstract is always better."

• An exact map of relations is required by SME. SME's mappings are therefore scored in a much more black-and-white way than Tabletop's. This problem has been recognized and addressed by a successor of SME, Falkenhainer's PHINEAS (1990).

• There is no way to focus computational resources in SME. For this reason, it would seem that SME would have a hard time scaling up to very large domains. In Tabletop, on the other hand, the ability to focus resources is a central design concern.

• SME is deterministic; Tabletop is stochastic.

Gentner's structure-mapping theory, SME, MAC/FAC, and PHINEAS have certainly contributed a number of significant insights to the modeling of analogy-making. But this body of work makes a number of assumptions:

1. A quasi-exclusive reliance on relational structure
2. That there could be a separate "representation module" (even along the MAC/FAC lines) that would be capable of supplying an a priori representation of the base and target domains independent of the mapping process
3. The appropriateness of a "brute-force" strategy of examining possible mappings, which, at least in its present form, would seem to lead to significant problems of scaling up

In my opinion, these assumptions cause these programs to miss some of the important aspects of analogy-making.

6.5 Burstein's CARL

Mark Burstein's work is an extension of Gentner's theory. The vehicle of his ideas is a program called CARL (Causal Analogical Reasoning and Learning). CARL learns about basic programming-language constructs "by reasoning from *several* analogies presented by a teacher" (Burstein 1986b). Burstein refers to six different "stages" in analogy-making:

1. A *memory-retrieval stage* leading to the identification of relevant situations
2. A *comparison stage* identifying connected sets of relations and objects in the base domain, as well as correspondences between the objects of the base and target domains
3. A *mapping stage*, in which, in the target domain, a partial model or relational structure is constructed, which represents a particular hypothesis about some behavior in the target domain
4. A *justification stage* for the above hypothesis

5. A *debugging stage*, in which the hypothesis is corrected

6. A *generalization stage*, in which "structures shared by analogically related domain models may be—abstracted to a more general structural principle

I do not believe that there are strict sequential phases to analogy-making. Rather, I
would argue that although there may be a *statistical* tendency to do certain things
before others, there is no sharp-edged distinction between stages. Of course, one can,
a posteriori, impose sequentiality on the process of making any specific analogy.
However, the Tabletop philosophy is that this kind of temporal breakdown must
emerge as a consequence of a deeper set of mechanisms, and for this reason, in
Tabletop there are no clear boundaries separating various stages in the overall task of
discovering an analogy. One stage does not cleanly terminate to make way for the
next one, as happens in Burstein's model. In Tabletop, there is a great deal of overlap
among the various "phases." The criticism raised earlier of Evans and of Falkenhainer,
Forbus, and Gentner for separating representation from mapping applies equally to
Burstein.

The one aspect of Burstein's work that relates to Tabletop is his incipient notion
of conceptual slippage. He clearly recognizes the need, in mapping one situation
onto another, to replace certain concepts by semantically close ones. This is unlike
Gentner's work in which, as I have pointed out, there is no model of conceptual
closeness. In describing CARL's operation, Burstein writes, "the action PTRANS ...
was replaced with the more general predicate representing an abstract TRANSfer action." Or again, "Only by *relaxing the match process* [my emphasis] so that the second-
order relation CAUSES could be placed in correspondence with links like IMPLIES,
could CARL ..." These are certainly examples of slippage (export slippage in the first
case, conceptual slippage in the second; see chapter 1 for details). Unfortunately,
however, readers are not told how, or under what circumstances, CARL perfoms
these slippages, nor is there any hint of a specific structure designed to mediate such
slippages with different and dynamically varying degrees of ease or likelihood, as
there is, of course, in Tabletop.

The main reason Burstein's work is an extension of Gentner's has to do with an issue that is central to the research reported in this book—namely, the importance of
context. In all of Gentner's examples, the relevant network of relations (i.e., set of
representations of a situation) is provided ahead of time by an unspecified representation module (i.e., a human). But, as I have pointed out many times, different
contexts should induce different representation networks. Assume that this were not
the case. Then the representation for "sun" in the wonderful Shakespearean metaphor
"Juliet is the sun" would presumably be the same as that used in making the insight-
lending scientific analogy between the solar system and the hydrogen atom. This
would presumably imply that "Juliet is a proton" would also be an excellent analogy
fusing literature with science! (See also [Kedar-Cabelli 1985].)

Burstein's model includes a set of "relevant actions" that allow it to select the appropriate sets of mappings from among the available candidates. Burstein thus recognizes that context affects the choice of the appropriate mappings, but his solution is
to *explicitly* supply the "relevant actions" that allow his program to pick the correct
mappings.

To my mind, Burstein's contribution has been to point out a major shortcoming of
Gentner's model. However, the fact that Burstein must supply his program with
"relevant actions" that allow CARL to select the correct set of mappings is not unlike

Gentner's simply handing SME the correct network of relations to begin with. Burstein's approach seems, therefore, to beg the question. What is the basis of the "relevant actions"?

In section 6.6, I discuss how Smadar Kedar-Cabelli attempts to solve this problem by introducing the notion of "purpose-directedness" into analogy making. Although I agree that this approach is valid in many cases, many analogies (like the reminding incidents described in chapter 1 involving a new lug bolt's being reminiscent of a gold tooth, or dogs' barking calling forth imagery of Hebbian cell assemblies, to say nothing of IQ-test-like or Copycat analogies) are simply purpose-free.

The Tabletop program relies on the interaction of perceptual tasks and a context-modifiable Slipnet, and this, I believe, goes a long way toward solving the problem that Burstein raises. Activation levels of nodes and dynamic conceptual distances in the Slipnet, determined by spreading activation and by activation received from codelets, reflect the prevailing context and guide the system to the discovery and construction of the relevant set of relations.

6.6 Purpose-Directed Analogies: Kedar-Cabelli

Smadar Kedar-Cabelli Considers her work to be an extension of Burstein's. She proposes a means of *automatically* deriving the relevant structural and functional features of the base and target situations needed to make an analogy between the two situations. The input that Kedar-Cabelli proposes giving to the system is the *explicit purpose* of the analogy.

Purpose-directed analogy is related to Kedar-Cabelli's work on explanation-based generalization (also called "purpose-directed generalization" in some of her earlier publications). "In adapting these techniques to analogy, the distinction between analogy and generalization has been somewhat blurred" (Kedar-Cabelli 1985).

The input to Kedar-Cabelli's program consists of a goal concept, its purpose, a target example, and a theory about the domain.

Kedar-Cabelli (1985), analyzes in detail an analogy between a styrofoam cup and a ceramic mug. In this example,

- The *goal concept* is HOT-CUP (a cup for holding hot liquids), a prototypical example of which is assumed to be known—in this case, a ceramic mug.
- The *purpose* of the analogy is to enable an agent to drink hot liquids.
- The *target example* is a Styrofoam cup.
- The *domain theory* consists of typical actions an agent could perform, along with a structural and functional model of the artifacts in the domain.

The program then determines, on the basis of an explanation of why the ceramic mug is a member of the category HOT-CUP, the reason that the Styrofoam cup is also a member of HOT-CUP. This explanation allows the base example (the ceramic cup) to be mapped onto the target example. Once this mapping has been established, the program then attempts to justify it. It is here, as in Burstein, that an incipient notion of conceptual slippage can be seen. Kedar-Cabelli writes, "[I]f it cannot justify (the mapping) using the explanation as it stands, it modifies the explanation to show that the target example is a member of the goal concept *in a slightly different way*" (my emphasis) (Kedar-Cabelli 1985). How Kedar-Cabelli proposes to carry out this modification is unfortunately anything but clear. In Tabletop, thanks to the Slipnet, this type of modification would be the result of a slippage between two active concepts that were close in the Slipnet.

A further disagreement between the present work and that of Kedar-Cabelli is that I do not share her view that all, or even most, analogy-making is a goal-directed process. Certainly, goal-directedness cannot be a *necessary* requirement of all analogy-making. Hofstadter, Mitchell, and French (1987) agree that knowledge of purpose sometimes helps to select a mapping from many possible mappings. But it is clear from examples drawn from microdomains like those of Evans's ANALOGY, Mitchell and Hofstadter's Copycat, and Tabletop that many analogy problems have compelling answers, despite the absence of any explicit purpose that they might serve.

A typical real-life example of an analogy that is strictly without explicit purpose was recounted to me by a friend. His girlfriend, who had never before swum a full mile without stopping, one day did the whole thing and then, without stopping, did one more lap. He met her at the edge of the pool as she quit after seventeen laps and said to her, "Congratulations—you just swam a guinea!" (Recall that a guinea in the old English monetary system was one pound—i.e., twenty shillings plus one shilling.) There was no joke or purpose here. Like being reminded of a gold tooth upon seeing a shiny new lug nut on the wheel of an old car, these perfectly good analogies—like most reminding incidents—just spontaneously came to mind.

6.7 A Connectionist Approach: Thagard and Holyoak's ACME

There have been very few attempts to date to apply connectionist techniques to computer modeling of analogy-making. The best-known case of this approach that I want to consider is ACME (Analogical Constraint Mapping Engine), the computer model created by Keith Holyoak and Paul Thagard (1989, 1995). This model combines first-order predicate-calculus representations with a Hopfield-net parallel-constraint-satisfaction algorithm. (Actually, Holyoak and Thagard claim to have been inspired by a network built by Marr and Poggio.)

Holyoak and Thagard compare their work to that of Winston (1980), which relied heavily on first-order predicate-logic representations of the base and target situations. Winston used a serial algorithm to carry out an exhaustive evaluation of all possible mappings between the base and target situations. Each mapping was ranked, and then the best one was picked. Obviously, if there are more than a few elements involved, this method becomes computationally intractable.

Since constraint satisfaction has proven to be a powerful weapon in the ongoing fight against combinatorial explosion, it would seem reasonable to suppose that parallel constraint satisfaction would be even better. The heart of ACME is thus a type of parallel-constraint-satisfaction algorithm, originally referred to by Marr and Poggio as a "cooperative algorithm."

ACME works as follows: Both the base and target domains are hand-coded as expressions of first-order predicate logic. (Of course, it is not true that the *full domains* are encoded; rather, tiny fragments of them have been preselected and encoded. This unconscious and fallacious conflation of a full domain with a tiny part of that domain pervades all research in which representations have to be hand-coded in advance.) The entities comprising both representations therefore consist exclusively of constants and predicates. A collection of nodes is created, such that each node represents a pairing of one entity in the base domain with a "logically compatible" entity in the target domain. ("Logically compatible" means simply that constants must be mapped to constants and n-place predicates to n-place predicates.) Each node has a real-valued activation level between -1 and 1, depending on the plausibility of the mapping hypothesis represented by the pairing of the two entities comprising the node. Links between the nodes in this network reflect four constraints:

> *Uniqueness* Each source element is mapped onto at most one target element. This is reminiscent of Gentner's criterion of clarity and Tabletop's disallowing of one-to-many or many-to-one mappings.
>
> *Relational consistency* The various pairings making up a mapping between base and target must tend to support each other. This means that if there is relation $P(a, b)$ in the base domain and a relation $Q(c, d)$ in the target domain and P is mapped to Q, then a must be mapped to c, and b to d, since these variables play corresponding roles in the two relations.
>
> *Semantic similarity* The greater the similarity of meaning of the mapped predicates, the greater the support for the mapping hypothesis. ACME incorporates a semantic network, called the "semantic unit," that encodes (fixed) conceptual distances, allowing these similarity ratings to be determined. This semantic unit (a network called WordNet (Beckwith et al. 1990)) "represents the system's prior assessment of the degree of semantic similarity between each pair of meaningful concepts in the source and target" (Holyoak and Thagard 1989).
>
> *Role identity* This restricts mapping hypotheses to those involving elements that play identical roles in the two analogous situations. (Role identity requires initial states to be mapped to initial states, goal states to goal states, and so on.) This constraint applies to problem-solving situations in which the problems are divided into initial states, goal states, sets of solution constraints, and operators.

Recall that a node is made for *every possible* pairing of entities in the base and target situations that satisfies the above constraints. Links are then drawn between all pairs of nodes. These links are weighted as follows: If the pairing in one node is supported (in the purely syntactic sense of relational consistency defined above) by a pairing defining another node, then the link between those two nodes is given a positive weight. Otherwise, the link is weighted negatively. In the above example, since the mappings $a \Rightarrow c$ and $P \Rightarrow Q$ are mutually supportive, the link between the corresponding nodes would be given a positive weight. On the other hand, if the mapping $P \Rightarrow Q$ does not support some other mapping, say, $s \Rightarrow t$, the link between these nodes would be negative. Once the network of nodes and links has been created and its links have been weighted, the system is initialized (the activation of the semantic unit is clamped at 1 and that of all other units set to 0), and activation is allowed to spread through the net. The system then settles to the activation pattern that presumably represents the best mapping between the source and target domains.

To ACME's credit, it attempts to make analogies in a bottom-up way, with a mapping emerging as the result of competition among conflicting pressures. (There are five simultaneous pressures, defined by the four constraints and the criterion of logical compatibility.) However, there are at least four major problems with the architecture of ACME, at least one of which blatantly belies the model's claim to cognitive validity.

First, symbols in ACME, like those in SME, are not grounded. This is exactly the same problem as the one that affected SME—namely, there is no procedural-declarative knowledge interconvertibility.

Second, WordNet allows conceptual halos, but its lack of modifiable link lengths does not allow *context-dependent* conceptual halos. This insensitivity to context means that the concepts represented by various predicates will *always* remain a fixed distance apart. This is a psychologically untenable assumption. The long-term memory richness is nice, but, aside from the problem of insensitivity to context, WordNet *still* suffers from the problem of empty symbols—ACME knows no more about what planets really *are*, or what "much weaker than" means than SME does. The problem, as I said above, is the impossibility of converting the declarative knowledge in the network to procedural knowledge about how it is to be used, and the total lack of connection between *concepts* and *instances* of those concepts.

Third, ACME's network consists of all logically compatible pairings between entities from the source domain and the target domain. Aside from the obvious problems of computational intractability, there is the question of cognitive plausibility. In the real world, what would it mean to consider *every logically compatible pairing* of entities in two situations? Consider, for example, an attempt to map Kennedy's assassination onto the attempted assassination of Ronald Reagan. Do we humans ever consider, even for the briefest of instants, mapping Kennedy onto Hinkley? Or Oswald onto Reagan's bodyguard who was shot? Or Jacqueline Kennedy onto Hinkley's gun? Of course not, but in the Holyoak and Thagard model, these nodes are every bit as "logically compatible" as the "Kennedy $\Rightarrow$ Reagan," "Oswald $\Rightarrow$ Hinkley," "Oswald's rifle $\Rightarrow$ Hinkley's handgun" nodes.

These nodes would all have to be created and processed by ACME if the situations were represented extensively and fully—that is, given the richness that people have when they think about those situations. Thus the nonsensical explosion of nodes is *absolutely unavoidable* if the situations are not boiled down a priori to tiny caricatures of themselves. Thagard and Holyoak therefore made the expedient choice—namely, they *do* reduce all situations to tiny caricatures of themselves beforehand. This effectively circumvents the problem of combinatorial explosion but leaves completely unanswered the vastly more complex question of how it would be possible for a computer to ever come up with these (apparently context-independent) caricatures. Considering all possible mappings is both computationally unfeasible (curiously enough, Holyoak and Thagard specifically criticize this aspect of an analogy-making program written by Patrick Winston in 1980 [Winston 1980]) and psychologically absurd.

In Tabletop, although such improbable mappings are, of course, theoretically possible, there is nothing resembling an exhaustive construction of all possible pairings followed by selection of the best set. In addition, the fact that Tabletop makes groups of objects and maps these groups to other groups (or sometimes to individual objects) means that, even for a tiny situation like a Tabletop configuration, there could be an enormous combinatorial explosion of mappings. Unlike ACME, which would consider all mappings from all possible objects and groups to all other possible objects and groups, Tabletop searches for good mappings probabilistically based on the salience of the objects or groups and the activation of nodes in the Slipnet.

The second criticism is not specific to ACME: the representation problem once again rears its head. The descriptions of both the source and the target situation are *fixed ahead of time*. There is no need to repeat once again the arguments concerning this problem.

6.8 Other Approaches to Analogy-Making

In any overview of related work, choices have to made about what research to cover. I have attempted to compare Tabletop only to research that shares some of the major concerns of Tabletop. For this reason, I have not considered programs that are concerned mainly with learning or with analogical retrieval. Nor have I considered programs whose approach is rooted in formal logic and for which cognitive plausibility is not an issue.

The first body of work, primarily concerned with learning and analogical retrieval, includes the research of Jaime Carbonell on derivational analogies (Carbonell 1990) and Roger Schank's research on retrieval of analogies from memory (Schank 1983). Research on case-based learning and explanation-based learning is not considered either, and for similar reasons: both areas are concerned mainly with the use of previously learned experiences rather than the building of representations of, and mappings between, two situations given in advance.

The second body of work excluded from these comparisons is work—essentially that of Winston (1980) and Greiner (1985)—based purely on formal logic. Neither Winston nor Greiner is concerned with the cognitive plausibility of their models. And, in the case of Winston's model, there is no concern for computational plausibility either.

Finally, a certain number of programs, even though they were not designed to do analogy-making per se, have much in common with the ideas underlying the architecture of Tabletop. One program, in particular, contributed significantly to the underlying philosophy of Tabletop: Hearsay II (Erman *et al.* 1980). In addition, Tabletop's Slipnet bears certain resemblances to Quillian's semantic network (Quillian 1968) and even more to the extensions of this original network made by Collins and Loftus (1975). Finally, ACT* (Anderson 1983) will be discussed. Although ACT* differs in many respects from Tabletop, the two programs do share certain significant features, among them a semantic network, spreading activation, decaying activation, and processes carried out by many smaller agents.

6.9 Quillian's Semantic Network

The implementation of a network whose nodes correspond to categories is due to Ross Quillian (Quillian 1968). In his network, each node corresponds to an English word. Quillian developed his semantic-network representation to aid in the modeling of natural-language understanding. In his system, there were five different types of links connecting the word nodes:

1. Superordinate links ("elephant ISA mammal") and subordinate links ("elephant HAS-INSTANCE Clyde")
2. Modifying links ("Clyde IS heavy")
3. OR links (linking disjunctive sets of meanings of a particular word)
4. AND links (linking multiple necessary attributes of an object)
5. Subject-object links ("elephant(s) LIKE oats")

In Quillian's network, there was a type of spreading activation, although today the term "spreading activation" has taken on a different meaning. What occurred in Quillian's network is now called "marker passing." Thus, as "activation markers" spread along legal paths through his network, they would "mark" each of the nodes encountered. In this way, Quillian's network was able to compare the meanings of different words. This was achieved by taking two distinct words and associating with each word a different marker (say, a blue marker for one word and a red marker for the other). The two words would then serve as starting points for marker spreading. Each node that was one link away from any blue marker was also marked blue; similarly, each node that was one node away from any red marker was also marked red; and so on, recursively. Marker passing stopped as soon as some node in the network was marked by *both* colors. The program then knew that the two words had the doubly marked category in common. On the basis of the red and blue marker pathways (which were always kept), the program could then say something about the relation between the two original words. A simple example might be a network that included the following branches: "Clyde ISA elephant ISA mammal ISA animal ISA living thing" and "Tweety ISA canary ISA bird ISA animal ISA living thing." If red-marker spreading were started from "Clyde" and blue-marker spreading from "Tweety," the two colors would first meet at "animal," and the program would thereby conclude that Clyde and Tweety were both animals.

There are major differences between Quillian's semantic network and Tabletop's Slipnet. Quillian's network, for example, does not guide or control active processing of the type carried out in Tabletop's Workspace. For one thing, there is no equivalent of working memory. The only processing that Quillian's network was concerned with was marker passing, whereas Tabletop's Slipnet actively drives a host of processes, such as releasing codelets to examine or build structures in short-term memory on the basis of concept-node activation levels. In Tabletop, the Slipnet was designed to guide processing, and this involves the state of the Slipnet as a *whole*, whereas Quillian was concerned only with finding where two marker traces intersected.

Another difference is the absence in Quillian's network of the notion of distance between nodes. It should be noted, though, that a distance measure corresponding to how strongly one concept is associated with others was not necessary for the purposes Quillian was pursuing.

Additionally, distances between concepts in the tabletop Slipnet vary according to features perceived in the context. Quillian's network had no such variability. Finally, there is a difference between spreading activation à la Tabletop and marker passing. Spreading activation is like heat spreading outward from a source: it is continuous, decays with time, and decreases in strength according to the distance from its source, whereas marker passing is discrete, does not decay over time, and is unaffected by distance.

6.10 Collins and Loftus

Since Quillian first implemented his semantic network, there have been numerous extensions and modifications of his work—so numerous in fact that it is sometimes hard to know exactly what *is* meant by "semantic network" these days. From the point of view of Tabletop, the most interesting extensions were provided by Collins and Loftus (1975). Their modifications include the following:

• An activation signal that attenuates according to the strength of the links as it travels outward from the source node. This is much like the notion in Tabletop of decreasing the amount of spreading activation as a function of the conceptual distance from the source node.

• Activation that decays with time. This is also a feature of the Tabletop Slipnet. However, in the Slipnet, the greater the conceptual depth (abstractness) of a node, the more slowly it loses its activation. There is no counterpart to this feature in Collins and Loftus's net.

• Organization of the network on the basis of semantic similarity. This is similar to the organization of the Slipnet.

The Collins and Loftus net could not be modified according to perceived context. This meant, for example, that, regardless of the situation activating the net, the conceptual distances would always remain the same. For this network, an orange crate, even when covered with a tablecloth, silverware, wine glasses, and roast turkey, would always be an orange crate and never a table—the distance between "orange crate" and "table" would always be too great.

6.11 Hearsay II

The Hearsay II speech-understanding program (Erman et al. 1980) was an inspiration for some central elements of the Tabletop architecture, probably the most important of which was the notion of continual interaction between top-down and bottom-up pressures.

Hearsay II receives as input a raw waveform produced by a human utterance. There are a number of "knowledge sources," each of which performs a certain task related to the perception of the raw waveform. One knowledge source is reponsible for segmenting the raw waveform into plausible time slices, another assigns phonetic labels to the given segments, another uses the phonetic labels to tentatively assign phonemes to labeled segments, another combines phonemes into hypotheses about syllables, another combines syllables into hypotheses about words, and so on. Each time a knowledge source performs some action, it posts the results of its action to a global "blackboard." The Hearsay II blackboard is much like Tabletop's Workspace. All of the knowledge sources are free to read the blackboard and to use the structures found on it. In this way, as increasingly higher-level structures evolve (e.g., phonemes, syllables, and, ultimately, words), higher-level knowledge sources can take advantage of the new information and perform their tasks.

This type of "cooperative" parallel processing is one of the most fundamental aspects of the Tabletop architecture. The knowledge sources in Hearsay II are akin to Tabletop's codelets, and the Hearsay II blackboard is similar to Tabletop's Workspace.

In some ways, Hearsay II resembles Tabletop more than Copycat does. In Hearsay II, several rival hypotheses about the data can exist at the same level, and an analogous fact holds for Tabletop, though not for Copycat. These differences between Copycat and Hearsay II are described by Mitchell (1990):

> In Hearsay-II, several rival hypotheses may coexist at each level—and the program evaluates all of them. Copycat constructs only one view at a time—but that view is malleable, and can be easily reshaped, given the right kinds of pressure. Humans cannot see the same high-level thing in two ways at once,

but, as with the famous Necker cube, they can switch back and forth between coherent perceptions with varying degrees of ease. Thus Copycat's method is more psychologically realistic than that of Hearsay-II. The latter method suffers from a potential combinatorial problem: competing hypotheses can exist for different pieces of a whole, so the number of compound hypotheses at higher levels can become very large.

Earlier, I described one of the basic differences between Copycat and Tabletop—namely, that Tabletop maintains a Worldview within its Workspace. Only structures in the Worldview are *perceived*, but there can be many other structures still *present* in the Workspace. In Copycat, once a structure loses a competition, it is removed from the Workspace. In Tabletop, by contrast, structures that compete for a place in the Worldview and lose are "demoted" (i.e., their evaluations are decreased), but they remain in the Workspace for a while, potentially able to compete again. Thus Tabletop's solution is something like a compromise between what happens in Copycat and what happens in Hearsay II.

Another difference between Hearsay II and Tabletop is how the program builds its structures: Hearsay II uses global information; Tabletop uses local information. Hearsay II's knowledge sources can "see" all of the information at a particular level of abstraction on the blackboard; Tabletop's codelets see only a small part of the Workspace.

Finally, Hearsay II had a type of parallel terraced scan implicitly incorporated into its architecture. Before a particular knowledge source could be invoked, pre-preconditions, preconditions, and conditions—each successively more complex and thus computationally more costly—had to be satisfied. All the conditions for all of the knowledge sources ran in parallel. This design served as the inspiration for parallel-terraced scans used in both Copycat and Tabletop.

6.12 Anderson's ACT*

Certainly one of the most ambitious cognitive-modeling efforts to date using semantic networks and spreading activation has been carried out by John Anderson. His program, ACT*, is touted as a full-blown theory of cognition (Anderson 1983). Since cognitive systems are themselves extremely complex, there is no reason to expect that a model of such systems would be less simple. Anderson's system, though, sometimes seems to be complex to the point of being ad hoc. However, ACT* has a set of underlying mechanisms that merit close examination, especially insofar as they resemble, at least to a certain degree, many of the mechanisms of Tabletop.

ACT* has a semantic network in which declarative knowledge is stored, a working memory in which active parts of the declarative store are processed, and a production memory in which the procedural knowledge of the system is stored and which interacts, via the working memory, with the semantic network.

The nodes in the semantic network represent what Anderson calls "cognitive units," which are essentially irreducible units of knowledge. These can be propositions, ordered strings, or spatial images. Specific situations are represented in this memory by linking together combinations of these cognitive units in short-term memory. Herein lies one of the major differences between ACT*'s semantic network and Tabletop's Slipnet. The nodes in Tabletop correspond, roughly, to *concepts*, whereas for

Anderson they are the small—and, he believes, basic—*pieces of knowledge* required to describe the world.

Furthermore, ACT*'s network, like all other semantic networks modeling long-term memory (with the exception of the Copycat and Tabletop Slipnets), has a static configuration. It is not subject to distortion based on what has been perceived in the environment. In addition, there is nothing in the ACT* semantic network that resembles the distribution of a concept over a *region*, with one node at its core. In other words, in ACT* there is no notion of conceptual halos around concepts, so there is no notion of conceptual slippage. Tabletop's Slipnet and ACT*'s semantic network are, nonetheless, similar in certain important respects:

- In both networks, nodes are activated by input from the environment.
- Activation spreads between nodes.
- Spreading activation is carried out in parallel throughout both networks.
- Activation of a node decays with time.

In addition to having a semantic network that corresponds to a certain degree to Tabletop's Slipnet, ACT* has productions in its production memory that correspond, roughly, to Tabletop's codelets. The major difference is that in all the examples given by Anderson (1983), the productions are very specific and domain-dependent. ACT*'s tasks perform at a high cognitive level, as opposed to Tabletop's codelets, whose actions are intended to be at a lower level.

6.13 Connectionism and Tabletop

In a sense, the recently developed connectionist models bear very little resemblance to the Tabletop architecture. The differences, in fact, are so great that one is justified in asking why these models should be considered "related work," while others, such as those by Winston, Carbonell, and Greiner, which deal specifically with analogy-making, are ignored.

The answer, in a word, is *emergence*. A bedrock assumption underlying the entire Tabletop project is that answers to analogy problems emerge from many small "subcognitive" activities. The work of the connectionists is similar in this crucial respect. They, too, believe that higher-level cognitive processes with semantic content, such as pattern recognition, must emerge from a multitude of low-level processes devoid of semantic content.

In an attempt to situate Tabletop along the spectrum running from traditional symbolic AI to connectionism, I will use the expression "semantic transparency" (Clark 1989) to designate systems in which the computational tokens explicitly manipulated by the program coincide with the cognitive-level representations. In short, the tokens of the system and the representations formed by the tokens have the same degree of semantic content. It is the degree to which systems are semantically transparent that will determine where on the symbolic/subsymbolic continuum they fall.

Physical symbol systems (Newell 1990) are, of course, the most semantically transparent systems, distributed connectionist systems the least. There are many varieties of connectionist systems, some of which—notably, the localist connectionist systems (Feldman and Ballard 1982)—are arguably as semantically transparent as traditional symbol systems, because the nodes in these systems represent concepts. The most widely used connectionist systems (e.g., feedforward backpropagation models and many recurrent networks), however, cannot be considered to be semantically transparent, because they are composed of meaningless elements.

Tabletop lies between these two extremes. The concepts in Tabletop can be thought of as semidistributed, because each of them, despite being centered on (and usually identified with) just one Slipnet node, is actually probabilistically distributed over a number of nodes. Slipping from one concept to another is equivalent to saying that the two concepts are "the same" in their respective situations. Thus if "fork" slips to "knife" or "left" slips to "right" in a particular analogy, they are perceived in that context as being "the same" in the sense that Eliza is doing "the same thing" Henry is doing, despite its not being *literally* the same (see chapter 1). It is this probabilistic "halo" of concepts surrounding each concept and to which each can slip that imbues concepts in Tabletop's Slipnet with a fluid, semidistributed nature. (For a more thorough discussion of this topic, see Chalmers [1991]; Hofstadfer 1995, ch. 5).

The differences between connectionist models and Tabletop are certainly far more significant than the resemblances. However, the connectionist research paradigm has had such a major influence in the last several years that when people hear the terms "net" (as in "Slipnet"), "emergence," and "spreading activation," they tend to assign to them their meanings in a connectionist framework.

Some of the major differences between Tabletop and the most popular type of connectionist net—the feedforward backpropagation network—are as follows:

- Slipnet nodes are not completely devoid of semantic content, whereas distributed-connectionist nodes are, or come close to that status.
- In Tabletop there is a clear distinction between types and tokens. There is a Slipnet in which concept types exist and a Workspace in which tokens—that is, instances of these types—are dynamically created, manipulated, and removed. In connectionist networks, there is no such type/token distinction, nor is there any analogue to a Workspace.
- In Tabletop there is a constant interaction between top-down pressures (from the Slipnet) and bottom-up pressures (from the Workspace); in connectionist nets everything is purely bottom-up.
- Tabletop's architecture is fundamentally stochastic at all levels of its operation. Except for the initial settings of the connection weights, most connectionist networks operate in a completely deterministic way. In other words, stochastic mechanisms play no active role in processing, whereas in Tabletop they play an essential and ongoing role in all processing. (Note that this is not true of all connectionist models. Boltzmann machines (Ackley, Hinton, and Sejnowski 1985), for example, do use ongoing stochastic decision making and have a notion of temperature that serves to guide this processing.)

In short, although I am in broad sympathy with the ideas of connectionism, I think there is a need for models that bridge the gap between purely bottom-up, fully distributed connectionist models and the purely top-down symbolic models of traditional artificial intelligence. Each paradigm has something to offer, and yet one sometimes has the impression that neither side is listening to the other. Tabletop and Copycat, lying squarely between both paradigms, may provide a meeting ground for people from both camps.

Chapter 7
Summary and Conclusions

In this book I have presented a general theory of analogy-making along with a computer model that attempts to implement the main ideas of that theory. Essentially, the theory derives from the key notion of *slippage*. In chapter 1, we see how slippage, in its various forms and in differing degrees, underlies a wide range of high-level perceptual capacities, ranging from simple object recognition to full-blown analogy-making. There is also a brief taxonomy, illustrated with a number of examples, of the various kinds of slippage and analogy-making. The remainder of the book is devoted to explaining Tabletop, the model that embodies many of the main ideas of this theory.

The second chapter begins by presenting a defense of microdomains in general and explains why they are a valuable—but largely ignored—tool for cognitive modelers. It goes on to explain and defend the Tabletop microdomain in some detail, and concludes with an overview of the differences between Tabletop and Copycat.

In chapter 3, the key features of the Tabletop architecture are discussed:

1. A concept network, called the Slipnet, that models long-term memory and a Workspace that models short-term memory
2. Processing that is carried out entirely by many small agents, called codelets
3. The absence of a global executive
4. Biased probabilistic mechanisms at all levels of processing
5. Gradual building up of perceptual "structures" in the Workspace (i.e., groups of objects and correspondence between groups and/or objects)
6. A context-dependent conceptual similarity metric, embodied by the link lengths in the Slipnet
7. A set of context-dependent, top-down search pressures, determined by the activations of nodes in the Slipnet and the salience of objects in the Workspace
8. Continual interaction between the Slipnet and the Workspace featuring
   - Bottom-up influences: the Workspace influences the Slipnet by selectively adding activation to nodes in the Slipnet, thus indirectly causing certain Slipnet links to shrink and others to grow
   - Top-down influences: high activation levels of nodes in the Slipnet, which cause certain types of relationships and structures to be preferentially sought and built
9. A notion of temperature, reflecting the amount and the quality of overall structure that the system has built, which in turn reflects how the system feels it has represented the table situation it is confronted with
10. The use of temperature to control the amount of randomness in decision making: the higher the temperature, the more random the decisions, the lower the temperature, the more deterministic

11. A "parallel terraced scan" that allows potentially more promising routes to be explored before less promising ones, without, however, totally excluding the possibility of exploring seemingly unpromising routes

Chapter 4 shows a fairly typical run of Tabletop up close and points out that the program can and does arrive at the same answer in a variety of ways. This chapter concludes with a few examples of the program's unpredictable behavior when the temperature is high.

Chapter 5 is the linchpin of the book. It shows how Tabletop actually performs. This chapter includes statistics that summarize about two thousand runs of the program on four families of problems that together constitute some forty-five different problems. The idea was to *gradually* and *systematically* vary the configurations presented to the program, adjusting, in each new configuration, such aspects as the positions of objects, the groups they form, the mutual proximity of salient objects, the categories of objects, and so on. In addition to studying the range and the frequencies of answers given by the program over the course of many runs of a particular problem, I also examined the structures built by the program in the Workspace and the average length of time taken to build them. By systematically varying the pressures and studying how this affected the program's performance, I was able to probe the program's "personality" quite extensively. This allowed me to build up a "performance landscape" of Tabletop. By systematically varying the pressures in the input space, I was able to determine some of the "ridges" in this abstract space where the program would switch from one preference to another. I argue for the utility—possibility even the necessity—of this kind of Turing-test-like methodology for other cognitive models and point out that no other current models of analogy-making, with the exception of Copycat, have been subjected to these kinds of systematic tests.

Chapter 6 compares Tabletop with other models of analogy-making, both past and contemporary.

7.1 What Is Different about Tabletop?

Traditional analogy-making programs claim to be reproducing famous scientific, literary, or philosophical analogies. Tabletop, on the other hand, merely models a microworld consisting of ordinary objects on an ordinary table. The "analogizing" that is done—touching an object on the table in response to the "Do this!" challenge—is of the most prosaic sort. Nonetheless, I believe that the mechanisms that underlie this type of simple analogy-making are the same as those underlying the more "exalted" analogies that most people think of when they think of analogy-making.

Unlike almost all analogy-making programs since Thomas Evans's ANALOGY (Evans 1968)—with the exception of Mitchell and Hofstadter's Copycat—Tabletop builds its own representations. A fundamental tenet of this work is that representation-building and correspondence-making are inseparable, interwoven processes. But true representation-building in real-world domains is an extraordinarily difficult problem. This is part of the reason that traditional analogy-making programs essentially ignore the problem of representation, relying instead on hand-coded representations of the situations to be put into correspondence. These hand-coded representations are then typically fed to a "mapping module" that syntactically discovers correspondences. These programs have no knowledge of the content of the situations they are faced with. In contrast, Tabletop *does* know something about the objects it is perceiving, because the Tableworld is a manageable microdomain. Its concepts are neither too rich nor too numerous to allow the program to gradually build up its own representation of the situations with which it is confronted.

Tabletop is fundamentally stochastic; all other traditional analogy-making programs are deterministic. Chapter 3 argues for the necessity of incorporating stochastic mechanisms into cognitive models. The simulated parallelism and the biased-random selection processes that permeate all levels of the architecture allow the program to focus its resources and confer on it the ability to scale up. In fact, perhaps more influential than any other single consideration in the design of this architecture was that it should be able to scale up.

Finally, the program's overall behavior is an outcome of the actions of a large number of "perceptual agents"—called codelets—which are responsible for gradually building up the representational structures that allow it to give an answer to the "Do this!" challenge. This "fine-grained" low-level approach, in which individual codelets are responsible for only small amounts of work, as opposed to an approach based on powerful, problem-specific functions, gives the program the flexibility it needs not only to produce the most obvious, reasonable answers but also, on occasion, to come up with very good but very unlikely—in a word, *creative*—answers.

7.2 Concepts: The Germs of Cognition

Research in cognitive modeling has just begun to scratch the surface of anything approximating true understanding of human cognition. It is reasonable to ask at what level we should attempt to understand minds. There is, of course, the neural level. To understand human cognition solely by describing events at this level (or, worse, at the level of synapses, as some propose) is—and will remain for a very long time—the stuff of science fiction. Accounts of the effects of brain trauma—losing the ability to read but not to write, losing the capacity to speak one language but not another, losing the ability to recognize an object but not its individual components, losing the capacity to recognize one's hand as belonging to one's body, and so on—serve as sober reminders of just how little we really know about how minds and brains are related. Understanding these kinds of high-level cognitive phenomena solely by reference to neural events may well be centuries away.

Should we perhaps study minds by studying such high-level cognitive skills as understanding newspaper stories, developing scientific theories, doing mathematics, or understanding natural language, music, and humor? These are some of the traditional domains of research in artificial intelligence and cognitive modeling. Again, I feel that research into these areas, while it may provide certain insights, is not yet in a position to provide any *fundamental* insights. Although research into these areas is certainly interesting and not to be discouraged, it is, in my opinion, premature. Research into these very high-level areas is somewhat like studying infectious diseases before the vectors of such diseases were known. To be sure, occasional insights could be made—for example, Semmelweis's institution of hand washing before delivering babies vastly reduced death from childbed fever—but no truly fundamental progress was possible until a theory of germs as the vectors of infectious disease had been developed by Pasteur and others.

The germs of human cognition are concepts. I believe that before fundamental progress can be made in understanding human cognition, we must understand much more about *concepts*: how they develop, how they evolve, and how they affect other concepts. This book is part of the attempt to better understand concepts and the mechanisms underlying their manipulation by the mind. I can only hope that this research might provide certain insights into the complex processes that underlie cognition and, in so doing, bring us just a little closer to the far-off goal of building truly intelligent machines.

References

Ackley, D. H., G. E. Hinton, and T. J. Sejnowski. 1985. A learning algorithm for Boltzmann machines. *Cognitive Science* 9(1): 147–169.

Ajjanagadde, V., and L. Shastri. 1989. Efficient interference with multi-place predicates and variables in a connectionist system. In *Proceedings of the Eleventh Annual Conference of the Cognitive Science Society*, 396–403. Hillsdale, N.J.: Lawrence Erlbaum.

Anderson, J. R. 1983. *The architecture of cognition*. Cambridge, Mass.: Harvard University Press.

Barsalou, L. W. 1989. Intraconcept similarity and its implications for interconcept similarity. In *Similarity and analogical reasoning*, ed., S. Vosniadou and A. Ortony, 76–121. Cambridge, England: Cambridge University Press.

Beckwith, R., C. Fellbaum, D. Gross, and G. A. Miller. 1990. *WordNet: A lexical database organized on psycholinguistic principles*. Cognitive Science Laboratory Report 42. Princeton University. Princeton, N.J.

Bongard, M. 1970. *Pattern recognition*. Rochelle Park, N.J.: Hayden Book Co., Spartan Books.

Burstein, M. 1986a. Concept formation by incremental analogical reasoning and debugging. In *Machine Learning: An artificial intelligence approach*, ed. R. S. Michalski, J. G. Carbonell, and T. M. Mitchell. Vol. 2, chap. 13, 351–70. Los Altos, Calif.: Morgan Kaufman.

Burstein, M. 1986b. *Learning and Explanation by Analogy*. Technical report. BBN Laboratories. Cambridge, Mass.

Burstein, M., and B. Adelson. 1987. Mapping and integrating partial mental models. In *Proceedings of the Ninth Annual Conference of the Cognitive Science Society*. Hillsdale, N.J.: Lawrence Erlbaum.

Carbonell, J. G. 1983. Learning by analogy: Formulating and generalizing plans from past experience. In *Machine Learning: An artificial intelligence approach*, ed. R. S. Michalski, J. G. Carbonell, and T. M. Mitchell, chap. 5, 137–61. Los Altos, Calif.: Morgan Kaufman.

Carbonell, J., ed. 1990. *Machine Learning: Paradigms and methods*. Cambridge, Mass.: MIT Press, Bradford.

Chalmers, D. J. 1991. *Subsymbolic Computation and the Chinese Room*. CRCC Technical Report No. 48. Center for Research on Concepts and Cognition, Indiana University, Bloomington, Ind. Also to appear in J. Dinsmore, ed. *The Symbolic and connectionist paradigms: Closing the gap*.

Chalmers, D. J., R. M. French, and D. R. Hofstadter. 1992. High-level perception, representation, and analogy: A critique of artificial intelligence methodology. *Journal for Experimental and Theoretical Artificial Intelligence* 4(3): 185–211.

Chapman, D. 1990. *Intermediate vision: Architecture, implementation, and use*. TELEOS Research Technical Report No. TR-90-06. Palo Alto, Calif.

Clark, A. 1989. *Microcognition: Philosophy, cognitive science, and parallel distributed processing*. Cambridge, Mass.: MIT Press, Bradford.

Clement, C. A., and D. Gentner. 1991. Systematicity as a selection constraint in analogical mapping. *Cognitive Science* 15(1): 89–132.

Clossman, Gray. 1987. *A model of categorization and learning in a connectionist broadcast system*. Ph.D. dissertation, Computer Science Department, Indiana University. Bloomington, Ind.

Coffey, W. R. 1983. *Great moments in baseball*. Mahwah, N.J.: Watermill Press.

Collins, A. M., and E. F. Loftus. 1975. A spreading activation theory of semantic memory. *Psychological Review* 82: 407–28.

Darden, L. 1983. Reasoning by analogy in scientific theory construction. *Proceedings of the International Machine Learning Workshop*. Monticello, Ill.

DeCesare, L. 1991. *The first ladies*. New York: Greenwich House.

Defays, D. 1986. *Numbo: A study in cognition and recognition*. CRCC Report No. 13. Center for Research on Concepts and Cognition, Indiana University, Bloomington, Ind. Also in Hofstadter, 1994. *Fluid Concepts and Creative Analogies*. New York: Basic Books.

Dreyfus, H. L. 1987. From micro-worlds to knowledge representation: AI at an impasse. In *Mind design: Philosophy, psychology, artificial intelligence*, ed. J. Haugeland. Cambridge, Mass.: MIT Press, Bradford.

Ebbinghaus, H. [1885] 1964. *Über das Gedächtnis (On memory)*, trans. H. A. Ruger and C. E. Bussenius. New York: Dover.

Erman, L. D., F. Hayes-Roth, V. R. Lesser, D. Raj Reddy. 1980. The Hearsay-II speech-understanding system: Integrating knowledge to resolve uncertainty. *Computing Surveys* 12(2): 213–53.

Evans, T. G. 1968. A program for the solution of a class of geometric analogy intelligence-test questions. In *Semantic information processing*, ed. M. Minsky. Cambridge, Mass.: MIT Press.

Falkenhainer, B. 1990. Analogical interpretation in context. *Proceedings of the Twelfth Annual Cognitive Science Conference*, 69–76. Hillsdale, N.J.: Lawrence Erlbaum.

Falkenhainer, B., K. D. Forbus, and D. Gentner. 1989. The structure-mapping engine. *Artificial Intelligence* 41(1): 1–63.

Feldman, J., and D. Ballard. 1982. Connectionist models and their properties. *Cognitive Science* 6(3): 205–54.

French, R. M. 1989. An analogy between Western legal traditions and approaches to artificial intelligence. *AI and Society* 3:229–55.

French, R. M. 1990. Subcognition and the limits of the Turing test. *Mind* 99(393): 53–65.

French, R. M., and J. Henry. 1988. La Traduction en français des jeux linguistiques de Gödel, Escher, Bach. *Méta* 33(2): 133–42.

French, R. M., and D. Hofstadter. 1991. Tabletop: An Emergent, Stochastic Model of Analogy-Making. In *Proceedings of the Thirteenth Annual Cognitive Science Society Conference*, 708–13. Hillsdale, N.J.: Lawrence Erlbaum.

Fromkin V., ed. 1980. *Errors in linguistic performance: Slips of the tongue, ear, pen, and hand*. New York: Academic Press.

Gan, Kok-Wee. 1994. An emergent, stochastic model for natural language processing and its application to Chinese word boundary disambiguation. National University of Singapore Department of Computer Science technical report (submitted for publication).

Gentner, D. 1980. *The structure of analogical models in science*. Technical Report No. 4451. Cambridge, Mass.: Bolt, Beranek and Newman.

Gentner, D. 1983. Structure-mapping: A theoretical framework for analogy. *Cognitive Science* 7(2): 155–70.

Gentner, D., and K. Forbus. 1991. MAC/FAC: A model of similarity-based access and mapping. *Proceedings of the Thirteenth Annual Cognitive Science Conference*, 504–9. Hillsdale, N.J.: Lawrence Erlbaum.

Gentner, D., and A. Markman. 1994. Similarity is like analogy. In *The Proceedings of the Workshop on Similarity at the University of San Marino*, ed. C. Cacciari. Milan: Bompiani (in press).

Gentner, D., M. Rattermann, and R. Campbell. 1993. Evidence for a relational shift in the development of analogy: A reply to Goswami and Brown (submitted for publication).

Gentner, D., M. Ratterman, and K. Forbus. 1993. The roles of similarity in transfer: Separating retrievablity from inferential soundness. *Cognitive Psychology* 25(4): 524–75.

Gick, M. L., and K. J. Holyoak. 1983. Schema induction and analogical transfer. *Cognitive Psychology* 15:1–38.

Glucksberg, S., and B. Keysar. 1990. Understanding metaphorical comparisons: Beyond similarity. *Psychological Review* 97(1): 3–18.

Goldstone, R. L. 1991. Feature diagnosticity as a tool for investigating positively and negatively defined concepts. In *Proceedings of the Thirteenth Annual Conference of the Cognitive Science Society*, 263–68. Hillsdale, N.J.: Lawrence Erlbaum.

Goldstone, R., D. Medin, and D. Gentner. 1991. Relational similarity and the nonindependence of features in similarity judgments. *Cognitive Psychology* 23:222–62.

Greiner, R. 1985. *Learning by understanding analogies*. Technical Report STAN-CS-85-1071. Computer Science Department, Stanford University. Stanford, Calif.

Hall, R. P. 1989. Computational approaches to analogical reasoning. *Artificial Intelligence* 39:39–120.

Haugeland, J., ed. 1987. *Mind Design: Philosophy, psychology, artificial intelligence*. Cambridge, Mass.: MIT Press, Bradford.

Hebb, D. O. 1949. *Organization of behavior*. New York: Wiley and Sons.

Hill, 1915. My wife and my mother-in-law. *Puck* no. 11 (November 6, 1915).

Hinton, G. E., and T. J. Sejnowski. 1986. Learning and relearning in Boltzmann machines. In *Parallel distributed processing*, ed. D. E. Rumelhart and J. L. McClelland, 282–317. Cambridge, Mass.: MIT Press, Bradford.

Hofstadter, D. R. 1979. *Gödel, Escher, Bach: An eternal golden braid*. New York: Basic Books.

Hofstadter, D. R. 1983. The architecture of Jumbo. *Proceedings of the International Machine Learning Workshop*. Monticello, Ill.

Hofstadter, D. R. 1984. *The Copycat project: An experiment in nondeterminism and creative analogies*. AI Memo No. 755, Massachusetts Institute of Technology. Cambridge, Mass.

Hofstadter, D. R. 1985a. Analogies and roles in human and machine thinking. In *Metamagical themas*, 547–603. New York: Basic Books.

Hofstadter, D. R. 1985b. On the seeming paradox of mechanizing creativity. In *Metamagical themas*, 526–46. New York: Basic Books.

Hofstadter, D. R. 1985c. Variations on a theme as the crux of creativity. In *Metamagical themas*, 232–59. New York: Basic Books.

Hofstadter, D. R. 1985d. Waking up from the Boolean dream: Subcognition as computation. In *Metamagical themas*, 631–65. New York: Basic Books.

Hofstadter, D. R. 1985e. A coffeehouse conversation on the Turing test. In *Metamagical themas*, 492–525. New York: Basic Books.

Hofstadter, D. R. 1987. *Fluid analogies and human creativity*. CRCC Technical Report No. 16. Center for Research on Concepts and Cognition, Indiana University, Bloomington, Ind.

Hofstadter, D. R. 1991. *A short compendium of me-too's and related phenomena: Mental fluidity as revealed in everyday conversation*. CRCC Technical Report No. 57. Center for Research on Concepts and Cognition, Indiana University, Bloomington, Ind.

Hofstadter, D. R. 1995. *Fluid Concepts and Creative Analogies*. New York, N.Y.: Basic Books.

Hofstadter, D. R., G. Clossman, and M. J. Meredith. 1980. *Shakespeare's plays weren't written by him, but by someone else of the same name. An essay on intensionality and frame-based knowledge representation system*. Technical Report No. 96. Computer Science Department, Indiana University, Bloomington, Ind.

Hofstadter, D. R., and L. M. Gabora, 1990. Synopsis of the workshop on humor and cognition. *Humor* 2(4): 417–440.

Hofstadter, D. R., M. Mitchell, and R. M. French. (1987). *Fluid concepts and creative analogies: A theory and its computer implementation*. Technical Report 10. Cognitive Science and Machine Intelligence Laboratory, University of Michigan, Ann Arbor, Mich.

Hofstadter, D. R., and M. Mitchell. 1988. Concepts, analogies, and creativity. *Proceedings of the Seventh Biennial Conference of the Canadian Society for Computational Studies of Intelligence*, ed. R. Goebel, 94–101. Edmonton, Alberta: University of Alberta.

Hofstadter, D. R., and M. Mitchell. 1991. *The Copycat project: A model of mental fluidity and analogy-making*. CRCC Technical Report 58. Center for Research on Concepts and Cognition, Indiana University, Bloomington, Ind. Reprint, J. Barnden, and K. Holyoak, *Advances in connectionist and neural computation theory*. Vol. 2: *Analogical connections*.

Hofstadter, D. R., and D. J. Moser. 1989. To err is human; to study error-making is cognitive science. *Michigan Quarterly Review* 28(2): 185–215.

Holland, J. H. 1975. *Adaptation in natural and artificial systems*. Ann Arbor, Mich.: University of Michigan Press.

Holland, J. H. 1986. Escaping brittleness: The possibilities of general-purpose learning algorithms applied to parallel rule-based systems. In *Machine learning: An artificial intelligence approach*, ed. R. S. Michalski, J. G. Carbonell, and T. M. Mitchell. Vol. 2, chap. 20, 593–623. Los Altos, Calif.: Morgan Kaufmann.

Holland, J. H., K. J. Holyoak, R. E. Nisbett, and P. R. Thagard. 1986. *Induction*. Cambridge, Mass.: MIT Press, Bradford.

Holyoak, K. J. 1984. Analogical thinking and human intelligence. In *Advances in the psychology of human intelligence*, ed. R. J. Sternberg. Vol. 2, 199–230. Hillsdale, N.J.: Lawrence Erlbaum.

Holyoak, K., and K. Koh. 1987. Surface and structural similarity in analogical transfer. *Memory and Cognition* 15(3): 456–468.

Holyoak, K. J., and P. Thagard. 1989. Analogical mapping by constraint satisfaction. *Cognitive Science* 13(3): 295–355.

Holyoak, K. J., and P. Thagard. 1995. *Mental Leaps*. Cambridge, Mass.: MIT Press.

Humphrey, G. 1963. *Thinking*. New York: Wiley and Sons.

James, W. [1892]. *Psychology, the briefer course*. University of Notre Dame Press, Notre Dame, Ind.

Johnson-Laird, P. 1989. Analogy and the exercise of creativity. In *Similarity and analogical reasoning*, ed. S. Vosniadou and A. Ortony, 313–31. Cambridge, England: Cambridge University Press.

Kahneman, D., and D. T. Miller. 1986. Norm theory: Comparing reality to its alternatives. *Psychological Review* 93(2): 136–53.

Kaplan S., and R. Kaplan. 1982. *Cognition and environment*. New York: Praeger Publishers.

Kedar-Cabelli, S. 1984. *Analogy with purpose in legal reasoning from precedents*. Technical Report LRP-TR-17. Rutgers University Laboratory for Computer Science Research. New Brunswick, N.J.: Rutgers University.

Kedar-Cabelli, S. 1985. Purpose-directed analogy. In *Proceedings of the Seventh Annual Conference of the Cognitive Science Society*. Irvine, Calif.

Kedar-Cabelli, S. 1988a. Analogy: From a unified perspective. In *Analogical reasoning*, ed. D. H. Helman, 65–103. Dordrecht, The Netherlands: Kluwer Academic Publishers.

Kedar-Cabelli, S. 1988b. Towards a computational model of purpose-directed analogy. In *Analogica*, ed. A. Prieditis. Los Altos, Calif.: Morgan Kaufmann.

King, S. 1986. *The Bachman books. Four early novels by Stephen King: The Running Man*. New York: New American Library.

Kirkpatrick, S., C. D. Gelatt, Jr., and M. P. Vecchi. 1983. Optimization by simulated annealing. *Science* 220:671–80.

Klima, E., and U. Bellugi. 1979. *The signs of language*. Cambridge, Mass.: Harvard University Press.

Kotovosky, L., and D. Gentner. 1994. Progressive alignment: A mechanism for the development of relational similarity. *Child Development* (in press).

Lakoff, G. 1987. *Women, fire, and dangerous things*. Chicago: University of Chicago Press.

Markman, A., and D. Gentner. 1993. Splitting the difference: A structural alignment view of similarity. *Journal of Memory and Language* 32(4): 517–35.

McClelland, J., and D. Rumelhart, eds. 1986. *Parallel distributed processing*. Cambridge, Mass.: MIT Press, Bradford.

McDermott, D. 1981. Artificial intelligence meets natural stupidity. In *Mind design*, ed. J. Haugland. Cambridge, Mass.: MIT Press.

Melz, E. R. and K. J. Holyoak. 1991. Analogical transfer by constraint satisfaction. *Proceedings of the Thirteenth Annual Conference of the Cognitive Science Society*, 822–26. Hillsdale, N.J.: Lawrence Erlbaum.

Meredith, M. J. 1986. *Seek-Whence: A model of pattern perception*. Technical Report No. 214. Computer Science Department, Indiana University, Bloomington, Ind.

Meredith, M. J. 1991. Data modeling: A process for pattern induction. *Journal for Experimental and Theoretical Artificial Intelligence* 3:43–68.

Meyer, D. E., and R. W. Schvaneveldt. 1971. Facilitation in recognizing pairs of words: Evidence of a dependence between retrieval operations. *Journal of Experimental Psychology* 90:227–34.

Mitchell, M. 1990. *Copycat: A computer model of high-level perception and conceptual slippage in analogy-making*. Doctoral dissertation. University of Michigan, Ann Arbor, Mich.

Mitchell, M. 1993. *Analogy-making as perception: A computer model*. Cambridge, Mass.: MIT Press.

Mitchell, M., and D. R. Hofstadter. 1989. The role of computational temperature in a computer model of concepts and analogy-making. *Proceedings of the Eleventh Annual Conference of the Cognitive Science Society*, 765–72. Hillsdale, N.J.: Lawrence Erlbaum.

Mitchell, M., and D. R. Hofstadter. 1990. The right concept at the right time: How concepts emerge as relevant in response to context-dependent pressures. *Proceedings of the Twelfth Annual Conference of the Cognitive Science Society*, 174–81. Hillsdale, N.J.: Lawrence Erlbaum.

Moser, D. J. 1989. *The translation of Gödel, Escher, Bach into Chinese*. CRCC Technical Report No. 31. Center for Research on Concepts and Cognition, Indiana University, Bloomington, Ind.

Nagel, E. 1961. *The structure of science*. New York: Harcourt, Brace and World.

Newell, A. 1990. *Unified theories of cognition*. Cambridge, Mass.: Harvard University Press.

Newell, A., J. C. Shaw, and H. A. Simon. 1959. Report on a general problem-solving program. *Proceedings of the International Conference on Information Processing*. UNESCO House, Paris.

Norman, D. A. 1981. Categorization of action slips. *Psychological Review* 88(1): 1–15.

Nosofsky, R. M. 1984. Choice, similarity, and the context theory of classification. *Journal of Experimental Psychology: Learning, Memory and Cognition* 10 (1): 104–14.

Novick, L. R., and K. J. Holyoak. 1991. Mathematical problem solving by analogy. *Journal of Experimental Psychology: Learning, Memory, and Cognition* 17:398–415.

Quillian, M. R. 1968. Semantic memory. In *Semantic information processing*, ed. M. Minsky. Cambridge, Mass.: MIT Press.

Reitman, W. R. 1965. *Cognition and thought: An information processing approach*. New York: John Wiley and Sons.

Rips, L. J. 1975. Inductive judgments about natural categories. *Journal of Verbal Learning and Verbal Behavior* 14:665–81.

Rosch, E., et al. 1976. Basic objects in natural categories. *Cognitive Psychology* 8:382–439.

Rosch, E., and B. Lloyd. 1978. *Cognition and categorization*. Hillsdale, N.J.: Lawrence Erlbaum.

Rumelhart, D. E., G. E. Hinton, and R. J. Williams. 1986. Learning internal representations by error propagation. In *Parallel distributed processing*, ed. D. E. Rumelhart and J. L. McClelland, 318–62. Cambridge, Mass.: MIT Press, Bradford.

Rumelhart, D. E., and J. L. McClelland, eds. 1986. *Parallel distributed processing*. Cambridge, Mass.: MIT Press, Bradford.

Schank, R. C. 1983. *Dynamic memory*. Cambridge, England: Cambridge University Press.

Schank, R. C., and D. B. Leake. 1989. Creativity and learning in a case-based explainer. *Artificial Intelligence* 40(1–3), 353–85.

Shepard, R. N. 1962. The analysis of proximities: Multidimensional scaling with an unknown distance function: I. *Psychometrika* 27:125–40.

Shrager, J. 1990. Commonsense perception and the psychology of theory formation. In *Computational models of scientific discovery and theory formation*, ed. J. Shrager and P. Langley, chap. 14, 437–70. Los Altos, Calif.: Morgan Kaufmann.

Skorstad, J., B. Falkenhainer, and D. Gentner. 1987. Analogical processing: A simulation and empirical corroboration. In *Proceedings of the American Association for Artificial Intelligence, AAAI-87*. Los Altos, Calif.: Morgan Kaufmann.

Smith, E. E. 1990. Categorization. In *An invitation to cognitive science*, ed. D. N. Osherson and E. E. Smith. Vol. 3: *Thinking*, 33–53. Cambridge, Mass.:: MIT Press.

Smith, E. E., and D. L. Medin. 1981. *Categories and concepts*. Cambridge, Mass.: Harvard University Press.

Smolensky, P. 1988. On the proper treatment of connectionism. *Behavioral and Brain Sciences* 11(1): 1–14.

Spellman, B., and K. Holyoak. 1992. If Saddam is Hitler then who is George Bush? Analogical mapping between systems of social roles. *Journal of Personality and Social Psychology* 62(6): 913–33.

Thagard, P. 1989. Explanatory coherence. *Behavioral and Brain Sciences* 12(3): 435–67.

Thagard, P., K. J. Holyoak, G. Nelson, and D. Gochfeld. 1990. Analog retrieval by constraint satisfaction. *Artificial Intelligence* 46(3): 259–310.

Thurstone, L. L. 1927. A law of comparative judgment. *Psychological Review* 34:273–286.

Turing, A. M. 1950. Computing machinery and intelligence. *Mind* 52(236): 433–60.

Turner, M. 1988. Categories and analogies. In *Analogical reasoning*, ed. D. H. Helman, 3–24. Dordrecht, The Netherlands: Kluwer Academic Publishers.

Tversky, A. 1977. Features of similarity. *Psychological Review* 84:327–52.

Tversky, A., and J. W. Hutchinson. 1986. Nearest neighbor analysis of psychological spaces. *Psychological Review* 93(1): 3–22.

Winston, P. H. 1980. Learning and reasoning by analogy. *Communications of the ACM* 23(12): 689–703.

Index